DRYLAND MANAGEMENT: ECONOMIC CASE STUDIES

edited by

John A. Dixon   *East—West Center*

David E. James   *EcoServices Pty Ltd*

Paul B. Sherman   *East—West Center*

LHBEC

EARTHSCAN PUBLICATIONS LTD   London

First published 1990 by
Earthscan Publications Ltd
3 Endsleigh Street, London WC1H 0DD

British Library Cataloguing in Publication Data

Dryland management: economic case studies.
  1. Arid regions. Natural resources. Management
  I. Dixon, John A. (John Alexander), *1946–*
  II. Sherman, Paul B. III. James, David E.

ISBN 1-85383-054-2 p/b

Production by David Williams Associates 01-521 4130
Typeset by Rapid Communications, London WC1
Printed and bound in Great Britain by
WBC Print Ltd, Bristol

Earthscan Publications Ltd is a wholly owned and editorially independent
subsidiary of the International Institute for Environment and
Development (IIED)

Contents

I. LAND IMPROVEMENT TECHNIQUES

II. FARM PRACTICES

III. RANGELAND MANAGEMENT

IV. IMPROVEMENT PROGRAMMES AT THE VILLAGE/LOCAL LEVEL

V. ENVIRONMENTAL MANAGEMENT AT THE REGIONAL LEVEL

VI. DAMAGE COST STUDIES

VII. MACRO/GLOBAL STUDIES

List of Contributors

Affiliations as of time of preparation of case studies

Jaap Arntzen	University of Botswana, Gaborone, and Institute for Enviromental Studies, Free University, Amsterdam, the Netherlands
Pitsanu Attaviroj	Office of Land Development, Ministry of Agriculture and Cooperatives, Bangkok, Thailand
Jan Bojö	Southern African Development Co-ordination Council, Maseru, Lesotho
Leon Braat	Institute for Environmental Studies, Free University, Amsterdam, the Netherlands
Robert Dumsday	La Trobe University, Bundoora, Australia
Hassan El Mangouri	University of Khartoum, Khartoum, Sudan
Richard Gigengack	University of Groningen, the Netherlands
Alison Gilbert	Institute for Environmental Studies, Free University, Amsterdam, the Netherlands
John Girt	Agriculture Canada, Ottawa, Canada
Liming Han	Northwest Agricultural University, Yangling, China
Dirk Hoekstra	International Council for Research in Agroforestry, Nairobi, Kenya
Göran Holmberg	Ministry of Agriculture and Livestock Development, Nairobi, Kenya
Catrinus Jepma	University of Groningen, the Netherlands
Flavian Kalikander	Ministry of Planning and National Development, Nairobi, Kenya

Farong Li	Northwest Agricultural University, Yangling, China
Rongao Li	National Environmental Protection Bureau, Beijing, China
Don MacRae	Department of Arts, Heritage and Environment, Canberra, Australia
Hans Opschoor	Institute for Environmental Studies, Free University, Amsterdam, the Netherlands
David Oram	La Trobe University, Bundoora, Australia
Franzi Poldy	Department of Arts, Heritage and Environment, Canberra, Australia
John Sinden	University of New England, Armidale, Australia
Society for the Promotion of Wastelands Development	New Delhi, India
Algia Sutas	Soil Conservation Service of New South Wales, Sydney, Australia
John Thomas	CSIRO Division of Water Resources, Perth, Australia
Guangsen Wang	Northwest Agricultural University, Yangling, China
David Wilcox	Western Australia Department of Agriculture, Perth, Australia
Weidong Wu	Northwest Agricultural University, Yangling, China
Timothy Yapp	Department of Arts, Heritage and Environment, Canberra, Australia

Foreword

Since its inception in 1972, and particularly since the United Nations Conference on Desertification in 1977, the United Nations Environment Programme has worked to assess the nature, extent and significance of desertification, and to identify and promote effective technological, policy and organizational means of com-bating desertification. In addition, UNEP has worked to make available (in co-operation with concerned institutions) training, technical co-operation and information on desertification control. It has been UNEP's belief that a major factor in the failure of govern-ments to give adequate policy attention and funds for desertification control is that the economic significance of dryland degradation, as well as of its rehabilitation, has not been clearly understood by them.

The Drylands Project began in 1985 following a major review of the UN Plan of Action to Combat Desertification (PACD), initially formulated by the UN Conference on Desertification in 1977. The 1985 review revealed that limited progress had been made in implementing the Plan. Adverse pressures of economic development had continued to outstrip the benefits of remedial actions being taken in dryland areas.

Dryland degradation and rehabilitation is a public policy area of vital significance, to which environmental assessment, economic-development planning techniques and social benefit-cost analysis can be applied. By 1985, a significant body of economic analysis had been developed that could be applied, in general, to deal with environmental and natural resource problems. It was then that UNEP, the Government of Australia and the East–West Center came together to initiate the process of evolving a systematic approach to analysing dryland degradation and rehabilitation issues within the framework of economic analysis. The present volume is a product of that collaborative effort.

The Drylands Project, with its focus on the role of economics in dryland management, is seeking to develop a systematic approach to dealing with the challenge of improved dryland management.

To date, this work has been guided by aglobal conference and three regional workshops involving over 300 participants from

45 countries, and generously supported by 14 international and national agencies between March 1986 and January 1987. The resulting objectives formulated for the Drylands Project are as follows:

- to focus attention on the need for better economic assessment of dryland degradation and rehabilitation and its role in decision-making;
- to pursue the problem within the context of overall development planning; *and*
- to demonstrate how the techniques of economic analysis can be used to guide the design and implementation of policies, programmes, projects and land management practices to prevent, arrest or reverse the process of dryland degradation.

The conference and workshops established a working strategy to achieve these objectives which included the preparation of the following documents:

- an Executive Report, *Drylands Dilemma*, aimed at senior level officials in governments, aid agencies and non-governmental organizations to heighten their awareness of the severity of dryland degradation problems and show the role economics can play in resolving them.
- *The Economics of Dryland Management*, aimed at project analysts, economists, planners and programme development officers, provides the information necessary for an understanding of the complex problems of drylands and explains how economic analysis can help resolve them.
- This volume, *Dryland Management: Economic Case Studies*, designed to complement the first volume by illustrating the application of economic principles and techniques. The case studies suggest solutions to various dryland management problems throughout the world.

Drylands Dilemma was released at the Governing Council of UNEP in June 1987. *The Economics of Dryland Management* was published by Earthscan in 1989.

Over 40 specialists from 12 countries have been actively involved in producing these documents. Technical leadership has been shared by Dr David James, a consultant to the Australian Government, who received a UNEP Global 500 award in 1988 for his work in environmental economics, and Dr John Dixon, a well-known environmental economist who is a Research Associate at the East–West Center, Hawaii. Paul Sherman, a project fellow at the East–West Center, was also involved throughout the production of these documents.

Summary proceedings of the conferences and workshops listed below were documented in a series of reports published by the Australian Government Publishing Service:

- International Conference on the Economics of Dryland Degradation and Rehabilitation, Canberra, March 1986.
- South and South-East Asian Regional Workshop on the Economics of Dryland Degradation and Rehabilitation, New Delhi, August 1986.
- Chinese Regional Workshop on the Economics of Dryland Degradation and Rehabilitation, Beijing, September 1986.
- African Regional Workshop on the Economics of Dryland Degradation and Rehabilitation, Nairobi, January 1987.

The main co-ordinating and sponsoring agencies for the Drylands Project are:

Australian Government
United Nations Environment Programme
East – West Center

Other project sponsors include:

African Development Bank
Australian International Development Assistance Bureau
Canadian International Development Agency
Commission of the European Communities
Commonwealth Secretariat
Economic and Social Commission for Asia and the Pacific
International Institute for Environment and Development
Norwegian Agency for International Development
United Kingdom Overseas Development Administration
United Nations Educational, Scientific and Cultural Organization
United States Agency for International Development

Proposals are currently under consideration for an ongoing commitment to the objectives of the Drylands Project.

Dr Don MacRae, Co-ordinator,
Drylands Project, Australian Government

Dr Mostafa K. Tolba, Executive Director,
United Nations Environment Programme

Dr Victor Hao Li, President,
East – West Center, Hawaii

Preface

Effective dryland management requires a combination of physical, social and economic analysis. As economists, our focus is on the economic dimensions of the decision-making process for improved dryland management. The principles and approaches to economic analysis of these resources are presented in our earlier book, *The Economics of Dryland Management* (Earthscan Publications, 1989). This companion volume presents 20 case studies illustrating the application of various techniques of economic analysis to selected dryland situations in nine countries on four continents.

Each study was prepared for this volume by researchers associated with the International Project on the Economics of Dryland Degradation and Rehabilitation. This multi-year project was co-sponsored by the Australian Government, the United Nations Environment Programme (UNEP) and the East–West Center. (The one exception is chapter 5 on soil conservation in the Kitui District of Kenya; based on a study carried out by G. Holmberg, it is used here with the author's permission.)

As editors, we have reworked many of the studies to bring out major points and, in some cases, shorten the presentation. Each study begins with a précis that highlights the contents of the study. In an effort to guide the reader, the 20 cases have been grouped into 7 sections; each section contains two to five cases on the section topic. The studies represent the wide diversity of dryland settings and the various economic approaches that can be used. By examining the section headings and the various case précis, readers can select those cases that are most relevant to their own interests.

We are indebted to all of the authors of the case studies for their valuable contributions and responses to our inquiries. In addition, a number of people reviewed all or several of the case studies. Professor Jack Knetsch of Simon Fraser University, British Columbia, Canada, reviewed the entire manuscript and provided valuable insights. Garrett Upstill, an economist working with the Australian Department of Arts, Heritage and Environment, helped in the initial phases of two of the African case studies: Sudan, and the Machakos study in Kenya. Uttam Dabholkar of UNEP was similarly helpful both as a reviewer and as our principal liaison in Nairobi. Mr Jan Bojö's case study of a soil conservation project in Lesotho has served double duty as a major case study in our earlier volume, and as an abridged case study here.

We were able to draw on the same excellent support staff involved with the first volume: research assistance was provided by Jane Fowler and Regina Gregory; word-processing by Mieke James and Mary Ruddle; editorial support by Helen Takeuchi; and artwork by Laurel Lynn Indalecio. We also acknowledge computer hardware provided by Rotating Memory Group (the Netherlands) and communications facilities from Narhex Ltd Australia.

Working with Earthscan has again been a pleasure. Neil Middleton, Managing Director, and Lavinia Greenlaw, Managing Editor, have helped turn a rather massive document into a published book of manageable size. Modern electronic communication, especially telexes and faxes, greatly assisted in bridging the 11-hour Honolulu to London time gap!

We are also grateful to our home institutions or firms for their support; the continuing involvement of Don MacRae of Australia and Yusuf Ahmad of the United Nations Environment Programme have been crucial in seeing the project through to this stage. Our greatest debt, of course, is to the authors of the 20 case studies whose contributions made this volume possible.

John A. Dixon, East–West Center
David E. James, Ecoservices Pty Ltd
Paul B. Sherman, East–West Center

Introduction

Drylands represent a sizeable portion of the earth's potentially arable land surface. They range from the hyper-arid regions found in classic desert areas of Africa and Asia to the more common semi-arid and subhumid areas that support extensive agricultural systems dependent on rainfall or irrigation. In between lies a continuum of land types, degrees of aridity, and patterns of land use. As one moves from the truly arid lands to progressively wetter regions, the dominant form of land use changes from extensive grazing of animals to permanent agriculture.

The proper management of drylands has been a topic of growing international concern for many years. The 1977 Nairobi Conference on Desertification, sponsored by the United Nations, resulted in the formulation of a Plan of Action to Combat Desertification (PACD). However progress under the PACD has been slow, and in 1984 a review of the Plan was carried out by the United Nations Environment Programme (UNEP). Among other findings, the review discovered a paucity of information on the economic implications of dryland degradation and a general neglect of economic assessment and planning procedures.

The reviewers identified the need to explore more fully the costs of land degradation and the economic benefits of reclamation, rehabilitation, and prevention. Specifically, UNEP saw the need to develop a set of guidelines which could alert public executives and high-level decision-makers to the value of economic analysis in dryland management and provide them with the techniques to undertake and implement such an analysis.

To meet these challenges, the International Project on the Economics of Dryland Degradation and Rehabilitation was established, co-sponsored by UNEP, the Government of Australia, and the East–West Center. Through a series of international meetings and workshops, an effort was made to focus attention on the problem and to develop written products to create awareness and demonstrate how the techniques of economic analysis can be used in the context of dryland management.

The first product of the project was an executive report, *Drylands Dilemma*, published in 1987. This document, aimed at senior-level officials in governments, aid agencies, and non-governmental organizations (NGOs), was designed to heighten awareness of the severity of dryland degradation problems and show the role that economics can play in resolving them.

The main output of the project, however, has been two books. The first volume, *The Economics of Dryland Management* (Dixon, James and Sherman 1989), is aimed at project analysts, economists, planners, and programme development officers. It explains the rationale for, and use of, economic analysis in assessing dryland management options. As a companion volume, this book illustrates the use of economic principles and techniques in addressing actual dryland problems in various countries around the world.

The Case Studies

The case studies presented here were prepared by researchers and officials from many countries. A number of the studies were first presented at the International Conference for the project held in Canberra, Australia, in March 1986. Other case studies were presented at the regional workshops held in New Delhi and Beijing (1986), and Nairobi (1987). Still others were either especially written for this book at the request of the editors, or were adopted from previously published studies.

The selected cases illustrate a range of dryland problems and economic techniques. Obviously, it is not possible to give examples for all of the analytical approaches presented in *The Economics of Dryland Management*, or to represent all the countries facing major dryland problems.

The Economics of Dryland Management presented analytical techniques usable at both the micro, project level as well as at the macro, regional or national level. The case studies in this volume cover a similar spread. Although the focus of both volumes is on economic analysis, the socio-cultural dimension of resource use is recognized as a key element in any successful project.

The 20 studies represent a total of nine countries on four continents (Africa, Asia, North America and Australia). They are organized into seven sections according to their main theme. The first two sections focus on economic analysis of farm-level or communal projects. Section I examines the use of land improvement techniques such as land levelling, earth shaping, and aerial seeding. These are evaluated with cost-effectiveness analysis as well as traditional benefit-cost analysis. Section II considers several farm practices largely within a traditional benefit-cost analysis framework. Agricultural techniques include the use of perforated plastic sheets to grow peanuts in China and terracing and alley cropping in semi-arid regions of Africa.

Rangeland is a major use in many dryland areas, especially in the more arid regions. Section III presents cases of rangeland management in both Australia and Botswana. The Arntzen study in Botswana evaluates the use of collective fencing while the Braat-Opschoor and Wilcox-Thomas studies (Botswana and Australia, respectively) both employ modelling techniques to analyse the dynamics of range management.

Village-level activities are frequently crucial in implementing projects involving common property or communal resources. The two cases from India in Section IV focus on the economic and social dimensions of resource management – one case revolving around reafforestation and the other on a small-scale, irrigation-based rural development programme. Both studies emphasize the need for a participatory approach to development that involves the inhabitants of the project area.

The last three sections take a broader, analytical perspective. Section V contains two Australian case studies illustrating regional environmental management models using a linear programming framework. Section VI contains three damage cost studies, one at the regional level and two at the national level. Such studies are a useful first step in assessing the economic magnitude of losses associated with land degradation. As seen in both the Canada and Australia cases, the direct economic costs of land degradation are large and growing. Lastly, Section VII illustrates the use of relatively new macro/global resource management models. In Chapter 19, natural resource accounting is used to analyse physical resource stocks and flows in Botswana. This technique shows considerable promise for helping national-level planners to better understand the use (and misuse) of the natural resource base. The last case study discusses the use of global models to better trace the interdependencies of today's world and understand the impacts of domestic policies on other countries' dryland resource use.

Using this book

Table I.1 presents a matrix of case studies and the various techniques or approaches illustrated. This matrix will help direct the reader to those cases that may be most useful as illustrations for a particular approach.

Table I.1: Matrix of cases and analytical techniques

Chapter, author	Country	Damage costs: National	Damage costs: Regional	Change in production	Environmental costs: On-site	Environmental costs: Off-site	Financial analysis	Social BCA	Cost-effectiveness analysis	Institutional/social focus	Modelling: Linear programme	Modelling: Simulation	Modelling: Other
1. Wang et al	China						□		□				
2. Attaviroj	Thailand			□	□	□	□	□	□	□			
3. Li	China				□	□	□						
4. Kalikander-Hoekstra	Kenya			□			□	□					
5. Holmberg	Kenya			□	□		□						
6. Wang and Han	China			□			□	□					
7. El Mangouri	Sudan			□			□	□					
8. Bojö	Lesotho			□			□	□					
9. Wilcox-Thomas	Australia									□			Grazing system
10. Arntzen	Botswana			□	□	□	□	□					
11. Braat-Opschoor	Botswana			□	□	□		□		□		□	
12. SPWD	India					□	□	□		□			
13. SPWD	India						□	□					
14. Dumsday and Oram	Australia											□	
15. Thomas	Australia		□										
16. Sinden et al.	Australia		□	□	□						□		
17. Sinden	Australia		□	□	□	□	□				□		
18. Girt	Canada	□				□							Natural resource accounting
19. Gilbert	Botswana					□							
20. Gigengack et al.	Global	□										□	

The editors have provided a short introduction to each section as well as a précis of each case study. All cases have been edited and reformatted to some extent, and a number have had to be substantially reduced in length. Nevertheless, we feel that these cases present a rich overview of a wide range of dryland resource issues and analytical approaches. They also illustrate what can be done in situations where data are scarce and/or time is a constraint.

This book should be used selectively and in conjunction with *The Economics of Dryland Management*. We welcome additional case study material that can be used to illustrate other dryland management problems and additional analytical techniques.

I
Land Improvement Techniques

Dryland management may require the use of land improvement techniques to increase the productivity of the land resource. Some techniques are discussed in Chapters 2 and 5 of *The Economics of Dryland Management*; they include land-forming or land-shaping practices, the use of irrigation, and a change in cultivation practices.

Any improvement will involve costs, either in terms of cash outlays or increased labour input, and these must be compared to the expected benefits from these land improvements. This section presents case studies of different land improvement techniques from China and Thailand.

The Thai study evaluates alternative means of reducing soil erosion. It examines several farming patterns that rely on both land shaping and changes in farm practices to reduce water-induced soil erosion and improve agricultural yields. It shows that land development is less cost-effective than conservation farming with limited capital works. This result is important since the high cost of land-forming and physical-erosion control structures limits the extent of their use.

The two Chinese cases are quite different. Wang *et al*. evaluate the economics of three different techniques for land levelling in a pump irrigation area. In this study, the environmental costs associated with topsoil movement and burial are evaluated in terms of maintaining a given level of yield. Off-site costs of eroded soil are also included. A sprinkler irrigation system for unlevelled land is used as a companion "shadow project" for comparison in this cost-effectiveness study.

The study by Li presents an overview of aerial seeding techniques used in arid and semi-arid regions of China. Aerial seeding is presented as a low-cost way to revegetate large areas of barren sand dunes. Results depend on the timing of seeding, the variety used, and the exact aerial technique. This approach has proved successful in vegetating many areas, slowing or preventing the movement of sand dunes, and producing useful products.

1
Economic Evaluation of Land Levelling in Weibei Dry Upland, Shaanxi, China

Guangsen Wang, Weidong Wu, and Farong Li

Précis

This is a case study about the Weibei dry upland irrigation project in the eastern part of Guangzhong, the central region of Shaanxi Province, China. In this study, the use of land levelling to develop irrigated agriculture was compared to irrigation without land levelling. An economic evaluation of the environmental effects associated with each plan was also made. In the analysis, the replacement cost, shadow project, and compensation cost techniques were used to estimate costs associated with the different options. Three different land levelling techniques (shaving head, ditching and reeling) were examined, and their present values were calculated using various discount rates. These results were then compared to a control case: unlevelled land that used sprinkler irrigation. Yields were assumed the same for all four options and the study is therefore an example of a cost-effectiveness analysis. The results indicate that land levelling is economically preferred over unlevelled land with a sprinkler system (the control case). Among the three levelling techniques examined, reeling was the least-cost option when all costs (direct and indirect) were taken into account.

Irrigation in the Weibei upland

The Weibei upland in the eastern part of Guangzhong, Shaanxi Province, China, is a semi-arid region. In this region severe weather conditions include frequent droughts. In addition, because of hilly topography and the concentration of rainfall within a short period, soil erosion in this area is very serious. Because of droughts and erosion, crop yields are low and unstable, resulting in low income levels and living standards for people. Land levelling and construction of an irrigation system are the main measures chosen to promote agricultural production in this area.

The Donglei Irrigation Project was approved by the Chinese government to irrigate 66,300 ha of dryland of Heyang, Dali, and Chengcheng counties. By the end of 1985, the principal part of the project and conveyance system for four irrigation districts had been completed. In order to make the most of the project and to promote agricultural productivity, a large-scale land levelling programme has been carried out in the area since 1984. In view of this background, the land levelling programme was chosen as the object of analysis for this case study. The study evaluates the production and environmental effects within an economic framework.

Significance of the Land Levelling Programme
The Donglei Irrigation Project uses electricity to pump water from the Yellow River at Donglei village up to the Weibei upland area for irrigation. Although the primary purpose of land levelling is to meet the needs of the irrigation system, land levelling can also serve to protect the land from soil erosion. Land levelling produces various socio-economic benefits:

* Levelled land economizes on electricity and water, which results in more efficient use of scarce resources and lower irrigation costs to farmers.
* Levelled land is easier to cultivate, thereby reducing energy needs from human labour as well as animal and machine power.
* The conversion of dryland to irrigated land will change the cropping system in the uplands, leading to increased output per unit area and increased farmers' incomes.
* Levelled land provides environmental and off-site benefits, leading to a more efficient and sustainable farming system.

Characteristics of the study area

Location and Physical Characteristics
The land levelling plan has been carried out in the Nanwuniou irrigation district which is the largest irrigation system of the Donglei Irrigation Project (Figure 1.1). The district, located in the northeastern part of Shaanxi Province, is 20 km long and 28 km wide and consists of ten townships with a total population of 128,000. The irrigated area is about 27,000 ha, or 40.6 % of the total land area in the region.

The cultivated land of the region is distributed over the loess steppe and terraces of the Huang-Wei Plateau. The soil is 200 – 300 m deep. The soil texture is porous, with a porosity of 40 –

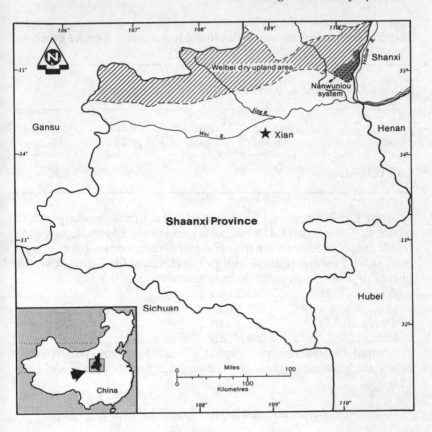

Figure 1.1: Location of the study site

50%, which is one of the main causes of soil erosion during the rainy seasons. Among the 27,000 ha of irrigated land, 57.2% is light loam and the rest is medium and heavy loam.

Average rainfall is 500 mm, and the annual evapotranspiration is 1,500 mm. Annual rainfall is unevenly distributed among seasons (Table 1.1). Droughts occur in spring and winter, and serious water erosion occurs mainly in the rainy season in late summer and fall.

Economic Features of the Region
The district is primarily an agricultural region with a grain-growing

---

Table 1.1: Average rainfall distribution among seasons

Season Month	Spring (3-5)	Summer (6-8)	Autumn (9-11)	Winter (12-2)
% of TOTAL	6	28	51	15

---

system. Grain crop yields averaged 1.16 tonnes/hectare (t/ha): wheat 1.35 t/ha, corn 1.11 t/ha, barley and pea 1.12 t/ha. Low yields result in low economic returns and low farm income. Farm household surveys show that the net per hectare profits (gross revenue minus all production costs) in the region are as follows:

Wheat	283 Yuan
Corn	155 Yuan
Barley and Pea	197 Yuan
Cotton	484 Yuan

Annual net income per capita is only 55 yuan, which is far below the provincial average. The average family plot is less than 1 ha.

Alternative patterns of land-levelling

In the past, land levelling had been practised in the upland area during farmland development. However, people only paid attention to the increase of crop yields, and overlooked the environmental changes resulting from the land levelling measures. It is our purpose in this case study to evaluate the costs and benefits of land levelling in a with-and-without format, including the environmental effects caused by various land levelling patterns in the irrigation project, so that the significance of land levelling can be better understood and proper patterns of land levelling chosen.

The three alternative techniques for land levelling considered were:

A. *Shaving Head:* This technique involves shovelling soil from the upper slope downward to the lower slope. Nearly all topsoil is buried by this levelling pattern.

B. *Ditching:* The field is divided into several long strips at intervals along the slope. The workers start by digging out one slot and taking the soil to the bottom of the slope, then the slot is filled with topsoil from the neighbouring strip. This process is repeated until the entire field is levelled. About two-thirds of the topsoil is buried by this technique.

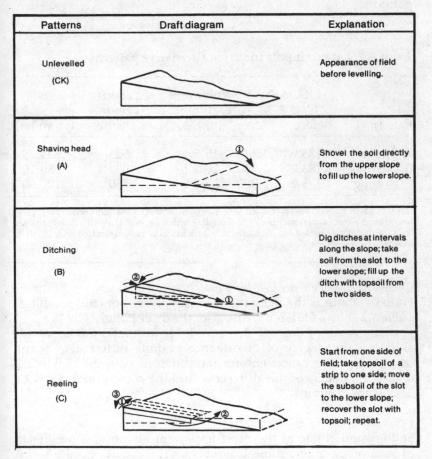

Patterns	Draft diagram	Explanation
Unlevelled (CK)		Appearance of field before levelling.
Shaving head (A)		Shovel the soil directly from the upper slope to fill up the lower slope.
Ditching (B)		Dig ditches at intervals along the slope; take soil from the slot to the lower slope; fill up the ditch with topsoil from the two sides.
Reeling (C)		Start from one side of field; take topsoil of a strip to one side; move the subsoil of the slot to the lower slope; recover the slot with topsoil; repeat.

Figure 1.2: Three land levelling patterns

C. *Reeling:* The field is divided into several long strips along the slope, and soil is moved in the following manner: topsoil is taken from the first strip to one side, immature subsoil of the slot is moved to the lower slope, then the slot is covered again with the topsoil. The procedure is repeated from strip to strip until the whole field is levelled. Only about one-third of the topsoil is buried with this technique.

Figure 1.2 sketches the procedures for the three land levelling patterns.

Table 1.2: Labour inputs for three alternative patterns

Pattern	Slope(°) Before	After	Volume of earthwork (m³/ha)	Labour (person-days/ha)	Cost* (yuan/ha)
A: Shaving	1:183.9	1:300	1575	525	824.25
B: Ditching	1:183.9	1:300	2572.5	630	989.10
C: Reeling	1:183.9	1:300	3570	750	1177.50

* Cost of labour per person-day is taken to be 1.57 yuan, which is generally used as the typical wage rate in water conservancy projects. It can be see that the labour inputs are different for the various patterns because much more earthwork has to be carried out for replacement of topsoil in patterns B and C.

Comparisons of the Three Levelling Patterns
Human labour is the main input in the process of land levelling. Table 1.2 shows the labour inputs for the three patterns.

Disturbance of the soil structure by land levelling is unavoidable, but the degree of disturbance is quite different in terms of topsoil preservation among the different patterns. Table 1.3 shows the details of this difference and the corresponding losses of available nutrients.

Environmental Effects
Soil erosion is one of the most important environmental effects of land preparation. Table 1.4 indicates the extent of soil erosion before and after land levelling in the dryland area studied. From the table, it can be seen that land levelling significantly reduces soil and nutrient losses in the long run. Levelling land can also reduce the consumption of energy used in agricultural production. Table 1.5 shows the savings of various types of power inputs after land levelling, with agricultural output being kept constant.

Table 1.3: Effects of land levelling patterns on soil nutrient conservation

Pattern	Topsoil Preserved (%)	OM (%)	QAN (ppm)	QAP (ppm)
Control	100	0.929	37.2	5.90
A: Shaving Head	5	0.460	5.0	1.77
B: Ditching	30	0.660	11.16	2.50
C: Reeling	70	0.750	26.06	4.13

Source: Field test data

*OM: Organic matter
QAN: Quick available nitrogen
QAP: Quick available phosphorus

Table 1.4: Soil erosion and water and nutrient loss before and after land levelling

Losses	Before	After	Decrease Due to Levelling (%)
Water (m³/ha)	570.00	262.50	53.9
Soil (t/ha)	7.77	1.99	74.4
N (kg/ha)	5.73	1.47	74.4
P (kg/ha)	10.84	3.29	69.7
OM (kg/ha)	84.87	21.86	74.3

Source: Field test data

Table 1.5: Estimated reduction in energy inputs as a result of land levelling (per ha)

Input	Days saved/yr
Labour	78.3
Animal power	25.2
Machine power	12.0

Economic analysis

An economic evaluation was made of the costs – both direct and indirect – associated with the three land levelling techniques. In addition, a control case is also considered where no levelling is carried out and sprinkler irrigation is used to increase production. A key assumption is that crop yields are the same under all *four* options – the three land levelling techniques and the control. As such, this is an example of a cost-effectiveness analysis whereby the goal is to irrigate the land at minimum cost.

Costs measured included both direct project costs and indirect, or usually unmeasured, environmental costs. A variety of valuation techniques were applied to measure the indirect costs, including replacement cost and compensation cost approaches.

In order to make an economic evaluation, one must first calculate the value of losses of nutrients, soil, and water caused by erosion before and after land levelling. This can be done with the replacement cost approach. Second, because the main aim of the land levelling programme is to complement the irrigation project in the upland area, a shadow project – sprinkler irrigation – is used for comparison. Last, land levelling will also result in the partial destruction of soil structure and loss of soil nutrients; these are negative effects of the plan, and the cost of compensating for these effects is therefore considered.

Costs
Soil erosion costs. Soil erosion occurs both before and after land levelling (see Table 1.4). The losses consist of two parts: the removal of soil and the loss of nutrients. The replacement cost approach (see Chapter 8 in *The Economics of Dryland Management*) considers the costs of physically replacing the lost soil and nutrients. This includes transferring sedimentary deposits in canals and reservoirs back to the fields, plus the cost of labour to spread the soil. These costs are valued at 2.00 yuan/t. The cost of replacing nutrient losses is valued using the market price of fertilizers (see Table 1.6).

Energy costs. Levelled land is easier to cultivate, and thus the required input of energy is reduced. This reduction of energy input with land levelling can be seen as a cost saving (see Table 1.7).

Shadow project expenditure. As mentioned, a sprinkler irrigation system is evaluated as a control (shadow project) that would produce the same irrigation benefits (and crop yield) as enjoyed

Table 1.6: Cost of replacing nutrients lost through soil erosion

Item[1]	Price (yuan)	Replacement cost[2] (yuan/ha) Before levelling	After levelling
Water (m^3)	0.06	34.20	15.75
Soil (t)	2.00	15.54	3.98
N (kg)	1.17	6.70	1.72
P (kg)	1.16	12.57	3.83
OM (kg)	0.43	36.49	9.40
TOTAL		105.50	34.68

1. As the soil is rich in K, the amount lost does not require replacement.
2. See Table 1.4 for quantities of nutrients, soil and water. Replacement cost is quantity × price.

Table 1.7: Reduction in energy costs due to land levelling

Item	Energy input saved (days/ha)	Averge value (yuan/day)	Cost saving (yuan/ha)
Labour	78.3	1.57	122.93
Animal power	25.2	1.20	30.24
Machine power	12.0	3.00	36.00
TOTAL	—	—	189.17

under land levelling. Considering the physical characteristics of the area, we assume that a moving sprinkler is adopted for which the fixed capital cost in the first year is 1,605 yuan/ha and the operating cost is 388.5 yuan/ha/yr. Since the irrigation cost for levelled land is 270 yuan/ha/yr, the additional annual operating cost of the shadow project is 118.5 yuan/ha. Therefore, the first year's cost is 1,605 + 118.5 = 1,723.5 yuan. In subsequent years, the additional cost is only 118.5 yuan/ha/yr.

Environmental costs. Land levelling will inevitably disturb the structure of soil and cause nutrient losses (see Table 1.3). Approximately 5 %, 30 %, and 70 % of the topsoil can be preserved by the three patterns of land levelling (shaving head, ditching, and reeling), respectively. In order to maintain soil fertility after

Table 1.8: Annual inputs required for soil maturation (per ha)

Pattern[1]	Year	Manure (t)	Urea (kg)	Calcium Super-phosphate (kg)	Irrigation Water (m³)	Deep Ploughing (person-days)
Control	—	37.5	300.0	375.0	750	—
A	1	75.0	450.0	750.0	1,500	150
	2	68.4	412.5	712.5	1,125	75
	3	59.6	375.0	675.0	1,125	—
	4	45.8	360.0	652.5	1,125	—
	5	40.5	315.0	465.0	1,125	—
B	1	60.7	375.0	637.5	1,500	—
	2	45.0	352.5	525.0	1,125	—
	3	42.2	322.5	487.5	1,125	—
C	1	41.3	375.0	461.3	1,125	—

Source: Field test data.

1. *Patterns*
Control = Sprinkler irrigation
A = Shaving head
B = Ditching
C = Reeling

Table 1.9: Market prices

Item	Average price
Manure (yuan/t)	2.00
Urea (yuan/kg)	0.54
Calcium superphosphate (yuan/kg)	0.14
Water (yuan/m³)	0.06
Wages (yuan/person-day)	1.57

levelling, measures must be taken to allow the subsoil to mature. The measures consist of increasing the fertilizer inputs and the volume of irrigation water, applying manure, and deep ploughing. It is estimated that the maturing of the subsoil with the application of these measures will take five years, three years, and one year, respectively, for the three different land levelling techniques.

Detailed yearly inputs and price data are given in Tables 1.8 and 1.9. Table 1.10 shows soil maturation costs for each of the three techniques for years 1 to 5. Since shaving head involves the greatest disturbance to and burial of topsoil, its soil maturation costs are highest. Reeling involves the least disturbance and the lowest costs.

Table 1.10: Maturation costs (yuan/ha/yr)

Year	A Shaving Head	B Ditching	C Reeling
1	489.00	168.65	82.68
2	310.05	86.85	0
3	149.20	59.80	0
4	110.35	0	0
5	49.20	0	0
TOTAL	1,107.80	315.30	82.68

Note: Costs were calculated as input × price; maturation costs of A, B, or C minus that of Control = Penalty.

Off-site costs. The erosion of upland fields also leads to downstream siltation of fields and reservoirs. The expenditure for clearing the silt is an off-site cost of the project. Soil erosion experiments show that the siltation caused by erosion from upland fields with land levelling has been 1.46 m^3/ha and 5.7 m^3/ha without land levelling. To clear 1 cubic metre of silt will take one person-day. The wage cost per person-day is assumed to be 1.57 yuan. Therefore, the off-site cost of silt removal created by unlevelled upland fields is 8.95 yuan/ha, and that of levelled land is only 2.29 yuan/ha.

Labour costs. The direct labour costs for land levelling are 824.25 yuan/ha for shaving head, 989.10 yuan/ha for ditching, and 1,177.50 yuan/ha for reeling (Table 1.2).

Total costs. Total costs of land levelling in year 1 for each of the three techniques, and the control sprinkler alternative, are given in Table 1.11. The three land levelling alternatives have associated environmental and project costs but show considerable savings when compared to the nutrient replacement, additional energy, and shadow project costs of the sprinkled, unlevelled alternative.

Table 1.11: Total cost for year 1 of alternative plans (yuan/ha)

| | Control | Levelling Patterns | | |
Item	(unlevelled with sprinkler)	A Shaving	B Ditching	C Reeling
Nutrient replacement	105.51	34.68	34.68	34.68
Extra energy requirements	189.17	0	0	0
Shadow project:				
Fixed input	1,605.00	0	0	0
Annual cost	118.50	0	0	0
Environmental costs	0	489.00	168.65	82.68
Land-levelling costs	0	824.25	989.10	1,177.50
Off-site costs	8.95	2.29	2.29	2.29
TOTAL	2,027.13	1,350.22	1,194.72	1,297.15

Table 1.12: Total cost for year 2 and subsequent years (yuan/ha)

Option	Year	Replacement Costs		Maturation Costs		Off-site Costs		Energy Costs		Total Costs
Control (unlevelled with sprinkler)	2+	105.50	+	0	+	8.95	+	189.17	=	303.62
Shaving head	2	34.68	+	310.05	+	2.29	+	0	=	347.02
	3	34.68	+	149.20	+	2.29	+	0	=	186.17
	4	34.68	+	110.35	+	2.29	+	0	=	147.32
	5	34.68	+	49.20	+	2.29	+	0	=	86.17
	6	34.68	+	0	+	2.29	+	0	=	36.97
Ditching	2	34.68	+	86.85	+	2.29	+	0	=	123.82
	3	34.68	+	59.80	+	2.29	+	0	=	96.77
	4+	34.68	+	0	+	2.29	+	0	=	36.97
Reeling	2+	34.68	+	0	+	2.29	+	0	=	36.97

The cost items in Table 1.11 recur in the following years except for the fixed project inputs. The replacement costs, off-site costs, the difference of the shadow project's operating costs, and extra energy costs are constant while the compensation costs will only happen during the soil maturation process, which will take from one to five years depending on which land levelling technique is used. Hence the total cost for year 2 and the following years can be calculated as shown in Table 1.12.

The Present Value of Total Costs
Time horizon. The time horizon is set at 15 years because of the following factors: (a) it takes a long time for the various results of the project to take effect; and (b) the length of land-use contract for peasant households has been set to at least 15 years according to the present practice in China. This latter fact is very important in determining the way cropland is used and cared for.

The discount rate. Taking the current level of return on capital investment and general interest rates into consideration, 7% was adopted as the discount rate in the calculation. This is also the rate that is generally adopted in water conservancy projects in China.

The present value. Using discount tables, the present values of expenditures for each year were calculated for a 15-year period using a 7% discount rate. The results are presented in Table 1.13.

Results

From Table 1.13, we can see that to maintain the same level of productivity, the present value of the total costs of any of the three land levelling patterns is less than that of not levelling (i.e., the sprinkler irrigation alternative). Thus we conclude that based on the assumptions presented, it is economically sound to carry out a land levelling plan in the irrigation project. Table 1.13 also shows that among the three levelling patterns, the present value of total costs is lowest for reeling. Taking a long-term point of view, reeling is the most suitable pattern and should be encouraged in the levelling plan. When the analysis was recalculated using different discount rates (from 5 to 20%), the results were unchanged: land levelling was still preferred to the non-levelling option, and reeling had the lowest level of present value of costs.

Among the three land-levelling patterns examined, reeling is the most desirable in terms of topsoil preservation and long-term effects. But in practice, the other two patterns are usually adopted for two reasons: (a) land levelling tasks are assigned by government

Table 1.13: Present value of costs of land-levelling alternatives and the unlevelled sprinkler system (yuan/ha) (7% discount rate)

Year	Control (unlevelled with sprinkler)	A Shaving Head	B Ditching	C Reeling
1	1,895.36	1,262.47	1,117.06	1,212.84
2	265.07	302.95	108.09	32.27
3	247.76	151.91	79.13	30.17
4	231.67	112.42	28.21	28.21
5	216.49	61.41	26.36	26.36
6	202.22	24.62	24.62	24.62
7	189.16	23.03	23.03	23.03
8	176.71	21.52	21.52	21.52
9	165.17	20.11	20.11	20.11
10	154.24	18.78	18.78	18.78
11	144.22	17.56	17.56	17.56
12	134.81	16.41	16.41	16.41
13	126.01	15.35	15.34	15.34
14	117.81	14.34	14.34	14.34
15	109.91	13.38	13.38	13.38
TOTAL	4,376.61	2,076.26	1,543.94	1,514.94

agencies to local people without clear instructions about the particular patterns of land levelling that should be adopted; and (b) people undertaking land levelling tasks are not those who contract the land for long-term use. Although land levelling jobs are paid for in terms of person-days and not in terms of hectares, people are not interested in adopting levelling patterns which require large amounts of labour. To implement reeling as the most desirable land levelling practice, we suggest that (a) clear clauses about land levelling patterns and task specifications be included in the government policy; (b) economic evaluation of different land levelling patterns be advocated and made known to all managers and participants of the project; (c) on-site inspection and technical aid be emphasized; and (d) allocation of land levelling tasks be made to bring together the interests of people who are responsible for the long-term effects of land levelling with those who do the levelling task. Alternatively, a specialized land levelling labour force should be organized so that management and expertise could be reinforced.

The economic analysis of land levelling patterns shows that there is a trade-off of labour inputs with non-labour inputs such as chemical fertilizers, manures, irrigation water and deep ploughing. Thus, the relative prices of labour inputs and non-labour inputs are critical in this analysis. It should be clearly understood that the conclusions in this case study are conditional and subject to adjustment.

2

Soil Erosion and Land Degradation in the Northern Thai Uplands

Pitsanu Attaviroj

Précis

This case study examines the economic dimensions of current and proposed land use practices in upland rainfed agricultural areas in northern Thailand. The study area has been occupied and used for upland cultivation for more than two decades and now suffers from land degradation. The study is concerned with the effects of land degradation, especially soil erosion, and examines both on-site and off-site effects. The main site of 1,300 rai (208 ha) is representative of the average situation in the northern upland region. Within that area, the study focuses on a site of 7 rai (1.12 ha), which is the size of the average farm (1 rai = 0.16 ha).

Three alternative land management systems are examined and compared: exploitive monocropping, land development alone, and conservation farming. The results of the analysis show that exploitive monocropping is an undesirable practice and that conservation farming systems generate the highest net benefits. The study also highlights the importance of the adoption rate of new cultivation techniques by farmers and calls for the rapid introduction of conservation farming systems in all upland areas of northern Thailand.

Description of the problem

Thailand depends heavily on its agricultural economy, which is largely based on cropping. It has been confronted with a growing rural population and consequent increase in the demand for additional land. As the useful lowland is largely occupied, this demand has been accommodated by substantial increases in the use of uplands.

There does not appear to have been an economically, socially and politically acceptable alternative to providing additional land. Much of the additional land has come from areas where the soils are both fragile and erosion prone. Historically, such lands have been cultivated by the "swidden" (slash-and-burn) system. Under low land-use pressure, this system has been stable and productive. However, increasingly intensive cultivation of this land, using traditional practices and cropping systems is leading to serious erosion. Coupled with the degradation of both soil structure and fertility, this is resulting in an unacceptable decline in production potential.

Management of the uplands of northern Thailand is largely exploitive. Weed control is usually less than ideal, and levels of production are generally low. Relay cropping and rotation of legumes with cereals are practised by few farmers; the majority of farmers grow only one crop each year.

The major limitation to production on these soils is poor management. In order to develop cropping systems that will be viable in the long term, it is necessary to find not only technical solutions but to ensure that techniques are appropriate, and that the social and economic conditions exist to encourage their adoption in practice.

The Royal Thai Government and its Ministry of Agriculture and Cooperatives, in particular, have been aware of the problem and its potential consequences since the early 1960s. Responsibility for dealing with the problem has been directed by the Ministry to its Department of Land Development (DLD). This case study reports the results of a land development and research project conducted by the Department of Land Development, with support from the Australian Government and the World Bank. The project is part of the Northern Agriculture Development Project and is known as the Thai-Australia-World Bank Land Development (TAWLD) Project.

Background

Physical environment
The study area is shown in Figure 2.1. Topography divides the northern region of Thailand into two sub-regions: the upper and lower north. The lower sub-region includes the alluvial plains and terraces that comprise the upper delta of the Chao Phraya River. It contains ten provinces: Kamphaeng Phet, Loei, Nakhon Sawan, Phetchabun, Phichit, Phitsanulok, Sukhothai, Tak, Uthai Thani, and Uttaradit. The topography of the upper sub-region is more extreme and embraces the higher terraces, lower plateaux, and hills and mountains of the northern portion of the region. The provinces here are Chiang Mai, Chiang Rai, Lampang, Lamphun, Mae Hong Son, Nan, Phayao, and Phrae.

The three major land forms are lowlands, uplands, and the

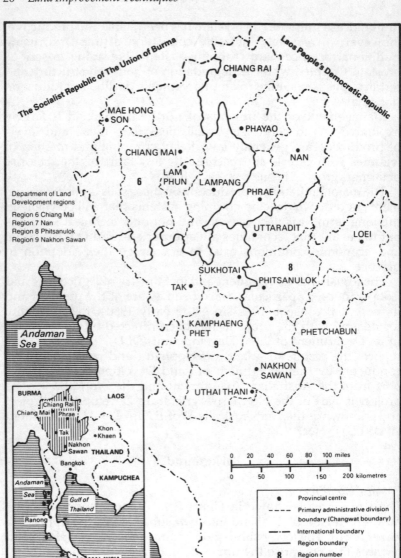

Figure 2.1: Study area of the TAWLD Project in Northern Thailand

highlands. The lowlands are generally fertile alluvial areas ranging from flat to gently undulating terrain. Lowlands occupy about 10 % of the total area of the upper north region, and 20 % of the lower north. The uplands comprise older alluvial deposits that occur as a series of terraces to about 500 metres above sea level, lying between the tributaries of the main rivers and along the foothills of the ranges. The highlands range in altitude from 500 to 2,500 m above sea level and from elevated flat plateaux to steep mountains.

The soils in the region vary with the topography. According to soil survey data, all soil series within the uplands have low fertility. Results of a soil fertility survey in the project area are more favourable, indicating that although most soils have low and declining organic matter levels, other factors are adequate or nearly so. Potassium levels are generally high, and while pH is low, phosphate responses may be expected on only a few soil types. Nitrogen is required by nonlegumes on all project soils, a reflection of low soil organic matter levels.

Available soil moisture capacity of most of the upland soils is low, and constitutes a major constraint to crop during periods of inadequate rainfall, which often occur in June and July. Management practices that conserve soil moisture or increase the water-holding capacity of the soils, or the use of supplementary irrigation, would help to take advantage of the full growing season.

Soil erosion is a serious problem. According to official surveys, about 28 % of the total area of the northern region is suffering from erosion, mostly severe or very severe.

During the wet season (April to September), 90 % or more of the annual rainfall occurs. The average annual rainfall over the region is about 1,200 mm but there are wide variations within the region, from about 950 mm at Tak to nearly double this amount (about 1,745 mm) at Chiang Rai.

The natural vegetation of the uplands is generally a secondary regrowth climaxing as an open stand of low deciduous *Dipterocarp* forest.

Current land use
Over the last nine years the area farmed in the northern zone has increased by 50 %, from 17.0 million rai (2.7 million ha) to 25.3 million rai (4 million ha). The largest increase in absolute area has been in rice production with an additional 3.5 million rai. However, other upland crops have shown a greater proportional increase (e.g., maize, 1.8 million rai, 43 %; mung bean, 1.6 million rai, 179%; and sugar, 0.3 million rai, 149%).

Fallow areas generally vary from 50% to all of the total land, depending on social, technical, and economic factors. Prior to development by the TAWLD Project, more than 47% of the uplands lay fallow. Project activities have resulted in a reduction of about 35% in the total area left fallow at most project sites.

Farm size and land tenure

In the uplands, the average size of farmland owned by the farmers is 9.19 rai per household although the actual land farmed by each household is 7.40 rai. In the lowlands, the average size of farmland owned by farmers is 7.41 rai, but the actual land area farmed is 7.58 rai.

In the upper north, many farmers own both paddy and upland plots. According to one survey, 67% of the households sampled were farming upland and lowland plots. This has a significant impact on investment of labour and capital. In the lower north, the average farm size is 30 rai.

The majority of farmers are *de facto*, if not legal, owners of at least some of the land they occupy. *De facto* owners buy, sell and rent land in virtually the same way as legal owners.

The proportion of households with no legal title to some of the land they cultivate varies from 43 to 84%. In some areas, even though land is "owned" by the household head and/or a member of his family, 95% of the farmers have an insecure title or no title at all. Only a relatively small amount of land in the north is occupied by leasing.

Social, demographic, and economic factors

The national census showed a total population of 10.7 million in the northern provinces. Population has grown from 7.9 million since 1970. The rate of growth has been falling and is now estimated to be below 1.6% per year. The population density varies from $18/km^2$ to more than $120/km^2$.

The average household has five people with a normal age distribution. Households with relatively large upland holdings have an average of 2 adult males and 2.6 full-time adult workers. According to surveys, 91% of household heads are male, and the average age of the household head is 44 years. Eight % have no education at all, 12% have less than four years of primary school, 73% have completed the first four years of primary school, and 7% have had more education. These social conditions differ between the upper and lower northern areas.

The following economic parameters are important:

- significance of commodities in family subsistence;

- potential production, anticipated farm gate prices, and the consequent gross cash income;
- availability and cost of necessary inputs (e.g., land, fertilizer);
- timely availability of labour;
- availability of necessary cash or credit, and the cost of credit;
- marketability of the product;
- risks and uncertainties in the seasonal conditions and the incidences of pests and diseases; *and*
- quality of transport and communications networks.

Environmental impacts
Increasingly intensive cultivation of the uplands using traditional practices and exploitive cropping systems is leading to serious erosion and the degradation of soil fertility. The most significant of the changes on-site is the depletion of organic matter and the decreased availability of phosphorus, nitrogen, potassium, and important trace elements. Field experiments also indicate an increase in soil bulk density and a decrease in infiltration rates with clearing and cultivation of land.

The composite effect of all these changes has been a decline in production potential, which varies with both soil type and the crops grown. The decline in yield over time has been more pronounced in rice than in corn. The decline in rice yield, furthermore, is not alleviated by fertilizer. Corn yield can, to a degree, be improved by fertilizer. This reflects the greater dependence of rice on high organic matter levels and good soil structure.

Serious off-site effects have also occurred. Siltation downstream has led to lower levels of water in reservoirs, depletion of hydroelectric capacity, degradation of the drainage system and consequent flooding as far away as Bangkok, and a reduction in river depth, impeding shipping and necessitating dredging operations.

Forestry losses have resulted from timber poaching, an increase in farm area, and reinstatement of farmland previously abandoned to bush fallow.

Approaches to development

The Thai-Australia-World Bank Land Development (TAWLD) Project
As early as 1967, the Thai government sought assistance from the Australian Government to tackle its problems of land degradation. Attention was initially directed to the upper north with its extensive areas of erosion-prone land. Since that time, the TAWLD

Project has developed with Australian and World Bank assistance. Project expenditures during 1980 – 87 were over US$14.6 million, including nearly US$9 million from the World Bank and US$5.7 million from the Thai government.

The TAWLD Project has been developing land by clearing it and providing soil conservation and access works. While such work reduces erosion, it does not prevent all degradation. Even with World Bank assistance, it has been possible to work on only 20,000 to 30,000 rai per year. The project has also been conducting a programme of research into related degradation problems.

Land improvement and conservation farming
Several alternative cultivation patterns and management practices are possible in the project area:

Exploitive monocropping. For more than two decades the increasing demand for land has been accommodated by expansion into the uplands. In general, the farmers have occupied and utilized areas of forest and secondary regrowth to supplement income from lowland farms. The exploitive practices adopted generally involve the burning of organic residues in the dry season, followed by mechanical or hand cultivation and sowing of the crop. Inputs of both time and materials are low. This alternative is considered the most likely to be adopted by the average farmer, left to his own devices. There is little incentive to conserve the land because the average farmer lacks either one or more of the following: tenure, technical knowledge and finance.

If exploitive monocropping continues, it can be expected to result in decreasing production and increasing problems from soil erosion and consequent siltation. Some land is already so severely degraded that its rehabilitation would be a long and expensive task, but most of the land is at the stage where the effects of erosion and degradation could be ameliorated.

Reversion to long-term swidden agriculture. Swidden (slash-and-burn) agriculture can provide a low-cost, stable alternative but it requires that land use pressure be substantially reduced. As this would mean relocating or otherwise employing many of the farmers, it is probably not politically, socially, or economically acceptable.

Land development alone. Soil erosion and land degradation are the two components responsible for declining production potential. On-site degradation in most circumstances is by far the more serious. The control or prevention of soil erosion alone does not solve the problem. Land development by itself seeks only to control the erosion. In all other respects, it is the same as exploitive monoculture. In the short term, most of the yield decline is attributable to degradation of the soil. Furthermore, such works are relatively expensive. While funding has been available from World Bank credit, it has been possible to maintain a significant programme. However, when the current credit is no longer available, capacity to undertake this activity will be significantly diminished.

Conservation farming. Conservation farming systems include measures such as contour ploughing, contour sowing, strip cropping, and the use of mulch to control erosion. They also involve green manure, cover cropping, and intercropping practices which contribute to erosion control and also maintain soil organic matter levels, improving and maintaining fertility at adequate levels. Provided the soils have not been unreasonably degraded, recovery of the land after treatment is fairly rapid in most areas.

Various cropping systems are suitable, based on rice or corn, or both in combination. The rotation must include a legume phase or phases and generate sufficient organic matter to ensure that the level of soil organic matter is maintained (approximately 10 t/ha/yr).

Generally, farmers plant approximately one-third of their land to rice and two-thirds to other crops. The rotation selected for this study is corn plus mulch followed by mung bean sown in late August, peanuts plus mulch followed by mung bean sown in late August, and blackbean (green manure) plus mulch followed by upland rice sown in June/July.

Economic analysis

Land use alternatives
Three main land use alternatives are evaluated in the economic analysis:

- continued exploitive monocropping with its consequent erosion and degradation;
- construction of physical works aimed at minimizing erosion alone; *and*
- controlling erosion and degradation through conservation farming practices either alone or in combination with physical works.

The planning horizon is 15 years. Discount rates of 5, 10, and 20% are used to translate future benefits and costs into present values. The sensitivity of results to different rates of adoption of the new strategies is also tested. Adoption rates of 5, 10, and 15% per year are used.

The study presents a comprehensive analysis of both on-site and off-site effects. Valuations of on-site benefits and costs are based on market prices and documented field data. Off-site benefits are measured as a reduction in off-site costs compared to those that would occur with exploitive monocropping.

On-site benefits and costs

On-site costs are the costs of production, and on-site benefits are the values of crops. For the alternatives involving land development, capital and maintenance costs are included.

For all alternatives, on-site benefits are based on average crop prices during 1980-83:

Crop	Price
Rice	2.90 baht/kg
Maize	2.26 baht/kg
Mung bean	6.36 baht/kg
Peanut	6.56 baht/kg

Exploitive monocropping. It is estimated that newly cleared forest land will yield 300 to 400 kg/rai of rice, with declining yields through time. The rate of decline is defined by the equation:

$$Y = 2689 - 492.8X + 41.34X^2 - .147x^3$$

where Y is the rice yield in kg/ha and X is the number of years.

This assumes initial yields of 358 kg/rai, declining to 120 kg/rai in year 9, the point at which farming becomes unprofitable. The analysis assumes half of the land is left fallow each year and that on reaching the lower yield, land is fallowed for five years. For corn, the decline in yields is slower than rice and differs with good and average soils. Equations for the time trends are:

$$\text{Average soils (tons/ha)} : Y = 2.7 - 1.75\log(X)$$
$$\text{Good soils (tons/ha)} : Y = 2.938 - 0.021X$$

The yields on average soils are assumed to commence at 432 kg/rai and reach 214 kg/rai in six years. It is estimated that 25% of the area farmed has good soils, and the remainder average soils. On-site costs for exploitive monocropping are low, as the only requirements are land preparation, seed, and labour.

Land development alone. As previously explained, this strategy seeks only to control soil erosion, not soil degradation. In the estimation of on-site benefits, it is assumed that farmers continue to exploit the land if assisted with land development regardless of tenure or utilization practices. Yield declines are thus assumed to be the same as exploitive monoculture; this is a strong assumption. However, intensity of land use increases. It is assumed that farmers use all of the land annually. The provision of access tracks is considered a benefit to landholders, but this benefit has not been quantified.

The main on-site costs are associated with initial capital works and ongoing maintenance of the land. Other farming costs are minimal, as with exploitive monoculture. Capital works include land selection, farm development, and access tracks. The Thai Government developed 124,400 rai up to 1985 at an average cost of 1,255 baht/rai.

In addition to capital costs, land development requires maintenance of access tracks and conservation banks. Project experience has shown that .021 km/rai of bank and .006 km/rai of track with maintenance costs of 4,623 baht/km and 4,495 baht/km, respectively, are necessary. Total maintenance costs per year are thus 124 baht/rai.

Conservation farming. Conservation farming practices can be undertaken with or without conservation works used in the land development option. Both situations are evaluated. The rate at which farmers can be persuaded to adopt such practices is important. To test the sensitivity of this, the analysis considers adoption rates of 5, 10, and 15% per year.

As for on-site benefits, research and on-farm demonstrations have produced the following yield estimates:

Crop	Year 1 (kg/rai)	Year 2 and on (kg/rai)
Corn	400	450
Mung bean	120	140
Peanut	250	250
Black bean	[green manure only]	
Rice	300	400

Conservation farming requires greater direct farm inputs than exploitive monocropping, and the associated costs are included in the analysis. Where conservation works are also adopted, the capital and maintenance costs are assumed to be the same as for the land development option.

Off-site benefits and costs

The off-site benefits of land development and conservation farming projects consist of reduced off-site damage costs, such as forest encroachment and siltation downstream of the project area.

Exploitive monocropping. During 1975 – 82, forest encroachment in northern Thailand occurred at the rate of 1.4 million rai/yr. Although some of this is due to timber poaching, 450,000 rai/yr were used as additional farm area. For this study, it was assumed that 200,000 rai/yr of forest were used to replace degraded lands. The annual cost in lost timber production from the area is estimated to be 330 million baht/yr, and it is assumed that under exploitive monocropping this loss would continue at the same rate.

The effect of sedimentation on the 4 major dams and 16 smaller reservoirs has been a depletion in storage capacity estimated at 18.18 million m^3/yr. Assuming a necessary annual water allocation of 2,500 m^3/rai of cropland, the storage depletion represents a potential loss of 7,272 rai of irrigable land per year (18.18 multiplied by $10^6/2,500$). The income lost from an irrigated rice crop was estimated at 552 baht/rai for a total of 4.01 million baht/yr.

A similar argument applies to the depletion of hydroelectric capacity. If the capacity of the dam to provide water for this purpose depreciates in proportion to sedimentation rate, the annual loss would be 1.706 million kwh. At a value of 1.50 baht per kwh, this amounts to a loss of 2.559 million baht/yr. This cost would accumulate annually, eventually totalling 38.385 million baht in year 15.

Sedimentation of the Chao Phraya River requires that 19 million m^3 of sediment be dredged from the first 18 km of the river every year, at a cost of 424 million baht, to keep the channel open to shipping. The additional cost of relieving the flood situation in Bangkok has not been included in the analysis because of the complexity of evaluating all effects.

Land development alone. A reduction in all off-site costs is assumed, consistent with the reduction in soil erosion. The universal soil loss equation is used to evaluate soil loss potential. Erosion rates are reduced by 29 to 39% through soil conservation works. A mean reduction of 34% is used in the analysis. Thus erosion-related costs in this option are approximately two-thirds of the costs in the exploitive monocropping case above.

Forest encroachment can still occur under land development alone, since soil degradation will continue. It is assumed that land will be allowed to revert to bush fallow when production falls to an unacceptable level.

Conservation farming. Off-site costs reflect the reductions in soil erosion and forest encroachment brought about by the change in land use. The adoption of conservation farming practices will reduce erosion by 67%. With the addition of contour banks at normal spacing, the reduction is 76 to 79%. A rate of 78% is used in the analysis.

As agricultural stability is attained under conservation farming, it is assumed that no further forest encroachment will occur, thereby avoiding the costs due to encroachment that occur under the other two options. This will be the case whether conservation farming is used alone or in conjunction with land development.

Table 2.1: Net benefits from land use alternatives in the northern upland region of Thailand (million baht)

Year	Exploitive monocrop	Land development alone	Conservation farming alone	Conservation farming plus land development
1	3,367	−5,394	2,851	−8,272
2	2,374	4,151	4,790	4,838
3	1,608	2,975	4,788	4,836
4	948	2,014	4,785	4,835
5	357	86	4,783	3,730
6	−184	463	4,781	4,832
7	−1,042	−895	4,779	4,831
8	−1,427	−1,308	4,777	4,829
9	−1,800	−1,695	4,775	4,828
10	−2,096	−3,033	4,772	3,723
11	−2,451	−2,282	4,770	4,825
12	−1,129	705	4,768	4,823
13	−1,956	−585	4,766	4,822
14	−2,587	−1,487	4,764	4,820
15	−2,549	−2,145	4,761	3,715

Results

Only a summary of the results of the economic analysis is presented here; full details appear in Attaviroj (1986). Time streams of net benefits for all the alternatives are shown in Table 2.1. The effect of the discount rate on the net present value (NPV) is described in Table 2.2. For options involving conservation farming, it is assumed that adoption of the new techniques is immediate.

Table 2.2: NPV of farming strategies over 15 years for the northern region of Thailand (million baht)

Discount rate (%)	Exploitive monocropping	Land development alone	Conservation farming −Land dev't	+Land dev't
5	−2,114	−4,244	47,757	35,582
10	1,147	−2,155	34,599	23,458
20	3,608	− 640	20,749	10,981

Note: Assumes that 8.9 million rai of upland are cropped.

Evaluation of alternatives

The calculations indicate that exploitive monocropping produces positive net benefits for five years and negative net benefits thereafter. Whether this system is economically viable depends on the discount rate. High discount rates put more weight on quick returns, and hence the high returns in years 1 to 5 outweigh the negative returns in the future.

For land development alone, the positive net benefits of years 2 to 5 do not outweigh the initial capital costs and the negative returns expected from year 6 onward, no matter what discount rate is used.

Conservation farming results in high net present values at all discount rates. It is unlikely, however, that such farming systems would ever be adopted without land development because steep land would require some conservation works. Despite the initial costs of necessary works, conservation farming systems with land development still produce high net benefits, although at higher discount rates the impact of capital costs and low on-site benefits in early years has a significant effect on NPV.

Failure to achieve 100% immediate adoption significantly lowers the net benefits of conservation farming over the 15-year period, as shown in Table 2.3. Substantial rewards from high rates of adoption appear to justify major expenditures on education and advisory programmes that encourage farmers to use conservation farming methods.

Table 2.3: NPV over 15 years for conservation farming with land development at adoption rates of 5%, 10%, 15% per year (million baht)

| Discount rate (%) | Adoption rate (%) | | |
	5	10	15
5	11,196	14,735	21,868
10	9,562	11,969	16,595
15	7,427	8,688	10,921

Policy implications

Based on the economic analysis conducted for this case study, conservation farming systems should be introduced in all areas of upland agriculture in northern Thailand as quickly as possible. Exploitive monoculture should be discouraged.

Land development should not be undertaken unless accompanied by the introduction of conservation farming systems. Works should not be constructed on lands with slopes of less than 5%; on steeper land, works should be constructed only as necessary to reduce the erosion hazard to acceptable levels.

Priority should be given to promoting conservation farming in areas currently being intensively farmed where degradation is occurring and the erosion risk is high. More generally, concern for soil degradation and erosion should be given a higher priority in the national programme and carried out on several fronts.

Comprehensive, well-orchestrated awareness programmes should be conducted through the schools and the media, particularly by television. This could be developed by a select committee comprising representatives from the National Economic and Social Development Board, the National Environment Board, the Ministry of Agriculture and Cooperatives, Department of Land Development and Department of Agricultural Extension, the Ministry of Education, and the Ministry of Interior.

A special promotional effort should be initiated through the Ministry of Agriculture and Cooperatives, Department of Agricultural Extension's Training and Visit System, aimed at increasing the rate of adoption of conservation systems and practices. Demonstrations of such systems being conducted by the Ministry of Agriculture and Cooperatives, Department of

Land Development, should be increased both to train all Ministry officers involved in the programmes and as an additional mechanism for educating farmers.

The Bank of Agriculture and Agricultural Cooperatives should be encouraged to provide suitable lines of credit to enable farmers to obtain the necessary additional inputs. The Ministry of Interior, Land Development, and the Ministry of Agriculture and Cooperatives, Forestry Department and Land Reform Office, must be encouraged to accelerate programmes aimed at providing adequate land tenure.

These initiatives may need to be supported by legislation or regulations that require farmers in particularly hazardous situations either to adopt some minimum conservation procedures or at least to cease using the most hazardous practices.

Acknowledgement

The author acknowledges assistance provided by the Kingdom of Thailand Ministry of Agriculture and Cooperatives, Department of Land Development, and the National Environment Board, and officers and staff of the Thai-Australia-World Bank Land Development Project, especially Mr W.F. Buddee.

Sources and references

Attaviroj, P. (1986),
"Soil erosion and degradation, Northern Thai Uplands: an economic study", paper presented to the International Conference on the Economics of Dryland Degradation and Rehabilitation, Canberra.
Central Office of National Census, Department of Provincial Administrations, Ministry of Interior (1983),
Circular relating results of the National Census dated 31 December.
Centre of Agricultural Statistics,
Agricultural Statistics (Bangkok: Office of Agricultural Economics (OAE), Ministry of Agriculture and Cooperatives), 1974–1983.
Charley, J.L., and J.M. McGatrity (1970),
"Soil fertility problems in development of annual cropping on swiddened lowland terrain in Northern Thailand", *Proc. International Seminar on Shifting Cultivation and Economic Development in Northern Thailand* (Bangkok: Chiang Mai University).
Ryan, K.T., and U. Taejajai (1985),
"Comparative soil erosion and amelioration rates in the swidden cultivation, permanent agriculture and forestry in Northern Thailand",

paper presented at the Workshop on Site Protection and Amelioration Roles for Agroforestry, Institute of Forestry Conservation, University of the Philippines, Los Baños, September.

Sathit Wacharakitti *et al*. (1984),
"The assessment of forest areas from Landsat imagery", paper presented at the Annual Conference, Royal Forestry Department, 6-14 November 1978, Bangkok.

Scholten, J.J., and W. Boonyawat (1972),
Detailed Reconnaissance Soil Survey of Nan Province, Soil Survey Division Report SSR-90 (Bankok: Department of Land Development).

Srikhajon, M., A. Somrang, P. Pramojanee, S. Pradabwit, C. Anecksamphant (1984),
"Application of the universal soil loss equation for Thailand" in *Proc. Fifth Asian Soil Conference*, 10-23 June, Bangkok.

Wischmeier, W.H., and D.D. Smith (1978),
Predicting Rainfed Erosion Losses: A Guide to Conservation Planning, US Department of Agriculture, Agriculture Handbook No. 537 (Washington DC: USDA).

3

Aerial Seeding in China

Li Rongao

Précis

China began development of aerial seeding techniques in the 1950s. During the past 30 years, the country has gained considerable experience in using this technique. Aerial seeding has been used in most of the provinces or autonomous regions for afforestation and/or establishment of pastures. In 1985, aerial seeding of grasses and trees covered more than 1.6 million ha in 14 provinces and autonomous regions, a 45% increase compared to 1984. The 30 years of experience have demonstrated that aerial seeding techniques are efficient, economical and labour saving. It is an effective means of afforestation in deserts and remote mountainous areas. This paper discusses the use of aerial seeding for grasses and trees in the arid and semi-arid region of China.

Ecological characteristics of the region

In China, arid and semi-arid regions account for one-third of the country's total area. These deserts and grasslands are largely located in the northwest, the northern part of north China, and the western part of the northeast. The main ecological characteristics of the region are as follows:

- *Poor precipitation and extended drought*: In the arid and semi-arid region, the climate is drought prone with very little precipitation. The extent of drought increases from the eastern part of the region, the semi-arid area, as one moves to the west; the Xinjiang Autonomous Region in the far west is the most arid area. The amount of annual precipitation declines from 200–400 mm in eastern Inner Mongolia, to 100–200 mm in the Zhunger Basin of western China. In the Talimu Basin of the Xinjiang Autonomous Region, precipitation is as low as 50 mm/yr. In the region, most rainfall occurs during late summer to early autumn. Thus, the rainy season is accompanied by high temperatures; the annual rate of evaporation is five times greater than the annual precipitation in the eastern part, and ten times greater in the west.

• *Extended photophase and temperature*: Because the region is in a temperate zone, clear skies are common. The region has an average annual photophase of more than 3,000 hours. Temperature is very low during winter, but high in summer. The average temperature of the warmest month (July) is often above 20°C. Temperature varies dramatically between day and night, conditions that favour plant growth and development.

• *Strong winds and wind erosion*: During winter and spring, strong windstorms frequently occur in the region. Windy weather often lasts for more than 100 days/yr. Under these conditions, combined with low annual precipitation and dramatically changing temperatures, the surface substrates become severely eroded and weather-worn. Erosion and sand accumulation by wind are substantial, resulting in rough ground surface and wide distribution of gobis, deserts, and sandy land.

• *Serious salinization of soil*: As a result of poor precipitation and lack of deep flushing and washing, soils of the region have a high content of various salts. In some areas with high groundwater levels, minerals accumulate in the upper surface of the ground through capillary action, leading to salinization of the soil. Salinization is fairly common in uncultivated deserts and grassland areas.

• *Xerophytic (drought tolerant) plants with sparse distribution*: Drought and poor precipitation have led to a natural selection of those plants xerophytically adapted in morphology and physiology. These plants predominate in desert and grassland areas; they are usually short, and their distribution grows sparser the farther one moves toward the hyper-arid areas.

Main aerial seeding techniques

China is a vast country with complex geography, varied climates, and a large variety of plant species. Since every plant species has its specific environmental requirements, aerial seeding techniques for plants must be adapted to local environmental conditions.

Influence of topographical features
There are many deserts in the arid and semi-arid region. The density, height and slope of sand dunes directly affect the results of

aerial seeding operations.

There are two types of unstable sand dunes in the Mao-Wu-Su Desert. The first type includes densely positioned dunes with a density index of 0.75 to 0.82. Basin areas between dunes are limited, and underground water is very deep. The second type of unstable sand dune includes barchans sparsely distributed with a density index of 0.5. Areas between barchans are large and underground water shallow.

Aerial seeding of *Hedysarum mongolicum* on the first type of desert resulted in an area survival rate of 9.4 to 25.7%, five years after seeding. The sand dunes were semi-fixed or fixed. In comparison, the barchan, or second type of desert, has a larger portion of areas with high moisture content in the soil. It is suitable for afforestation, since plants grow rapidly to form relatively large groups of seedlings. Aerial seeding on this type of desert often produced better results than on the densely distributed dunes. The five-year area survival rate of *H. mongolicum* over the barchans was 76.3 to 83.1%, and the barchans appeared to be fixed. After a windy season in the following year, an area survival rate of 64.9% was still maintained. These results indicate that the success of aerial seeding is very dependent on the topography of the seeding area – the more dense the distribution of sand dunes, the lower the survival rate.

Along the peripheries of Teng-Ge-Li Desert, there is a type of sand dune characterized by low height, flat topography and many depressed areas. Wind erosion and accumulation of sand are not very severe. Plants growing on the dunes serve as a barrier, preventing dispersion of seeds sown from the air, and thereby promoting plant growth.

In contrast, another type of dune in the same area includes barchans positioned in parallel chains. This type of barchan is characterized by greater height (usually 7 to 10 m high), a 15 to 20° slope on the side facing the wind, and lack of obviously depressed areas between barchans. Wind erosion and accumulation of sand are severe, and naturally developed vegetation is scarce. Results of aerial seeding experiments over these barchans showed that the survival rate was eighteen times lower than that of seeds planted on the flat type of dunes. Thus, the flat type of sand dune provides better conditions for aerial seeding.

Selection of appropriate plant species

Plant species used for aerial seeding in arid and semi-arid regions should be well adapted to the environment of the region. They should be native plants tolerant of drought, wind erosion and coverage by sand, and with high natural productivity. If the plants are to be sown as pasture grass, they should also be nutritious and palatable to domestic animals. Moreover, the plants should have large quantities of vegetative biomass above ground. Naturally, the plant species used will vary from location to location.

In 1978, five plant species – *Hedysarus fruticosum, Artemisia sphaerocephala, Melilotus albus, Astragalus adsurgens*, and *Caragana korshinskii* – were sown from the air in a comparative study conducted in Inner Mongolia. The results showed that the area survival rates of *H. fruticosum* and *A. sphaerocephala* were 46 and 46.8%, respectively, higher than that of other species. More than 72% of the *H. fruticosum* seedlings appeared on unstable sand dunes. The height of these seedlings averaged 16 cm, and the main roots extended to 50 cm. The area survival rate of the plant in the fifth year was 30%, of which 31.2% were found on unstable sand dunes. The survival rate of *A. sphaerocephala* in the fifth year was 20%.

In the Xinjiang Autonomous Region, experimental results of aerial seeding on more than 200 ha in 10 counties showed that a pasture grass, *Kochia prostrata*, is most suited for desert and that another grass, *Elymus sibiricus*, is most suited for central mountainous regions. From 1980 to 1983, *K. prostrata* was sown from the air on more than 11,000 ha with a 65% area survival rate. In 1983, *E. sibiricus* was sown from the air on 600 ha with a 60% survival rate. These results illustrate the importance of suitable native plant species for successful aerial seeding.

Timing and the success of aerial seeding
Aerial seeding at the appropriate time can lead to fast seed germination and high rates of seedling emergence. Based on experience, appropriate timing for aerial seeding is determined largely by factors such as precipitation, temperature, and wind.

For example, flights were conducted to sow *H. fruticosum* in Inner Mongolia in mid-June 1980. The seeds were mostly covered with wind-blown sand several times, 10 days after seeding. The seeds were then watered by a rain of more than 50 mm during late June to early July. These events led to an early germination of the seedlings. A survey in mid-July 1980 showed an area survival rate of 66.3% throughout the seeded area. Based on several years of experiments, mid-June has been found to be the best season for aerial seeding in this region. This period is just prior to the rainy season, with favourable conditions of wind direction, wind speed, and precipitation for seed coverage and moisture requirements for germination.

In Yulin District, Shaanxi Province, seeds of *Hedysarum scoparium* and *H. mongolicum* can germinate in two or three days if temperature in the upper sand level exceeds 10°C after coverage of the seeds, and if precipitation of 5 to 10 mm is available. In nature, these prerequisites can be fulfilled even in late April. Experiments have indicated, however, that seedlings would be killed by wind erosion in the windy season of April, although a good germination of seeds may be obtained. It has also been found that seedlings from the seeds sown in early May are subject to insect damage. On the other hand, germination would be reduced if seeds were sown after mid-June, since the lack of wind-borne sand at that time would leave many seeds bare on the ground. Therefore, the most suitable season for aerial seeding in this region is during mid- to late May.

On Tianshan Mountain of the Xinjiang Autonomous Region, aerial seeding of *Elymus sibiricus* over the pastures on central hills of the northern slope can be conducted during early winter, early or late spring, or late autumn. The results have all been satisfactory. In the central hills of the South Mountain of Urumqi, however, the rainy season is during June, July, and August. Synchronization of sufficient rainfall and high temperature secures an average of 62% area survival rate for the seeds sown in mid-May, which is just prior to the rainy season. These examples illustrate that plant species require different seeding patterns based on local conditions.

Mixed seeding of shrubs and herbaceous plants

Mixed seeding not only assists the plants in becoming established in various ecosystems, but also provides a solution to the problem of a deficiency of seed source for aerial seeding. The method can also increase density of seedlings in a given area, thus increasing the plants' resistance to wind erosion.

Results of experiments conducted in Yi-Jin-Huo-Luo Banner of Inner Mongolia in 1978 showed that when three plant species – *H. fruticosum*, *A. sphaerocephala*, and *M. albus* – were seeded together at a rate of 14.5 kg/ha, the area survival rate for the year of seeding and for five years after seeding were 69.2 and 53.7%, respectively. In comparison, the rates for *H. fruticosum* seeded alone were 80.5 and 28.5%, respectively, for the seeding year and five years after. A replication experiment conducted in 1980, in which *H. fruticosum*, *A. sphaerocephala*, and *A. adsurgens* were seeded together versus *H. fruticosum* seeded alone, showed a similar trend in the area survival rate as in the previous experiment. It is thus considered that mixed seeding of more than two species has the double advantages of higher survival rates and a reduced individual seed requirement. This method should be adopted for extension on a larger scale.

Determining the appropriate operational width and flying altitude

The operational width (the width of area to be covered in one pass) of a seeding flight is affected by flying altitude, wind speed, and weight of the seeds. During 1980 to 1982, aerial seeding of *Kochia prostrata* was conducted in the Xinjiang Autonomous Region. The designed flight operation width was 40 to 50 m, while the actual operation width was 37 to 45 m. It led to 23.5% of the seeding area being left without seeds. Since 1982, the designed operation width has been modified to 30 to 35 m, while the actual operation width has been 41.5 m for flight operations covering more than 6,000 ha in 11 seeding areas of the region. An overlapping band between two flights increases the density of seeds along the peripheries. It has been repeatedly demonstrated that 30 to 35 m is the most reasonable operation width in this region.

Flying altitude is positively correlated with operation width. Generally, operation width increases as the flight altitude increases. Higher flying altitudes, however, will increase the time needed for seeds to fall to the ground, thereby subjecting them to greater dispersion by the wind. This causes the seeds to disperse beyond the expected seeding range, resulting in blank lines in the seeding area and the need for repeated operations. Results of several years of experiments suggest that the best flying altitude is 40 to 50 m.

In addition to implementation of correct operation width and flying altitude, maintenance of the seeded area is crucial to the long-term effectiveness of aerial seeding.

Costs and benefits of aerial seeding in China

The main costs of aerial seeding are for seeds and planes. Seeding 1 ha of *H. mongolicum* requires 15 kg of seeds, at a total cost of US$20 ($1.3/kg). Plane costs depend on the distance from the airport to seeding sites. In our experience, plane costs average $0.6 to $0.75/ha when the distance from airport to site is 10 to 15 km. In addition, maintenance costs of seeded areas are $5.1/ha. Thus, the total cost of aerial seeding, excluding labour, is $25.7 to $25.9/ha.

In comparison, surface seeding by hand would involve planting, seedling cultivation, seedling transportation, and transplanting at a total cost of $60 to $200/ha, depending on location of the afforestation project. Thus, the cost for aerial seeding is substantially lower than that for surface seeding. Moreover, aerial seeding is 300 times faster than surface seeding. One Y-5 model plane can sow 1,000 ha/day, while on the surface, a person can only plant 3.33 ha/day.

Unstable sand dunes can be semi-fixed or completely fixed several years after aerial seeding. The height of sand dunes can also be reduced to some extent. Along the eastern peripheries of Teng-Ge-Li Desert, the extent of vegetation coverage has increased from 0.2 to 17.2% four years after aerial seeding of *A. sphaerocephala* and *Calliganum mongolicum*. Improvements in vegetation coverage has provided a better habitat for wildlife and general enhancement of the ecosystem.

In Yulin District, Shaanxi Province, 66.5 ha of *H. mongolicum* and *H. scoparium* fruited three to five years after aerial seeding. Based on an estimated coverage rate of 7.4%, about 2,000 kg of seeds valued at $2,700 can be harvested. This income far exceeds the original investment in aerial seeding.

Administrators of a pasture in Urumqi of the Xinjiang Autonomous Region invested $6,530 to sow *E. sibiricus* from the air on more than 100 ha. Three years later, 528 tons of hay were harvested, giving an income of $17,600. This, plus the $15,200 from selling seeds, gives a total gross return of $32,800, which is five times the original investment. (Note that labour costs are not included in this example.)

Currently, there are still large areas of uncultivated mountains, wild lands, and deserts suitable for afforestation. Most of them are sparsely populated and located in remote areas without easy access. Therefore, aerial seeding techniques offer great promise for afforestation of these areas.

Sources

Jin Zhaoshou (1984),
  "Air-seeding of *Hedysarum fruticosum var.* and *Hedysarum scoparum* – case study in Yulin Sandy Area, Shaanxi Province", *Journal of Desert Research*, vol.3, no.3.
Li Binsheng *et al.* (1984),
  "Techniques of experiment of air-seeding in the sandy area in Yulin", *Journal of Desert Research*, vol.4, no.2.
Wang Yunzhong *et al.* (1983),
  "Experiment on air-sowing of sand-fixing plants in the Mao-Wu-Su Desert", *Journal of Desert Research*, vol.3, no.1.
Wu Jingzhong (1985),
  "Effect of sand stabilization by air-seedings – experiment on mobile dunes at eastern edge of Tengger Desert, West of Inner Mongolia", *Journal of Desert Research*, vol.5, no.1.

II

Farm Practices

A variety of technologies to increase farm productivity are widely available; others are at various experimental stages. It may seem somewhat paradoxical that improved farming systems, with proven positive results, are so often ignored by the farmers who would benefit most from such techniques. Economic analysis of farmer behaviour often reveals why this can be the case.

Farmers' perception of risk, their time preference, and their selection of time horizons may lead to seemingly "irrational" behaviour. Social customs may create a reluctance to try new crops and technologies. Conflicts often exist, especially in developing countries, between cash cropping and subsistence agriculture. Land tenure and use rights may inhibit the introduction of improved practices. Access to credit markets may be limited or non-existent. Availability of labour, especially during certain seasons, may also be a constraint. Economic assessment of these factors often suggests appropriate forms of public action such as improved extension schemes, field demonstrations, and direct financial incentives.

It is important, nevertheless, to consider new farm

practices within the context of specific situations. What may be appropriate to a capital-rich country or region may be inappropriate elsewhere. Economic analysis of farm practices should be conducted for specific areas and social groups – only then the particular circumstances and obstacles to improvement can be addressed. If there is to be any likelihood of success, the benefits to farmers must be demonstrated before widespread introduction is attempted.

There is a double inducement for public agencies to involve themselves in improvement programs where benefits accrue both on-site and off-site. In many instances, the off-site benefits of new farming techniques are substantial. Public policy should take these into account, and appropriate incentives should be established.

The case studies in this section deal with many of these issues. The Chinese study of peanut production shows how farmers can benefit from a simple plastic mulching technique which increases yields and at the same time conserves water. In Kenya, on-site and off-site benefits have been observed in pilot studies by Kalikander and Holmberg. In the Sudan, food shortages may be alleviated by mechanized farming. The case study by El Mangouri suggests that significant financial and general economic benefits can be obtained from mechanized farming. Finally, Bojö shows how economic analysis can be applied to soil conservation programmes in dryland areas, with a case study of Lesotho. The direct financial benefits to farmers, the off-site benefits, and the role of risk are all addressed.

4
Dryland Management: the Machakos District, Kenya

Prepared by the editors from materials from Flavian Kalikander and D.A. Hoekstra

Précis

This study examines the Machakos District, a dryland region in Kenya, east of Nairobi. As in many other areas in Kenya, the major challenge in the Machakos District is to promote sustainable agricultural activity through soil and water conservation and improved farming practices. Farming in the district is largely for subsistence, with little cash for health requirements, education, clothing, pesticides, and fertilizers. The majority of the farmers face soil erosion problems, usually sheet or gully erosion.

An important programme designed to improve economic conditions is the Machakos Integrated Development Programme. MIDP has sought to boost agricultural production and raise living standards through an integrated approach covering cropping practices, soil and water conservation, forestry and grazing management, and the provision of infrastructure. At the farm level, a promising new method of agroforestry known as alley cropping is being introduced. Alley cropping involves the cultivation of maize and beans among hedgerows of trees. It results in higher yields, a mixture of products including fuelwood, reduced soil erosion, and retention of nutrients. The method also appears to be economically viable, as this study shows.

The management challenge

The Machakos administrative district east of Nairobi (see Figure 4.1) is a semi-arid area with high susceptibility to land degradation. Migration to the area and population growth in recent decades have led to intensive farming of lands that were traditionally used for nomadic pastoralism. The population is now 1.1 million, although carrying capacity for subsistence farming was estimated to be only 530,000 (see Table 4.1).

Environmental and agricultural problems faced by the region are soil erosion and decreasing soil fertility, devegetation, and

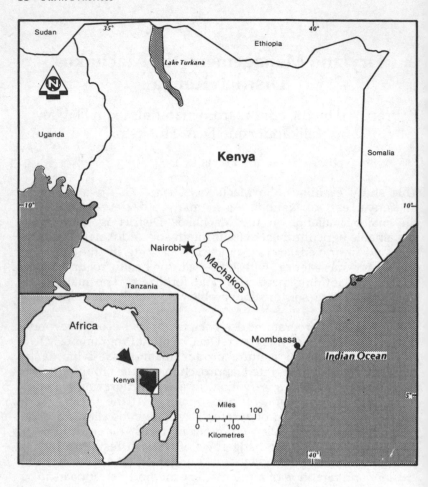

Figure 4.1: Map of Kenya showing Machakos District

Table 4.1: The Machakos District: basic data

Area	14,156 km^2 (of which approx. 10,000 km^2 is under crops and pastoralism)
Population	1.1 million
Rainfall periods	March-May (long rains), November-December (short rains)
Vegetation period	50-85 days/season
Rainfall maximum rates	Up to 110 mm/hr
Altitude	610-2,000 m
Mean temperature	21-23°C
Evaporation	1,600-2,000 mm/yr
Land use	Permanent rainfed agriculture using both rainy seasons; livestock grazing
Cropping systems	Rotation/fallow/intercropping
Soil tillage	Ox plowing with concomitant sowing
Weeding	Hand hoe or ox plow
Manuring	Livestock manure, no mineral fertilizer
Storage	Extensive storage losses
Livestock	Zebu cattle, goats, sheep
Utilization of animals	For milk, meat; for draft power; as crop insurance
Erosion	Severe on steep slopes, despite some terracing and contour plowing
Family size	Average 3 adults, 6 children
Farm size	Average 2 ha arable, 3 ha grazing
Diet	Mainly maize and pulses
Distribution of labour	Women have large role in farm work, fetching wood and water; men frequently take off-farm work
Marketing	Crop surpluses plus cash crops such as cotton, coffee

appreciable risk of crop failure associated with uncertain rainfall. In general, food production from the district has not matched population growth in recent years, and food assistance from the central government is frequently needed.

The management challenge is to promote sustainable agricultural activity – through means such as soil and water conservation and improved land use – and raise the standard of living of local inhabitants and help integrate the district into the rest of the economy.

Physical and socio-economic environment

Physical environment

The Machakos District has a total area of 14,156 km², of which 10,000 km² are under crops and pastoralism. Rainfall is bimodal and irregular. There are two distinct rainy seasons: the so-called long rains from March to May, and the more reliable short rains from November to December. Annual precipitation varies from 50 to 1,250 mm. Torrential downpours are common (up to 110 mm of rain per hour), and these aggravate erosion problems on cultivated slopes. Rainfall also varies with altitude and locality (Figure 4.2). Zone 1 has adequate rainfall and is intensively cultivated for subsistence and cash crops. Zones 2 and 3 are semi-arid and involve subsistence farming and pastoralism. The risk of crop failure in the semi-arid zones is high, with a significant reduction in crop yields. In Zone 2 crop failures occur in three out of ten seasons, and in Zone 3, in six out of ten seasons.

Much of the district's terrain consists of steep slopes. Soils are typically shallow and well drained, and have low organic content and fertility. Vegetation is predominantly of the savanna type, with perennial grasses dominating the more temperate zones. In the higher rainfall and higher altitude areas, the savanna vegetation merges into bushland and moist woodland.

Land use

Machakos is an agricultural district. Total farmland is about 10,000 km², of which 78% is small farms and 22%, large farms. Only 10% of the area, which is under intensive management for crops such as coffee, fruits and vegetables, cereal and beans, has high agricultural potential. The remaining area carries food crops such as maize, sorghum, millet, beans, and pigeon peas. Uncropped land is used as natural pasture for livestock, mainly cattle, sheep, and goats.

The typical farm is about 5 ha, with 2 ha used for cultivation of crops and 3 ha for grazing livestock. Cattle, goats, and sheep are important for meat and milk, as a source of draft power in tillage, and as a form of insurance against crop failure. The average farm supports about three adults and six children.

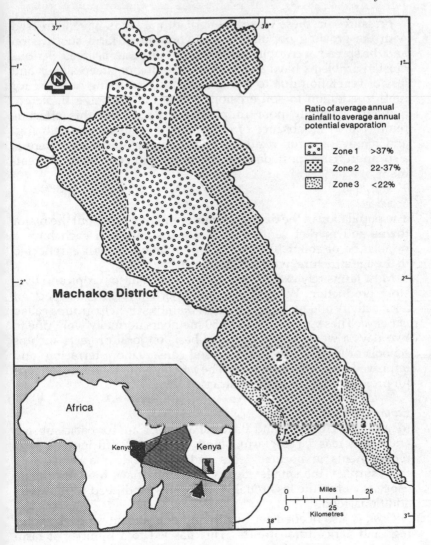

Figure 4.2: Agroclimatic zones of Machakos District

Pressures on these marginal agricultural lands have increased with the growing population and consequent farm subdivision and the spread of cropping onto traditional pastoral areas. Serious erosion problems have arisen from cropping on steep slopes and loss of vegetation due to overgrazing and gathering of wood for fuel. In addition to soil erosion, soil fertility is being depleted. Soils are naturally poor in plant nutrients, and this effect is reinforced by an absence of crop rotation, little or no fertilizing, and removal of crop residues from low-potential soils. There is also appreciable pest damage to crops without chemical treatment.

Social factors

The population in the district is predominantly rural, but the major towns and market centres of Machakos and Athi each have a population of about 10,000. High population growth is reflected in the age structure, with 62% under 20 years old.

Most farms rely exclusively on family labour for crops and livestock production. Women play an important role in all aspects of farm activity and in the traditional Akamba self-help groups called *mwethya*. These groups of 15 to 50 members normally work one to two days a week on a communal basis on local projects such as schools or local services and on soil conservation, terracing, and improved farm infrastructure. The *mwethya* are, therefore, a focus for project initiatives in the district.

Economic factors

Most of the cropping and pastoral activities are for basic subsistence. Whereas larger farms tend to be self-sufficient in food requirements in normal years and are able to market part of their surplus, the smaller farms frequently have food shortfalls, especially after the less reliable long rains, and need to purchase additional food.

Cash is also needed for health and educational services, clothing, and agricultural inputs. This has led to a number of farm workers seeking off-farm work, frequently outside the district, to supplement family income.

Marketing of commercial crops and surplus agricultural produce, mainly maize and beans, takes place through agents who in turn sell to the National Cereals and Produce Board.

Labour is the major constraint in farm production. Each day several hours generally need to be put aside for wood gathering and, particularly in the dry season, for travel to local water sources to provide water for domestic and livestock purposes. There are peak labour requirements during planting, weeding and harvesting times.

The absence of capital and cash limits the opportunity for introduction of new farming technologies and greater use of fertilizers and pesticides. With unreliable rainfall and the risk of crop failure, farmers often use limited cash resources to invest in livestock as a source of insurance rather than undertake risk-prone investment in land improvement. A high priority is thus to improve the reliability of cropping and security of farm income, and thereby relieve environmental pressures caused by overgrazing.

Programmes for economic improvement

General development plans

The main aim of Kenyan policies at the national and regional levels has been to provide the food and energy requirements of the rapidly growing population. Kenya's Fourth National Development Plan (1979 – 83) gives particular importance to the basic principle of widespread participation; the need to alleviate poverty; the objective of reducing inequality; the use of the district as the basic unit for development planning and implementation; the need to improve opportunities and services available to those living in semi-arid lands; and the focus on small farmers as a target for agricultural development and alleviation of poverty.

Kenya's Energy Plan complements the Government's Food Policy (aimed at broad food self-sufficiency) with greater emphasis on private wood production. At present Kenya's demand for fuelwood exceeds the sustainable yield. Deforestation of marginal land is a major contributor to erosion and land degradation.

The Machakos Integrated Development Programme (MIDP) has been formed in the context of Kenya's general plans for national development, and food and energy policies. It has sought to raise agricultural production and living standards through an integrated approach including improvement in reliability and yield of cropping practices; soil and water conservation works; forestry and grazing management; and improvement in infrastructure and social services.

Management objectives

The problems of the semi-arid region of Machakos District are typical of many arid and semi-arid areas in Kenya and elsewhere in Africa. What was previously sustainable livestock grazing land providing a stable lifestyle for local people has been put under stress by migration to the area, local population increases, and accompanying increased food demand. The low and irregular rainfall means that farming is risky. The need for livestock for draft power, food, and insurance against crop failure, accompanied by a reduction of pastoral area due to increased cropping, has put greater stress on pasture and natural vegetation. Risks of degradation lie in the declining fertility of marginal cropping land and the overgrazing of the pastoral areas.

The management challenge is to achieve continuing and sustainable development of these regions as population increases so that they are not classic famine relief cases in times of rainfall deficiencies.

Regional development requires consideration of a number of factors such as improving yields and reliability of crop production, improving the quality of livestock for food and draft power, afforestation or agroforestry for wood fuel energy needs, soil and water conservation, and improving rural water supply as well as marketing, roads, and social services.

Assistance by the public sector is needed to improve the information, marketing, and services available to individual farmers. These include control of soil erosion, reafforestation and provision of infrastructure such as water reservoirs and wells to benefit groups of farmers.

Assessing farmers' needs

An awareness of the constraints and context within which individual farmers seek to optimize their use of farm resources provides a basis for design and analysis of regional projects and for determining research needs. One approach to understanding behaviour and predicting the results of technical changes is the modelling approach (the representative farm model). Another approach is to conduct surveys of farmers, techniques, farm requirements, and the way in which behaviour is affected by local conditions.

An understanding of farmers' behaviour provides a basis for developing projects and programmes tailored to the needs of local populations and particular locations. Smaller scale projects so designed have a better record of success than large-scale projects often designed without reference to local social and environmental factors.

Farming research

Agronomy and livestock research can make a major contribution to raising yields and reducing the risk of crop failure, although this needs to be tested in the field and followed through with appropriate extension services. A critical factor is the need to use limited and variable water resources.

Key areas of research include improved cropping systems; improved crop varieties; dryland tillage practices; protection of crops from pests; agroforestry systems (e.g., alley cropping); pasture improvement; and dry season feed for livestock (e.g., legume evaluation).

In Machakos District, there have been a number of pilot projects and research activities investigating ways of improving farm technology and land use in the region. The next section gives a detailed analysis of the potential benefits from alley cropping.

Alley cropping

In 1983, a diagnostic and design study was carried out by the International Council for Research on Agroforestry (ICRAF) to determine the potential role of agroforestry in the Machakos District. Based on the findings of that study, an alley cropping system was proposed to deal with the problems of soil erosion and loss of soil fertility. Since little or no information was available then on such a system for semi-arid conditions, a simulated ex-ante economic analysis was conducted to determine if there was any scope for an introduction of alley cropping. The analysis given here is a summary of that study and its findings (Hoekstra 1983). As a follow-up to that study, the Drylands Agroforestry Research Project was introduced in 1983 in the Machakos District. Research on alley cropping systems on the research station as well as on farms was initiated under that project. It should be noted that the results of that research have modified some of the assumptions of the original study; however, a definitive analytical report on those results is not yet available.

In traditional systems, beans and maize are grown twice a year, with average yields per season of about 200 kg of beans and 800 kg of maize per hectare. Average yields are not likely to change greatly, as the nutrient content and organic matter in the soil have already reached minimum levels, but there may be considerable variation in yields, depending on rainfall.

Alley cropping involves planting hedgerows of trees (e.g., *Leucaena leucocephala*) spaced approximately 2 m apart. Crops such as beans and maize are grown in between, still twice a year. Land occupied by the trees is unavailable for annual crops. With a 2m spacing for hedgerows, the land area will be divided 50% for trees and 50% for crops. The trees, however, help to conserve moisture and nutrients.

For each of the first three seasons, 100 kg of beans and 400 kg of maize per hectare can be expected. Thereafter, seasonal outputs are assumed to increase to 200 kg of beans and 1,075 kg of maize. Fuelwood is obtained after the third season, when the trees can be lopped. Leaves and twigs are returned to the soil as nutrients, and the timber is used as fuelwood. It is assumed that approximately 900 kg of fuelwood per hectare can be obtained for each seasonal cut. After 10 years, the hedges require replanting.

Table 4.2: Net benefits of traditional beans/maize cultivation (Sh/ha)

Year	Season	Labour costs	Material costs	Total costs	Gross revenue	Net revenue
1	1	698	480	1,178	1,720	541
	2					
2	1					
	2					
3	1					
	2					
4	1					
	2					
5	1					
	2					
6	1					
	2					
7	1					
	2					
8	1					
	2					
9	1					
	2					
10	1					
	2					

Note: Each year has two plantings of a mixed beans/maize system.

Table 4.3: Net benefits of alley cropping system with full response to nutrients (Sh/ha)

Year	crop	Labour costs	Material costs	Total costs	Gross revenue	Net revenue
1	1	807	440	1,247	860	(387)
	2	440	280	720	860	139
2	1	374	240	614	860	245
	2	515	240	755	2,196	1,440
3	1					
	2					
4	1					
	2					
5	1					
	2					
6	1					
	2					
7	1					
	2					
8	1					
	2					
9	1					
	2					
10	1					
	2					

Note: Each year has two crops of a mixed beans/maize system, with fuelwood also produced from the tree component.

Economic analysis of alley cropping

Economic analysis of alley cropping involves a comparison of the "with" situation (where hedgerows are introduced) and the "without" situation (a traditional beans/maize production system). Hoekstra's comparative analysis is presented in Tables 4.2 and 4.3. The analysis assumes a price of 3 Sh/kg for beans, 1.4 Sh/kg for maize and 0.1 Sh/kg for fuelwood. The time horizon is 10 years, with two growing seasons per year.

Alley cropping reduces the amount of land available for beans and maize, but this is compensated for by higher yields and a supply of fuelwood. Seedlings are assumed to be supplied by the government or grown by farmers themselves. Additional labour is required for planting, and the availability of labour may constrain the rate at which the technique can be introduced. Draft power and seed requirements, on the other hand, are reduced and, in the longer term, labour requirements will also be lower. The farmer is thus faced with a trade-off involving higher initial inputs and reduced yields, but longer term reductions in inputs combined with higher yields. Clearly, the farmer's time horizon and rate of time preference are important elements of the decision.

Hoekstra's best estimates of NPV per hectare for the two systems are shown in Table 4.4. Assuming a 12% discount rate, traditional beans/maize agriculture gives a NPV of 6,293 Sh/ha. Alley cropping results in a NPV of 12,859 if the crops respond fully to recycled nutrients, and 10,247 if a lower response is obtained. Bean yields are assumed to be 200 kg/ha with a full response, and 100 kg/ha with a reduced response.

Table 4.4: Estimated present value (Sh) of net benefits per hectare from alternative farming practices (12% discount rate)

	A	B	C
Optimistic assumptions	11,410	14,691	17,855
Best estimate	6,293	10,247	12,859
Pessimistic assumptions	1,176	5,804	7,863

A = Traditional farming
B = Alley cropping
C = Alley cropping with full response to nutrients

Source: Hoekstra (1983)

According to these estimates, alley cropping is clearly superior to traditional agriculture. The superiority of alley cropping is unaffected by changes in key variables. For example, under both optimistic conditions (20% increase in revenue and 20% decrease in costs) and pessimistic conditions (20% decrease in revenue and 20% increase in costs), the NPV for alley cropping is higher than that of traditional agriculture.

Changing the discount rate also does not affect the outcome. Even with discount rates over 30%, alley cropping generates a higher NPV than traditional methods.

Policy implications

The preceding analysis assesses alley cropping mainly from the farmer's viewpoint. A broader approach is needed to assess such land improvement practices from a societal viewpoint. For example, the reduction of soil erosion may result in off-site benefits, by preventing downstream damage to crops and siltation of reservoirs.

It should also be remembered that alley cropping is still in an experimental stage and has to be tested and evaluated under full farm conditions. Alley cropping is not likely to be attractive in areas with higher soil fertility or low erosion rates.

Although alley cropping is apparently superior to traditional agriculture even at high rates of discount, this will have varying significance for individual farmers. Where farmers are able to borrow funds, the institutional rate of discount may be applied, but in the case of subsistence farms, any short-term reduction in output may be unacceptable. The success of the method may well depend on the degree of optimism or pessimism with which farmers view the future, the urgency of food supply, and the perceived risk of crop failure. Government support or special loan facilities may be required to help farmers survive the first three seasons.

Reference

Hoekstra, D.A. (1983),
   "An economic analysis of a simulated alley cropping system for semi-arid conditions, using micro computers", *Agroforestry Systems*, vol.1, pp.335–45 (The Hague: Martinus Nijhoff).

5

An Economic Evaluation of Soil Conservation in Kitui District, Kenya

G. Holmberg

Précis

The use of terraces to conserve soil and moisture is widespread in many parts of Kenya. This study evaluates the economic benefits and costs of farm terracing from the perspective of both the individual farmer and society. Terracing results in large yield increases and also promotes crop diversification. The return to additional labour inputs to terracing is high. A major obstacle to terracing, however, is the initial investment. The use of group labour to construct terraces is one solution to this problem, particularly for poorer farmers.

Background

Since 1974 Kenya's soil conservation efforts have been receiving active support from the Swedish International Development Authority (SIDA). The area covered and the number of technical assistants and soil conservation officers trained have expanded rapidly. Up to 60,000 farms per year now undertake soil conservation measures, and about 365,000 farms have been terraced during the past decade.

Past studies of soil conservation practices had focused on high rainfall, fairly productive areas. Since few studies had been carried out in semi-arid districts, Kalia (a sublocation of Kitui district) was chosen for this study (Figure 5.1).

This study evaluates a soil conservation project in a semi-arid area to understand the constraints that farmers face as well as the expected economic returns of soil conservation. Because of resource limitations, the study uses a random sample of farmers in one location.

The study area
Kalia sublocation is 10 km² in area with gently undulating slopes (2 to 5%). The soil is a complex of well-drained very deep clays of varying colour and consistency.

The annual rainfall in the area is 800 to 1,000 mm, and the average

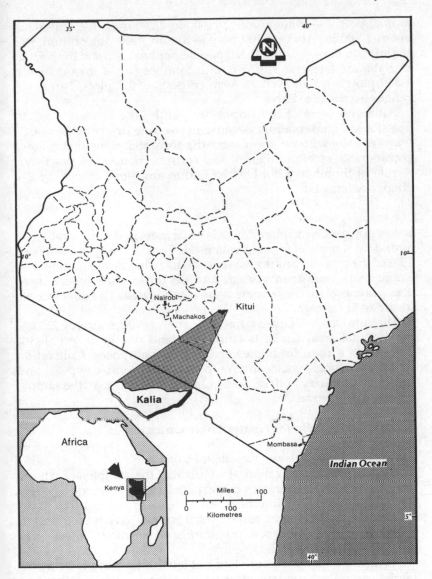

Figure 5.1: Location of Kalia sublocation in Matinyani location, Kitui District

annual potential evaporation is 2,000 to 2,200 mm. The altitude is about 1,100 m. About 3,700 people live in Kalia sublocation; the population density is about 370 people per km^2. Most of the people in Kalia are farmers. The 791 farm families in the area cultivate 1,239 plots, and an average farm consists of 1.5 plots. Farm size ranges from 0.12 to 20 ha.

Although most of the slopes are gentle, the farmers need to practice soil conservation. Because of the long dry periods, which leave the soil without cover, and the torrential rains that follow, considerable erosion occurs if soil conservation is not practised. A rule of thumb in Kitui District is that any slope exceeding 2% should be terraced.

The sample of farmers
It was not possible to interview all the farmers in the sublocation so a random sample of farmers was used. For the study, a sample of 15% of the plots in the area was chosen by using random numbers. These plots were then visited, and on those plots where there was a homestead, the farmers were interviewed. The final sample included 81 farmers.

The interviewed farmers have an average farm size of 2.0 ha. Of the total area, 1.5 ha is cultivated land, 0.4 ha is grassland, and 0.1 ha is used for homestead or other purposes. Cultivation is still traditional – maize intercropped with beans, cowpeas, and pigeon peas during both seasons. Only a few farmers in the sample cultivate in pure stands.

Present pattern of resource use

Status of soil conservation on the sampled farms
The major soil conservation structures in the sample are cut-off drains and *fanya juu* terraces constructed by the farmers. The terraces have developed into benches measuring 0.3 to 1.0 m high, with grass planted on the top edges. Terraces have been found to be effective in retaining soil, moisture, and nutrients as well as in changing the degree of the slope.

As most of the terraces are laid out level, they have to be maintained carefully, especially after heavy rains. As there is always a low point on a level terrace, water concentrates at that point and, when a heavy rain occurs, water flows over the terrace edge. Sometimes the terrace breaks and a heavy waterstream flows down the farm, washing away the topsoil and breaking lower terraces. If the farmer does not maintain the terraces, gullies will soon form.

The cut-off drains in the area are primarily dug to conserve water. The run-off area served by the cut-off drain is usually the homestead, so there is no real need for cut-off drains to divert water from the fields.

Farmers are generally paid for digging cut-off drains on their own farms but in the Kitui District, the Ministry of Agriculture has stopped this practice. The Ministry staff argues that the benefits the farmers receive from the cut-off drains are enough to encourage them to construct the drains themselves. Instead, the staff encourages group work by giving the farmers hand tools for soil conservation work. However, the Ministry of Agriculture pays for cut-off drains on communal land.

Most of the farmers interviewed were aware of the need for soil conservation, and as many as 64 farmers (80% of the sample) have started some kind of soil conservation work; 52 farms are fully terraced (Figure 5.2). But the fact that a farm is fully terraced does not mean the farm is erosion free. On almost half of the terraced farms, one or more terraces are in poor condition. Some of the farmers do not maintain terraces and instead renew them every third or fourth year. Terrace maintenance is especially important, as they are used for grazing after the harvest.

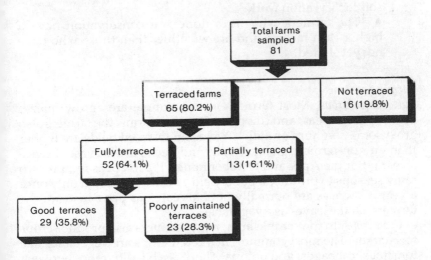

Figure 5.2: Soil conservation on sampled farms

In this study the farmers cultivating terraced farms will be called "soil conservation (SC) farmers", and those cultivating non-terraced farms will be called "non-terraced (NT) farmers".

In Kalia sublocation, almost every cut-off drain serves just one farm, meaning that the farmers must construct the cut-off drains themselves or pay casual labourers for digging them. Most of the farmers in the sample employ casual labour when they do soil conservation work, paying 100 to 3,000 Sh, with an average of 1,100 Sh/farm.

Farmers who did not construct terraces or did an incomplete job said that the main reason was lack of money, lack of a work group, or no perception of a problem.

The following conclusions can be drawn based on interviews with farmers and a general discussion of the situation in Kalia:

- The farmers believe soil conservation work is not possible without employing casual labourers or working in groups.
- Poor farmers who do soil conservation work are more dependent on group work to construct the terraces than are other farmers in the area.
- The farmers who have started terracing their farms are more progressive than those who have not yet started any soil conservation work.
- The farmers who have done soil conservation have a higher cash income and are wealthier than those who have not yet started.

Farming systems

Subsistence crops. Most farmers in the sample area grow maize, beans, pigeon peas, and cowpeas. On a few farms, the farmers also grow some sorghum or millet. Yields on terraced fields are higher than on non-terraced fields. Maize and beans are harvested twice a year (after the April and October rains). Pigeon peas require two rainy seasons to produce a good yield and are harvested only once a year. Cowpeas are normally not harvested as peas; instead, the farmers eat the leaves as a vegetable.

Cash crops. In the sample area, many farmers also produce crops for market. The most common marketed crops are vegetables like tomatoes, cabbages, and onions. There is a big difference between the SC and NT farms; as many as 45% of the SC farmers cultivate some kind of cash crop, while only one of the NT farmers does so.

Fruit trees. Every farmer except one has at least one fruit tree. Most of the farmers have more than one species of fruit tree. The most common fruit trees cultivated are orange, banana, guava, mango, and papaya.

Most of the fruit trees, especially the orange trees, are still very young. Interest among the farmers in orange trees has grown because the expected profit is much higher than from any other tree in the area.

Livestock. Kitui District is traditionally a district with many cattle and goats. The study area is no exception; only five farmers in the sample (6%) have neither cattle nor goats. The average livestock-owning farmer has three cattle, three goats, and several hens.

All farmers in the sample graze their cattle and goats. Usually, terrace edges are grazed during the dry season. Maize stalks and banana residuals are used by all farmers as fodder; one farmer also used branches and leaves from leucaena trees. None of the farmers interviewed bought any kind of fodder.

Use of inputs. There was a slight difference in input use between the two groups of farmers. Generally, SC farmers used more inputs than NT farmers, but use of improved seeds, fertilizers, and chemicals was low throughout the sample.

For example, the use of improved Katumani maize seed was not very common. Only 13 farmers (18%), all of whom had done soil conservation, bought the improved Katumani seed. Only 10 farmers (12%) used fertilizer; the average use rate is less than 40 kg/ha.

All farmers who kept livestock applied the manure to crops, but the total amount available was insufficient to meet all of their needs. Two of the SC farmers who did not have access to animal manure cut the grass on the terrace edges to make compost for manuring their crops. Pesticides were most commonly used on cash crops or fruit trees.

Measured yields

Yields were measured using selected sample areas in the fields. These sampling sites were distributed over the upper, middle, and lower terraces. The sampled areas were marked with pegs and string or by tying string around the maize. The areas were selected during the weeding season, and the farmers were told not to harvest the maize or beans inside the marked areas.

Unfortunately, lack of rain prevented normal harvests during the first two seasons. The third season (October 1984 to February 1985) had excellent rain but, due to a shortage of seed, only limited areas were planted. This experience demonstrated the difficulty in using single-year data as a base in semi-arid areas since wide yield variations are experienced due to rain or seed shortages. As seen in Table 5.1, the October 1983 season was a failure because of lack of rain. Yields were extremely low compared to the good October 1984 season (harvested in February 1985). Although the data are not statistically significant, the terraced areas yielded consistently higher quantities than the non-terraced areas.

Table 5.1: Actual yield from harvested area in Kalia sublocation (kg/ha)

| | SC Farms | | | NT Farms | | |
Crops	Upper Terrace	Middle Terrace	Lower Terrace	Upper Terrace	Middle Terrace	Lower Terrace
Maize						
October 1983	166	177	280	120	97	172
October 1984	1,584	1,527	1,261	548	825	502
Beans						
October 1983	50	50	70	17	19	46
October 1984	214	135	158	176	80	146

As a result of these unusual circumstances, the economic analysis of soil conservation measures used historical yield data to estimate gross revenues from terraced and non-terraced fields. These calculations are discussed in the next section.

Calculation of the financial benefits and costs of soil conservation

In order to calculate the economic benefits of soil conservation, a model of SC and NT farms in the area must be developed. The following information is needed:

   i)   land use in the area;
   ii)   physical soil conservation technique adopted;
   iii) soil conservation crops grown;
   iv)   yields from the different crops in the area; *and*
   v)   number of, and production from, livestock on the average farm.

Information on the first three points was collected through interviews with the farmers. Yield data for the different crops were collected through interviews and by measuring the yields on the fields. Since it was not possible to get information on livestock productivity, these data were estimated.

Yields from different crops
The main constraint to increasing yields of food crops in the area is lack of water. When farmers practise soil conservation, they also conserves the water, which means that yields will increase. Soil conservation also helps conserve topsoil. As explained earlier, yields were measured but, since the rains either failed or were abnormally good, figures from the field measurements are not representative of an average year.

Based on interviews, historical yield data were obtained. These data, combined with measured yields, resulted in the yield estimates presented in Table 5.2. For maize and beans the yield is the same for both crops (the April and October rains), while pigeon peas produce only one harvest per year. Yields for fodder grass are hard to estimate since most farmers graze the grass during the dry season.

Table 5.2: Estimated yields

	NT Farms		SC Farms	
Crops	*kg/ha*	*kg/farm*	*kg/ha*	*kg/farm*
Maize	350	525	542	814
Beans	150	225	285	428
Pigeon Peas	150	225	285	428

The yields from fruit trees are not very high due to unfavourable conditions in the area. There is no difference in yield per tree between SC and NT farmers. Based on the interviews, the following annual yields have been estimated: mangoes, 2 bags/tree; oranges, 1 bag/tree; bananas, 1 bundle/tree; guavas, 1 carton/tree; papayas, 15 kg/tree.

There was no difference between SC and NT farmers in the number of forest trees. Almost every farmer in the area had many trees on his farm, so that in the future they do not need to buy firewood. Wood production would be enough for firewood but not enough to supply the farmer with timber and poles.

Number and production from livestock
The production of livestock products was very low. The farmers keep cattle and goats not for production of milk and meat, but as

a reserve to be used when the crops fail and as a sign of wealth. As a result, they are not overly concerned about the feeding as long as the cattle and goats survive. Using the information farmers provided during the interviews, production is estimated as follows: 3 cows, 1 calf/yr and 1 litre milk/day; 3 goats, 2 kids/yr; and hens, 1 cull hen/yr and 75 eggs/yr.

Farm models used in the calculation
Instead of the SC/NT distinction, three farm models were developed to represent the range of practices found in the sample:

1. A farm without soil conservation practices.
2. A farm with average soil conservation practices.
3. A farm with a superior level of soil conservation practices.

The main benefits and costs associated with the different farm models are listed below. (Not all benefits or costs are relevant to each model.)

Benefits
- Increased yields of traditional food crops due to conservation of topsoil and water.
- Added income from soil conservation crops planted on terrace edges and cut-off drains.
- Prevention of further topsoil loss so that the topsoil will be available for cultivation by future generations.

Costs
- Production costs for the traditional food crops and labour costs for cultivation.
- Costs for maintaining soil conservation structures, largely terrace and cut-off drains.
- Production costs for the added soil conservation crops.
- Increased labour costs for cultivation.
- Average value for annual cost of the soil conservation investment (interest and depreciation).

Total revenues for all three farm models were calculated based on yields, market prices and information provided by the farmers. The results, presented in Figure 5.3, show that farms with a superior level of soil conservation practices yielded a total revenue nearly twice as large as from farms with no soil conservation.
Between models 1 and 2, the largest increases are in the value of subsistence and fruit crops. Between models 2 and 3, the increase

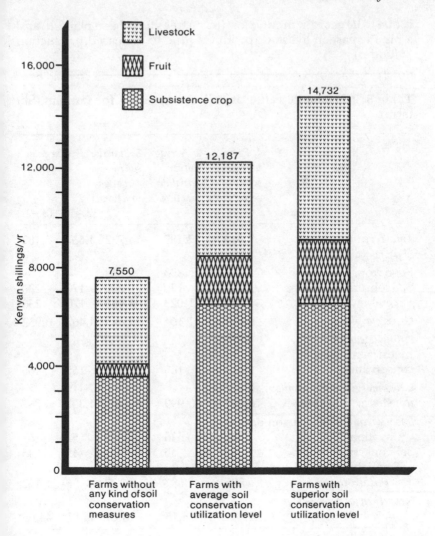

Figure 5.3: Estimated total revenue from the different farm models

is due to larger fruit production (more trees have been planted) and a big increase in livestock products (due to increased production of fodder).

Table 5.3: Economic value of soil conservation for farmers (Sh/ farm)

	1. Farm without soil conservation	2. Average soil conservation practices	3. Superior soil conservation practices	Marginal analysis	
				(2.–1.)	(3.–1.)
Total revenue	7,550	12,187	14,732	4,637	7,182
Variable costs					
Food crops	853	853	853	—	—
Soil conservation crops	—	170	230	170	230
Total variable cost	853	1,023	1,083	170	230
Gross margin	6,697	11,164	13,649	4,467	6,952
Annualized costs					
Investment in soil conservation	—	165	165	165	165
Gross margin minus annualized investment (net return)	6,697	10,999	13,484	4,302	6,787
Labour requirement (person-days)					
Cultivation	585	636	692	51	107
Soil conservation work	—	45	45	45	45
Total labour requirement	585	681	737	96	152
Net return for person-day of labour	11.44	16.15	18.29	44.81*	44.65*

*Net return to the *additional* labour required under models 2 and 3.

Just looking at the increase in revenues is not enough, as the *costs of production* have also increased. First of all, *variable costs* (other than labour) have to be considered. In our analysis, since there is no increase in the use of inputs, variable costs will remain the same for all three models for the subsistence crops. The only increase in variable costs will be for the added soil conservation crops, such as fodder grass and trees. Subtracting variable costs from total revenue yields the gross margin for each of the three models (Table 5.3).

In order to calculate a net return, the fixed costs associated with soil conservation practices must also be taken into account. Most farmers in the area pay for soil conservation work; it is necessary to distribute (annualize) the costs for the investment over the period the investment will last. In this approach, the cost for the investment is defined as the average sum of money spent by the farmers on terraces and cut-off drains. Annual costs are calculated based on an interest rate of 15% and a lifespan of 20 years. Investment costs have averaged 1,100 Sh per farmer in the area; thus, annualized costs are 165 Sh.

Labour requirements for farm activities are based on published statistics and the farmer interviews. For maintenance of soil conservation structures, labour figures given by the farmers have been used as there are no other data available. Table 5.3 presents all of this data in a comparison of the three farm models. While variable costs increase only slightly with greater levels of soil conservation, total revenues increase sharply. Since models 2 and 3 also require increased investment and more labour input, the net return per person-day is a useful measure.

The net return per person-day is around 11 Sh in the zero conservation model; this is close to the payment of casual labour in the area. The net return per person-day rises to 16 Sh in model 2 and 18 Sh in model 3.

The *marginal return* to increased labour input in models 2 and 3 is quite high – about 45 Sh per person-day. (This figure is found by comparing the returns under the average and superior soil conservation practices, columns 2 and 3 in Table 5.3, with the "without soil conservation" returns in column 1.) This is far above the usual level of payment for casual and other unskilled labour in the area. Therefore, it is profitable for farmers who are working partly as casual labourers to concentrate on improving their own farms instead. There is, however, one drawback: the farmers will not receive any payment before the next harvest.

Another problem is that farmers must finance the construction of soil conservation works on their own land. Although the annualized cost is low and rapidly returned, cash and credit constraints may prevent many farmers from undertaking these measures.

Social analysis of soil conservation

As shown above, investments in soil conservation are very

profitable for the individual farmers. A social analysis, however, requires that all the benefits and costs to society also be taken into account.

The benefits and costs for the farmers have already been listed; additional social benefits and costs are listed below:

Benefits
1. *Preservation of topsoil* for future generations. Although not quantifiable at the moment, this is an important social benefit.

Costs
1. *Technical assistance*: The terraces and cut-off drains are normally planned by technical assistants in the area. The technical assistants are also responsible for spreading the soil conservation message to the farmers. On average, two technical assistants have been working with the soil conservation programme in Kalia. Since the project started in 1977, 14 person-years have been invested. One person-year costs 20,000 Sh; technical assistance, therefore, has cost 280,000 for the entire period.
2. *Training*: The project pays for training of the technical assistants, chiefs, subchiefs, and farmers in the area.
3. *Tree seedlings*: Most of the costs for tree seedlings are paid for by the farmers themselves because they purchase seedlings from other farmers. There are social costs, however, for the forest and fodder trees that are given free to farmers.
4. *Fodder grass*: In the beginning, there was a need for bulking up areas; but because there is now an abundance of grass in the area, a farmer can get it free from other farmers.
5. *Hand tools*: The project is supporting some groups by providing them with hand tools.

The total costs for items 2 through 5 during the project period is estimated at 100,000 Sh, plus technical assistance costs of 280,000 Sh for a total of 380,000 Sh.

In addition, the following adjustments are made to crop prices and labour costs:

Maize, which is a traded good (an import substitute), will be valued at the CIF border price. Beans, peas, and the soil conservation crops are not import substitutes and will be valued at local market prices.

In the first calculation, the benefits of soil conservation were measured in terms of net return per person-day. In calculating the social benefits, the prices of labour should be the opportunity cost of labour. If there is no alternative occupation, the opportunity cost of labour would be zero. However, since using a zero cost for labour is unrealistic, the current cost for casual labor has been chosen as the labour cost.

Production

With 65% of the farms now terraced in Kalia, there is an increase of around 45% in the production of food crops. If the nutritive food value of the added soil conservation crops is also considered, the increased production through present soil conservation measures has made it possible to feed about 50% more people in the area than would be the case without any soil conservation measures.

The value of the increased production totals 2,619,000 Sh, a 40% increase over the non-terraced level of output. Subsistence crops account for a large share of this increase. Maize, for example, accounts for more than 700,000 Sh worth of the increase when valued at the import price.

Table 5.4 presents a summary of the social analysis. Gross revenue, appropriately priced, is given for both options – no terracing and a 65 percent level of terracing. There is only a modest increase in production costs due to planting of soil conservation crops.

Of the total investment of 945,000 Sh in soil conservation measures, 565,000 Sh is paid for by the farmers. This is mainly payment for casual labour; about 40,000 person-days have been put into soil conservation works during the project (over a period of seven years). On average, this is equivalent to 16 full-time jobs per year. As there is a shortage of capital available for investments in Kenya, the interest on the invested money has been estimated at 15%. With a 20-year lifespan of the investment, the annualized cost for the investment will be 118,000 Sh.

Subtracting the annualized cost of the soil conservation measures from the net product value leaves a net return of 2,367,000 Sh/yr.

With the soil conservation measures, labour requirements will increase 10%, or 49,000 person-days per year. (This increase comes almost equally from increased cultivation labour needs, 26,000 person-days, and from labour to maintain soil conservation works, 23,000 person-days.) Therefore, a marginal return of more than 48 Sh per increased person-day of effort has been created, considerably larger than the local wage rate for casual labour.

Table 5.4: Economic value of soil conservation in Kalia subloca-tion for society (thousands of Sh/yr)

Item	Zero soil conservation model	Present pattern (65% terraced)	Increase
Gross revenue			
Value of production	6,703	9,322	2,619
Production cost			
Food crops	675	675	—
Soil conservation crops	—	134	134
Total production cost	675	809	134
Gross Margin	6,028	8,513	2,485
Investment			
Public investment			
Technical assistance		280	280
Other costs		100	100
Farmers' investment in soil conservation		565	565
Total investment		945	945
Annualized cost of the investment (15% interest, 20-year life)		118	118
Net return	6,028	8,395	2,367

Summary

The results of the study indicate that soil conservation measures are profitable from the farmers' perspective as well as to society. Production has increased from the construction of terraces and cut-off drains. Increased yields of traditional crops and produc-tion from newly introduced crops have resulted in increases of 40 percent or more in gross revenues.

Employment has also increased markedly. Not only is labour required to construct the soil conservation structures, but additional farm labour is required to maintain structures and produce the increased yields. Each year an additional estimated 49,000 person-days of labour are required, equivalent to 160 full-time jobs. Since the gross revenues generated by the project are as high as 48 Sh/person-day (several times the going wage rate for casual labour), the soil conservation measures are financially rewarding to the farmers.

The total investment cost in soil conservation measures is distributed between the government (technical assistance, some tools) and the farmers (largely their own labour or hired labour). Although returns to investment are high with a rapid pay-back period, credit or labour constraints may prevent some farmers from making the initial investments that are required.

The study also identified several areas for improvement in the programme.

- One problem is the maintenance of terraces and cut-off drains. More emphasis should be put on maintenance in the extension work and in training courses and seminars. Maintenance of soil conservation structures during slack periods should be an important message of the extension service.

- Many farmers find it hard to dig *fanya juu* terraces with available family labour; it is important, therefore, to encourage group work in areas where there is a need of *fanya juu* terraces. The poorest farmers are particularly dependent on group work to carry out soil conservation. Group work could be encouraged by putting more emphasis on group work in extension courses and seminars; by issuing more hand tools to groups; and by training the group leaders in soil conservation and equipping them with soil conservation tools.

- There is a problem feeding livestock during dry periods. Fodder trees and other fodder species should be introduced. Since farmers graze the terraces during the off-seasons, fodder trees have to be protected from grazing.

Reference

Adapted from:

Holmberg, G. (1985),
   An Economical Evaluation of Soil Conservation in Kalia Sub-Location, Kitui District (Nairobi: Ministry of Agriculture and Livestock Development, Soil and Water Conservation Division).

6
Economic Evaluation of Dryland Peanut Growing With Perforated Plastic Mulch

Guangsen Wang and Liming Han

Précis

This paper deals with the economic evaluation of a new technique of peanut growing in rainfed farming areas: flat cultivation of peanuts covered with perforated plastic sheets. Material and labour inputs as well as compensation for environmental losses are taken into consideration. The "replacement cost" approach has been adopted for evaluating environmental effects associated with the new technique and thereby carrying out the comparison of economic benefits derived from cultivation of peanuts with and without plastic mulch. Since all inputs in the two cases are only used for one peanut growing season, no discounting has been done in this study. The main emphasis is on the evaluation of technical and economic benefits; social and political factors are only briefly mentioned.

Peanut growing with perforated plastic mulch

Peanuts are a legume crop with a very strong adaptability to the environment. They are particularly suitable for poor soil in rainfed areas. The growing of peanuts using perforated plastic mulch is a new measure to cope with dryland conditions and make better use of the land resource.

Effects of plastic mulch
The use of plastic mulch has several beneficial effects, including the following:
Raising soil temperature. The temperature of the topsoil is increased by the direct heating of sunlight and the buffering effect of the plastic covering to moisture evaporation. Test results have shown that the utilization rate of solar energy can be raised 20 to 33%, and temperature of the soil can be raised 3° to 6°C. Since raising soil temperature can partially compensate for

low air temperatures, peanut plants can germinate, emerge, and develop earlier and faster, with the result that the growing period of peanuts can be shortened by 5 to 10 days.

Retaining soil moisture and improving soil texture. The increased temperature difference between upper and lower soil layers brings about the movement of soil moisture from the deeper layers to the upper soil layers where it gradually condenses. As soil temperature rises, vapourization of soil moisture is also accelerated. When this vapour reaches the plastic sheet cover, drops of water are formed, which will eventually return to the soil. Thus, loss of soil moisture will be reduced and, in turn, the available soil moisture content is increased. Test results have indicated that soil moisture in the 0- to 30-cm layer is about 2.5% higher during the seedling stage of peanut growth with perforated plastic covering than in uncovered soil, and soil moisture in the 0- to 10-cm horizon is 4.5 to 5% higher.

In addition, the new technique makes soil looser and improves the physical as well as chemical properties of soil tilth. This is because a soil surface that is protected by the plastic sheet avoids being directly splashed by raindrops, thereby reducing soil crusting; also, expansion and contraction movements are accelerated which makes the soil looser.

Accelerating nutrient decomposition and plant absorption. With the raising of soil temperature, increased moisture, and improved texture, soil organisms thrive and aerobic decomposition intensifies. In this way, the decomposition of organic matter in the soil is accelerated, and the availability of nutrients in the soil horizons increases greatly. Experiments have determined that the soluble nitrogen content in the peanut field with perforated plastic covering is 1.438 mg/100 g higher than that in peanut fields without the plastic mulch, and the available phosphorus is 0.605 mg/100 g of soil higher than in untreated fields. At the same time, the absolute uptake of nitrogen, phosphorus, and potassium by peanut plants has increased significantly so that the nutrient conditions of the peanut plants have improved as well.

Promoting plant growth and improving its yields and qualities. Perforated plastic mulch creates a good environment for the growth of peanuts – the seedlings grow vigorously with more differentiation of flower buds. As a result, the number of flowers per peanut plant is greatly increased. The initial, terminal, full-bloom, and mature stages of peanuts are brought forward by 5 to 10 days. Density of nodules on the root system are increased, and the peak period of leaf area index comes earlier with a higher rate of photosynthetic production. Therefore, average peanut weight and the number of peanuts per plant increases, and peanut yield per hectare is increased.

Factors influencing adoption of the technique

Whether a new agricultural technique will be accepted depends mainly on its potential for improving crop yields and quality, as well as its suitability within the agricultural system and its potential for enhancing sustainability and stability. Perforated plastic covering can meet such criteria in the following aspects.

Suitability to dryland farming. The major constraint of agricultural production in dryland areas is rainfall. Although peanuts are relatively drought tolerant, lack of soil moisture is still a major constraint to high yields. By raising and preserving soil moisture in the topsoil, perforated plastic mulch can make fuller use of the scarce water resource in dryland areas to realize relatively high crop yields. Test results have shown that in average years, peanut yields can be increased by 40% with the use of perforated plastic mulch.

Enhancement of soil fertility. Dryland areas are generally poor in soil fertility and lack readily available nutrients, organic matter, and soil moisture. Plastic mulch can increase the nitrogen-fixing ability of peanut plants. Experiments have determined that the average amount of nitrogen fixed by peanuts in the whole growing period with perforated plastic covering is 1975 mg/plant versus 1937 mg without plastic mulch, an increase of 2%.

Increasing returns to growers. Because of natural and economic constraints, income levels in rainfed agricultural areas are generally very low. Peanuts, a high-yielding, oil-bearing crop, compares favourably with rapeseed, which is the major cash crop in rainfed uplands. Tests have shown that with perforated plastic covering, peanut yields can reach as high as 546 jin/mu (2 jin equals 1 kg, 15 mu equals 1 ha; this is equivalent to 4,095 kg/ha). Priced at 0.5 yuan/jin on the market, the production value is 273 yuan/mu, which is equivalent to 500 jin of rapeseed. And yet, it is unusual to harvest even 400 jin/mu of rapeseed. The introduction of high-yielding peanut cultivation techniques is therefore important to the increase of farmers' incomes in the upland areas and their standard of living.

General background of the area and source of data

The technical data quoted in this paper come from the Comprehensive Experimental Area of Qianxian County, Shaanxi Province, China. The Experimental Area is operated jointly by the Northwest Agricultural University and the Science Commission of Qianxian

County. It is located in the northern part of the Guanzhong Plain and is also a part of the Weibei upland. It consists of 11 townships with a total area of 488 km^2 and a population of 128,000. Most of the arable lands are found on terraced surfaces and gully slopes. Forest coverage is very sparse, so water-induced soil erosion is high, with an average amount of 16 to 27 t/ha/yr. Gullies are common and the landform appears to be very broken. The major soil type is yellow loam, which comprises one-third of the total area. The climate is not adequate for double cropping so the general practice is to grow three crops every two years. The major crops are winter wheat, rapeseed, sorghum, and millet. At present, agricultural yields are low but there is a great potential for development.

Historically, rapeseed has been the major oil-bearing and nitrogen-fixing crop in the Weibei upland area. The acreage of rapeseed has been about 40,000 mu, or one-tenth of the total crop area. However, production records show that rapeseed is a high-cost and low-yielding crop compared to peanuts.

Table 6.1: Peanut cultivation by selected peasant households

Head of peasant household	Area (mu)	Soil type	Cultivation measures	Yield per mu (jin)
Chang Zhongxiao	0.3	Yellow loam	Flat cultivation, no plastic covering	548
Pu Junzhang	1.1	Yellow loam	Flat cultivation, no plastic covering	434.8
Pu Wenhui	0.9	Yellow loam	Flat cultivation, no plastic covering	417.2

In order to examine the costs and benefits of growing peanuts, the agronomists in the Experimental Area conducted peanut cultivation tests for the first time in May 1984. Three peasant households were also contracted to carry out the tests of peanut cultivation not covered with perforated plastic sheets. The controlled tests of peanut cultivation with and without perforated plastic covering were conducted in the experimental plots. The year 1984 was normal with rainfall of 598 mm, slightly higher than average. Results obtained from the tests were very encouraging. It was demonstrated that peanuts grow well under rainfed conditions, especially with perforated plastic covering. The peasant households in this area were so encouraged by the test results that in 1985, after just one year, the area sown to peanuts had reached about 1,000 mu. It is anticipated that peanut growing will continue to increase rapidly in the coming years. The test results are summarized in Tables 6.1 and 6.2.

Table 6.2: Controlled experiment of peanut cultivation, Qianxian

Cultivation pattern	Area (mu)	Density (plants/mu)	Soil type	Yield per mu (jin)
Flat cultivation with perforated plastic mulch	0.27	10,000	Yellow loam	546.3
Flat cultivation without perforated plastic mulch	0.27	10,000	Yellow loam	352.3

In this case study, only the two experimental plots are examined. The arrangement of the plots is shown in Figure 6.1.

1. Flat cultivation of peanut without perforated plastic mulch.

2. Flat cultivation of peanut with perforated plastic mulch.

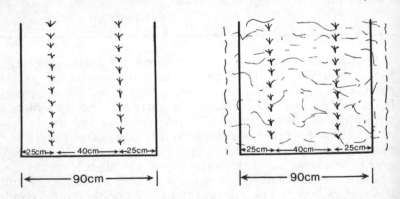

Figure 6.1: Arrangement of experimental plots

Valuation of costs

In this study, flat cultivation of peanuts without plastic mulch is the conventional way of peanut growing, while flat cultivation of peanuts with perforated plastic covering is the new technical measure to be evaluated. The expenses of each of the cultivation methods are examined.

Material and labour expenses
Flat cultivation without plastic mulch. The major expense items for growing peanuts without plastic covering fall mainly in the following five categories: fertilizers, seeds, agricultural chemicals, tractors and draught animals, and human labour.

1. *Fertilizers.* No organic fertilizer was applied; instead, chemical fertilizers were applied once after land preparation at a rate of 10 jin of urea and 20 jin of ammonium primary phosphate per mu. The market prices of urea and ammonium primary phosphate are 0.28 and 0.38 yuan/jin, respectively.

   Total fertilizer expenses
   = (10 × 0.28) + (20 × 0.38)
   = 10.40 yuan/mu

2. *Seeds.* Forty jin of peanuts in the shell per mu is used for seeds; the market price of these peanuts is 0.70 yuan/jin; thus, we have

   Seed expense
   = 40 × 0.70 = 28 yuan/mu

3. *Agricultural chemicals.* Agricultural chemicals were applied four times during the growing season. For the soil treatment prior to sowing, 3 jin of Rogor powder per mu were used with a price of 0.15 yuan/jin, that is, .45 yuan/mu. Rogor spraying was also carried out once in the seedling stage with an estimated expense of 0.29 yuan/mu, and once again in the flowering stage, which cost another 0.29 yuan/mu. During peanut growth, chemicals were used to prevent rats from causing damage to the plants, with an estimated cost of 0.1 yuan/mu. Agricultural chemical expenses are thus calculated as follows:

$(3 \times 0.15) + 0.29 + 0.29 + 0.1$
$= 1.13$ yuan/mu

4. *Tractors and draught animals.* Prior to sowing, deep ploughing was done by tractor which cost 2.5 yuan/mu. Land preparation was done by draught animal with a cost of 3 yuan/mu. Tractor and draught animal expenses, therefore, totaled 5.5 yuan/mu.

5. *Human labour.* Four items were included at a local wage rate of 1.5 yuan/person-day. Sowing: dibbling by hand with one person opening ditches and one person dibbling, 4 person-days/mu. Hoeing: carried out twice at 0.3 person-days/mu or 0.6 person-days required altogether. Harvesting: 4 person-days/mu. Sun drying the peanuts: 2 person-days/mu for picking and sunning. Total labour expenses are then:

$(4 + 0.6 + 4 + 2) \times 1.5$
$= 15.9$ yuan/mu

The material and labour expenses (yuan/mu) for flat cultivation without plastic covering can be summarized as follows:

Fertilizers	10.40
Seeds	28.00
Agricultural chemicals	1.13
Tractors and draught animals	5.50
Human labour	15.90
TOTAL	60.93 yuan/mu

Flat cultivation with plastic mulch. For cultivation with perforated plastic covering, the costs of fertilizers, seeds, agricultural chemicals, and tractors and draught animals remain unchanged. Human labour expenses increase somewhat. A new item is the expense of plastic sheets.

1. *Labour expenses.* Perforating the plastic sheets required 4 person-days/mu, totaling 6 yuan. There is, however, a reduction of 0.6 person-days in the labour expense for hoeing, a savings of 0.9 yuan/mu. Thus, the total labour expense becomes:

15.9 + 6 − 0.9
= 21 yuan/mu

2. *Plastic sheet expense.* In the study, 7.4 jin/mu of white and transparent plastic sheets of 90-cm width and 0.012-mm thickness were used in the experimental plots. The market price of these sheets is 3.16 yuan/jin; thus, we have

Plastic sheet expense
= 7.4 × 3.16
= 23.38 yuan/mu

The material and labour expenses for flat cultivation with plastic mulch can be summarized as follows:

Fertilizers	10.40
Seeds	28.00
Agricultural chemicals	1.13
Tractors and draught animals	5.50
Labour	21.00
Plastic sheets	23.38
TOTAL	89.41 yuan/mu

Valuation of environmental factors
The environmental effects of plastic mulch have three aspects: soil temperature enhancement, moisture preservation and soil fertility improvement. Owing to lack of data, the valuation of environmental factors is made only for soil moisture and nutrients.

Valuation of soil moisture loss. Soil moisture content was kept identical for the two experimental plots before sowing. Field tests determined that the moisture retentive capacity was 15.27% on weight basis and that 1 m^3 of soil weighed 1.24 t. Thus, soil moisture content in the 2-m soil horizon/mu is calculated as follows (note that one mu is equal to 666.67 m^3):

Soil moisture content
= (2 × 666.67 × 1.24) × 15.27/100
= 252.48 t/mu

Annual rainfall was 589 mm in 1984. By converting each millimetre of rainfall into 0.67 tons/mu of water, we have the amount of rainfall water:

589 × 0.67
= 394.63 tons/mu

It was determined that water consumption of peanuts is significantly different for different yield levels. Within the yield range of 500 to 600 jin per mu, water consumption in the production of every 100 jin of peanuts was 48.9 t, while within the yield range of 300 to 400 jin/mu, the water consumption per 100 jin of peanuts was 53.7 t. Thus, the amount of water consumption for the two cases can be calculated as follows:

1. Water consumption for production of peanuts with covering
      = 48.90 × 546.3/100
      = 267.14 t/mu
2. Water consumption for production of peanuts without covering
      = 53.7 × 352.3/100 = 189.19 t/mu

After harvesting, soil moisture in the two experimental plots was determined. The moisture retention capacity of the peanut plot with plastic mulch was found to be 18.31%, while that of the plot without plastic was 16.49%. The moisture content in the 2-m soil horizon is calculated as follows:

1. Test plot with plastic mulch
      = 2 × 666.67 × 1.24 × 18.31/100
      = 302.74 t/mu
2. Test plot without plastic mulch
      = 2 × 666.67 × 1.24 × 16.49/100
      = 272.65 t/mu

The non-productive soil moisture loss in the two cases can be calculated as follows:

1. For test plot with plastic mulch
      = (252.48 + 394.63) − (267.14 + 302.74)
      = 77.2 t/mu
2. For test plot without plastic mulch
      = (252.48 + 394.63) − (189.19 + 272.65)
      = 185.3 t/mu

If the non-productive soil moisture loss in the whole growing period is compensated for with supplementary irrigation, and

the amount of water for one irrigation is 45 t/mu at a cost of
13.5 yuan, moisture replacement in the two cases is as follows:

1. Moisture replacement per mu with plastic mulch
    = 77.2/45 × 13.5 = 23.2 yuan
2. Moisture replacement per mu without plastic mulch
    = 185.3/45 × 13.5 = 55.6 yuan

Valuation of soil nutrient loss. Prior to sowing, soil properties and
readily available nutrient contents in the two plots were kept identical. It was determined that the readily available N content in 0- to
30-cm soil tilth was 35.7 ppm prior to sowing and the available P was
11.8 ppm. Thus, the nutrient content in 0- to 30-cm soil tilth/mu
before sowing is calculated as follows:

>   Available N
>   = 0.3 × 666.67 × 1.24 × 1,000 × 35.7/1,000,000
>   = 8.85 kg/mu
>   Available P
>   = 0.3 × 666.67 × 1.24 × 1,000 × 11.8/1,000,000
>   = 2.93 kg/mu

The amount of chemical fertilizers applied to both the experimental plots before sowing was 10 jin/mu of urea and 20 jin/mu of
ammonium primary phosphate. The N content in urea is 44%. For
ammonium primary phosphate, the content of N is 21% and P is
52%. The amount of chemical fertilizers applied per mu can be
converted into pure N and P as follows:

>   Converted into pure N
>   = (10 × 44/100) + (20 × 21/100) = 8.6 jin = 4.3 kg/mu
>   Converted to pure P
>   = (20 × 52/100) = 10.4 jin = 5.2 kg/mu

Experiments have determined that the actual harvest density
is 7,850 plants/mu in the case of flat cultivation of peanuts
with perforated plastic covering, and the amount of biological
fixation of nitrogen per peanut plant is 1,975 mg on the average.
In the case of flat cultivation of peanuts without perforated plastic
covering, the actual harvest density is only 7,357 plants/mu and
the amount of biological fixation of nitrogen per plant averages
1,937 mg. Thus, the amount of nitrogen fixation per mu in the two
cases is as follows:

1. Nitrogen fixation with plastic mulch
   = (7,850 × 1,975)/1,000,000 = 15.5 kg/mu
2. Nitrogen fixation without plastic mulch
   = (7,357 × 1,937)/1,000,000 = 14.2 kg/mu

It was determined that the yield formation of every 100 jin of peanuts needs 6.8 jin of pure N and 1.3 jin of pure P on the average. Thus, the nutrients required per mu for the yield formation of peanuts in the two cases are calculated as follows:

1. Pure N required in the case of plastic mulch
   = 546.3/100 × 6.8 = 37.15 jin = 18.57 kg
   Pure P required in the case of plastic mulch
   = 546.3/100 × 1.3 = 7.1 jin = 3.55 kg
2. Pure N required in the case without plastic mulch
   = 352.3/100 × 6.8 = 23.96 jin = 11.98 kg
   Pure P required in the case without plastic mulch
   = 352.3/100 × 1.3 = 4.58 jin = 2.29 kg

The amount of remaining nutrients in the two experimental plots is different after peanut harvesting. It has been determined that the readily available N in the plot with plastic covering is 13.95 ppm and the readily available P is 13.79 ppm, while in the plot without plastic covering the figures are 24.95 ppm and 13.93 ppm, respectively. Thus, the residual amounts of pure N and P per mu in 0- to 30-cm soil tilth of the two plots are calculated as follows:

1. Pure N residue in the plot with plastic mulch
   = 0.3 × 666.67 × 1.24 × 1,000 × 13.95/1,000,000
   = 3.46 kg/mu
   Pure P residue in the plot with plastic mulch
   = 0.3 × 666.67 × 1.24 × 1,000 × 13.79/1,000,000
   = 3.42 kg/mu
2. Pure N residue in the plot without plastic mulch
   = 0.3 × 666.67 × 1.24 × 1,000 × 24.94/1,000,000
   = 6.19 kg/mu
   Pure P residue in the plot without plastic mulch
   = 0.3 × 666.67 × 1.24 × 1,000 × 13.93/1,000,000
   = 3.45 kg/mu

The total amount of nutrient loss in the two cases are calculated as follows:

1. Total N loss in soil tilth with plastic mulch
   $= (8.85 + 4.3 + 15.5) - (18.57 + 3.46)$
   $= 6.62\,kg/mu$
   Total P loss in soil tilth with plastic mulch
   $= (2.93 + 5.2) - (3.55 + 3.42)$
   $= 1.16\,kg/mu$
2. Total N loss in soil tilth without plastic mulch
   $= (8.85 + 4.3 + 14.25) - (11.98 + 6.19)$
   $= 9.23\,kg/mu$
   Total P loss in soil tilth without plastic mulch
   $= (2.93 + 5.2) - (2.29 + 3.45)$
   $= 2.39\,kg/mu$

Assuming that the N loss will be compensated by applying urea (with a market price of 0.56 yuan/kg and an N content of 44%), and that the P will be compensated by applying a different fertilizer, super-phosphate (priced at 0.16 yuan/kg with a P content of 12%), we have the following nutrient replacement costs:

1. Replacement costs for nutrient loss in the plot with plastic mulch
   $= (6.62/0.44 \times 0.56) + (1.16/0.12 \times 0.16)$
   $= 9.98\,yuan/mu$
2. Replacement costs for nutrient loss in the plot without plastic mulch
   $= (9.23/0.44 \times 0.56) + (2.39/0.12 \times 0.16)$
   $= 14.93\,yuan/mu$

By summarizing the preceding calculation of production expenses and compensation of environmental factors, we obtain a detailed list of costs for the two cultivation techniques (Table 6.3):

Conclusion

The introduction of perforated plastic mulch into peanut cultivation increased the financial expenditures of the grower by 28.78 yuan/mu, because labour cost increased from 15.90 to 21.00 yuan and a new cost item, plastic sheets, was added. This kind of cost analysis, however, is incomplete and often misleading because the environmental factors of peanut growing as a natural system were not taken into consideration.

After accounting for compensations for soil moisture and nutrient losses as well as the material and labour expenses, it was found that the total cost of peanut growing with plastic mulch is 122.59 yuan/mu, which is less than the total costs of the conventional way of cultivation. The difference is as follows:

131.46 − 122.59
= 8.87 yuan/mu

Since the output of peanut cultivation with plastic mulch has been proved to be much higher than that without, the overall benefit-cost analysis shows even larger net benefits. The differences between the two measures in terms of yields, production value and costs, and net benefit per mu are as follows:

	With plastic mulch	Without plastic mulch	Difference (with − without)
Yield (jin/mu)	546.3	352.3	194
Value of production (yuan/mu)	273.15	176.15	97
Cost of production (yuan/mu)	122.59	131.46	−8.87
Net benefit (yuan/mu)	150.56	44.69	105.87

The net benefit of the use of plastic mulch, including environmental factors, is more than 105 yuan/mu. However, if only direct out-of-pocket costs and the value of output are compared, the financial benefit is reduced to 68.54 yuan/mu. Thus, the correct inclusion of the value of environmental factors has a major effect on increasing net returns of the new technique and thereby increasing the attractiveness of using plastic mulch.

Table 6.3: Total costs (yuan/mu) for peanut growing with and without plastic covering

Item	Without	With
Fertilizers	10.40	10.40
Seeds	28.00	28.00
Agricultural chemicals	1.13	1.13
Tractors and draught animals	5.50	5.50
Labour expense	15.90	21.00
Plastic sheets	—	23.38
Compensation of soil moisture loss	55.60	23.20
Compensation of nutrient loss	14.93	9.98
Total	131.46	122.59

7
Dryland Management in the Kordofan and Darfur Provinces of Sudan

Hassan El Mangouri

Précis

Sudan, the largest country on the African continent, is heavily dependent on agricultural activities. Increasing population and intensive use of its land resources have resulted in widespread land degradation and a decline in agricultural productivity. The provinces of Kordofan and Darfur, comprising a mixture of arid and semi-arid areas, are typical of lands in the Sudan-Sahelian region. Overgrazing, overcropping, deforestation, and shifting agriculture have caused widespread resource degradation and declining food production. During the severe drought of the 1980s, two-thirds of emergency food aid to Sudan went to Kordofan and Darfur provinces. Long-term development of the land and increased productivity are essential to avoid repeated crises. This study examines land improvement options and farm practices. The main programmes addressed are integrated village development, rehabilitation of degraded rangeland, afforestation, and mechanized farming. Detailed financial and benefit-cost analyses are presented for mechanized farming, which offers good economic prospects for the use of these dryland areas.

Background

Sudan, in land area the largest country on the continent of Africa, covers some 2.5 million km^2 and stretches from 4° to 22° N. It has a population of some 23 million (1986) and an annual population growth rate of about 2.2%. It is primarily an agricultural country with 75% of the labour force engaged in cropping, pastoral and forestry activities.

The major crops grown for domestic consumption are sorghum, millet, sesame and sugarcane. Principal export commodities are cotton, peanuts and gum arabic (Sudan is the leading world producer for this product of the dryland *Acacia senegal* tree). In 1982, non-subsistence agricultural production accounted for some 63% of exports and 33% of gross domestic product (GDP).

The agricultural sector is characterized by a marked dualism between high-income irrigated and mechanized rainfed agriculture in the central region, and traditional subsistence cropping and extensive pastoralism in other areas.

The arid and semi-arid areas of the country experience high variations in rainfall typical of the whole Sahelian zone. The drought conditions since 1970 have severely affected food production in Sudan and made it a major focus for famine relief. The western provinces of Darfur and Kordofan have been particularly afflicted by the drought. The provinces cover a dryland area of some 880,000 km² and have a population of about 6 million, most of whom are engaged in subsistence cropping and pastoral activities (see Figure 7.1).

While the drought has been the dominant factor in reducing food production in recent years, its effects have been intensified by human activities. Many of the problems encountered in managing the Darfur-Kordofan region are common to other countries in the Sahel: vulnerable ecosystems, population pressures, rainfall variability, erodible soils, and often conflicting interests of nomadic pastoralists and settled farmers.

Factors affecting economic development

The physical environment
The climatic and vegetational zones that run from east to west throughout the Kordofan-Darfur provinces constitute the basis for the characteristic Sahelian societal patterns. These zones are the desert and semi-desert areas (200 mm annual average rainfall per year), the arid area (200 to 400 mm) with a growing season of one to two months per year, and the semi-arid area (400 to 800 mm) with a growing season of approximately 3 months (see Figure 7.1).

The key agricultural variable is rainfall. Rain predominantly falls in the summer months of June and July although there is considerable variation in annual totals. The temperature in the region ranges from a mean maximum of 39° to 42°C in the hottest months to a mean minimum of 8° to 13°C in the coolest months.

Within the two provinces, there are several agricultural regions. These are the clay plains extending from eastern Sudan into the case study area and which are amenable to mechanized farming and sorghum crops, and the sandy "goz" on the stable dune belt which is the major rainfed cropping zone. The sandy soils are suitable for growing crops although they are excessively well drained and easily eroded. Long fallow periods of 8 to 15 years are needed to restore fertility to exhausted soils. Supplementary water for settlement and agricultural needs is obtained by wells.

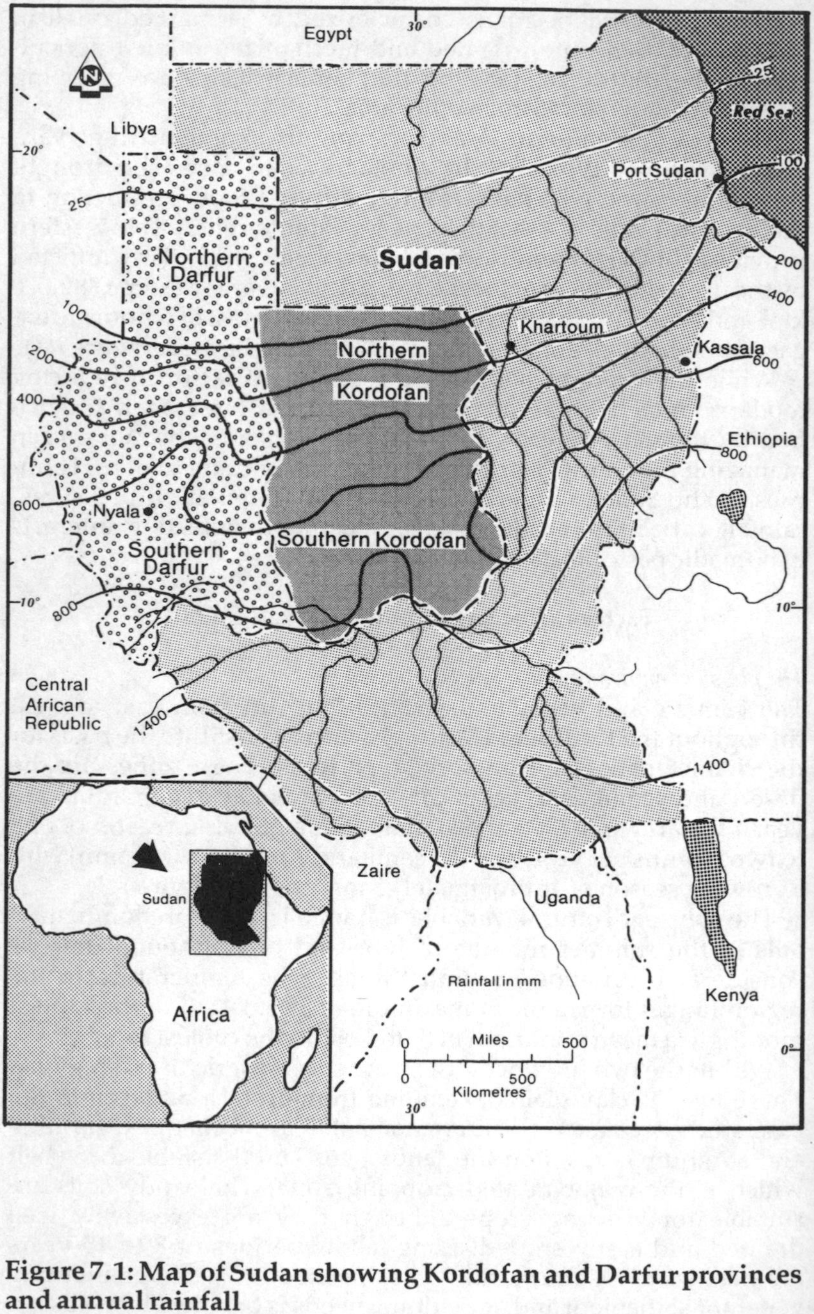

Figure 7.1: Map of Sudan showing Kordofan and Darfur provinces and annual rainfall

Social and economic factors
The Kordofan-Darfur provinces have a relatively low population density of about 7 persons/km². Although 90% of the population is rural-based, the majority reside in settlements with permanent water supplies. Only 5% of the population are nomadic pastoralists with camels or cattle.

Exchange of goods between people is facilitated by a system of weekly markets. The region is poorly served with transport to other parts of Sudan, which limits development and the effective marketing of crops and livestock. Poor communication also limits direct involvement of the Khartoum government in regional development. There is a railway from Khartoum to Nyala, but there are few all-weather roads.

Land tenure systems
In the traditional Sudan savanna economy, neither land nor labour is traded for money. Under the communal land tenure system, grazing land is open to all. Exclusive rights to cultivate accrue to the individual who clears the land and who then has the right of use or allocation to others. When the land is exhausted and left fallow, the rights revert to the community two years after the last cultivation, and the cultivator is allocated rights to new fields. The net effect is a disincentive to resource conservation leading to mining of the soil and environmental destruction.

Dryland degradation
The arid and semi-arid savanna zones of the Kordofan and Darfur provinces face pressure from three main sources: cultivation, pastoral activity, and wood requirements – all exacerbated by a growing population.

Of primary concern is the *extension of cropping areas* well into the marginal lands of low and unreliable rainfall. There is clear evidence of declining productivity in Northern Darfur province as the area under millet production has increased threefold from 1960 to 1975 (Ibrahim 1978). Clearing of the savanna in these areas for cropping exposes the land to increased risk of desertification.

Pastoral activity is an additional concern. Livestock numbers have increased by 100 % between 1970 and 1980. Overgrazing and devegetation of pastoral lands have contributed to serious erosion problems. There has been an increasing tendency towards year-long grazing on land suitable only for seasonal grazing; one example is the excessive use of land by local and nomadic stockholders near newly sunk wells.

Finally, there is the demand for *wood for fuel* and construction purposes, leading to a clearing of the savanna, a destabilization of the soils and subsequent wind erosion. Ibrahim (1978) has estimated the annual consumption of wood per family in the Northern Darfur region to be some 330 trees of middle height per year. One-seventh of this is used for fuel, with the remainder being employed for building huts and enclosures.

In addition, environmental pressures have accelerated the processes of degradation in this region, manifesting themselves in a number of ways:

- *Movement of the desert margin*. On-site and satellite evidence suggests that the desert has moved southward in the past few decades.
- *Encroachment of sand dunes*. In several areas of Northern Kordofan and Northern Darfur, moving sands have claimed consolidated sandy clay soils and some settled areas. This is exacerbated by the removal of ground vegetation, which exposes sandy soil to wind movement and leads to sand accumulation.
- *Decline in agricultural production*. Offsetting the growth in area under cultivation has been a decline in productivity per hectare. This has been associated not just with lower yields of poorly endowed land but also decreasing yields on intramarginal lands, reflecting losses in plant nutrients, losses in topsoil by wind erosion, or in some cases loss of cultivable area.
- *The pressures of overcultivation, overgrazing, and devegetation intensify in times of drought*. Settled farmers and nomadic herdsmen depend on assured water supplies and adequate crop yield and forage. During poor years farmers may become semi-nomads, putting significant pressures on land over which they trek and in which they seek relief.

Development programmes

The desire to control desertification and to put agriculture on a sustainable and structurally sound basis has made the provinces a primary target area for the Government of Sudan Desertification Control and Rehabilitation Programme and programmes sponsored by international agencies. Programmes introduced to assist traditional farmers in Kordofan and Darfur include the following.

Integrated village development

This programme was established to address the phasing out of traditional farming systems in which land is cropped and then abandoned for a fallow period. Successive cropping of land has reduced its ability to revert to natural cover and resist soil erosion.

Two complementary strategies developed by the Government of Sudan include integrated crop farming and ranching on clay soil areas which are not susceptible to wind erosion; and village-level land use plans in sandy soils with rainfall greater than 450 mm.

Rehabilitation of severely degraded rangeland

The deterioration of rangelands results from the increase in livestock population, uncontrolled fires, cultivation of marginal lands and uneven distribution of watering points. In Northern Kordofan and Northern Darfur, programmes are being established to demonstrate the rehabilitation of rangelands through natural regeneration and selective seeding of desirable species.

Restocking of greenbelt for desertification control

The Sahel greenbelt extends across the African continent south of the Sahara between 12° and 15°N. This programme ran from 1981 to 1983 with the main purposes being desertification control and rural development – these to be achieved through the planting of *Acacia senegal* and the subsequent production of gum arabic by the farmers. Project activities included training courses on planting and seeding with follow-up by extension services on the tending of trees and tapping of gum. A total of 26,000 *feddans* was planted with *Acacia senegal* (one *feddan* is equal to 0.42 ha).

Mechanized farming

In recent years, there has been a move toward mechanized farming. Referred to as "mechanized rainfed farming", it is a system of crop production run exclusively for commercial purposes. It contrasts with traditional farming methods. Land is leased from the state by individual investors, and most of the finance for starting operations is provided either by the state or foreign-based funding agencies in the form of commercial loans.

Economic assessment of mechanized farming

Mechanized farming techniques

Mechanized rainfed farming requires the use of modern tractors and machinery. Preparation of the land involves clearance of trees and other vegetation by machines and labour, with simultaneous ploughing and sowing by tractor with disc plough and planters. Hand labour is required during the weeding and harvesting seasons. Farm size is usually 1,000 to 1,500 *feddans* (420 to 630 ha).

Since 1973 the area under mechanized farming has increased threefold. More than 8.5 million *feddans* were being used in 1985. The technique has been introduced primarily on the clay plain that stretches across Sudan from Kassala to the Darfur provinces where soil is difficult to cultivate by hand. The sandy "goz" soil is less suitable for mechanized farming because of wind erosion problems associated with large-scale clearing. About 80% of the area cropped by this technique is under sorghum and 20% under sesame; some cotton is also grown.

Mechanized farming is favoured on the claylands because of the soil and climatic conditions and the low population density of the area. Machinery is much more efficient than hand or oxen cultivation in heavy cracking clays, particularly since rainfall is generally limited to the months of June to September. A relatively large amount of power is needed during a short period following the first rains. The scarcity of perennial sources of water and a relatively low population density in the clayland areas also favour capital-intensive farming methods.

According to the International Labour Organization (ILO), (1976), advantages of mechanized farming, apart from employment of a sparsely settled land that is difficult or even impossible to work without mechanization, are that it makes a valuable contribution to expanded food supplies for domestic consumption and export. It does not demand as many public services as irrigated or traditional farming. It mobilizes private investment and, compared with other modes of agriculture, progresses rapidly.

Various problems, however, do have to be addressed. In some instances mechanized farming has led to the destruction of timber resources, a decline in soil fertility, and increased risk of desertification resulting from overcultivation.

The environmental effects of mechanized farming depend on the operation of individual farms and the attitude to longer term versus shorter term management. To use the method successfully, 25% of each farm area should be kept in fallow, but this is not always done. Measures are generally not taken to leave uncleared strips of land as protective barriers or to plant *Acacia* trees for wood or gum production. This reflects a lack of research and understanding of impacts of large-scale farming. One effect of major disturbances to the ecosystem has been the removal of natural predators such as snakes and cats, and consequent crop damage by rats and birds. The disappearance of insect-eating birds has led to infestation of crops by some pests.

There is some evidence that the productivity of mechanized areas has been declining over time. For example, data on the average yield of sorghum in the Habila mechanized farming scheme in Southern Kordofan indicate that productivity has fallen from 0.341 t/*feddan* in 1973 – 74, to 0.199 t/*feddan* 1983 – 84. Higher yields in crop production have been achieved by increases in the land area under cultivation. This result, however, should not be surprising, as average yields will generally decline as marginal land is brought into production. Variability of output also makes it difficult to establish a definite trend.

Financial and economic analyses of mechanized farming

A *financial analysis* of sorghum production by mechanized farming shows that profits can be made. Calculations for a 1,000-*feddan* farm producing sorghum are presented in Table 7.1. Gross annual returns are LS59,500 (measured in 1985 prices 1 LS = US$ 0.4) and net returns are LS15,014. Average gross returns are LS59.5/*feddan* (US$ 56.6/ha) and average net returns are LS15.0/*feddan* (US$ 14.3/ha). Applying these figures to all 8.5 million *feddans* under mechanized cultivation, a total farm product of approximately LS505 million (US$ 202 million) and a net farm product of LS128 million (US$ 51 million) should be attainable from this form of production.

An *economic analysis* of mechanized farming is presented in Table 7.2. The calculations are based on the financial analysis of a 1,000 *feddan* farm shown in Table 7.1, over a 20-year period, using a discount rate of 10%. Instead of an annualized figure for maintenance and depreciation, the capital costs for land clearing are shown separately in Year 1. The cost of roads is an additional capital cost. Machinery must be replaced every eight years, and thus involves a recurring expenditure. Operating and maintenance costs for production exclude land rent, interest on capital, and depreciation. Marketing costs are the same as in the financial analysis, but local taxes are excluded since these constitute a transfer payment.

Table 7.1: Sorghum production by mechanized agriculture – financial analysis (1,000-*feddan* farm, average yield 1.7 sacks/*feddan*) (1985 prices in Sudanese pounds, LS)

Production costs	
Land rent	1,000
Land clearance	3,500
Seeds	2,500
Plowing and sowing	3,250
Weeding	2,500
Harvesting	3,700
Food for labourers	3,500
Maintenance & depreciation at 10%	2,500
Management	1,500
Interest on capital	2,186
Unforeseen expenditure	500
TOTAL	26,636
Marketing costs	
Sacks and springs	4,675
Finishing and loading	1,700
Transport – field to camp	425
Transport – camp to market	6,800
Local taxes	4,250
TOTAL	17,850
Production plus marketing costs	44,486
Annual net returns	
Gross return (LS35/sack)	59,500
Less total cost	44,486
NET RETURN	15,014

Note: 1 *feddan* = 0.42 ha, LS2.5 = US$1

The present value of net benefits for the 1,000-*feddan* operation is estimated to be LS188,382 (US$ 75,353). The equivalent annualized net economic return is LS22,127 (US$ 8,850).

Interpretation of results
From both public and private perspectives, mechanized farming offers sound investment opportunities, although the venture can

Table 7.2: Sorghum production by mechanized agriculture – economic analysis
(1,000-*feddan* farm; average yield 1.7 sacks/*feddan*) (1985 prices, 10% discount rate)

Year	Land clearing costs	Road costs	Machinery	O&M[1] costs	Marketing	Total costs	Gross revenue	Net benefits	Discount factor	Net present value
1	3,500	25,000	16,000	17,664	13,600	75,764	59,500	-16,264	.909	-14,783
2				17,664	13,600	31,264	59,500	28,236	.826	23,322
3				17,664	13,600	31,264	59,500	28,236	.751	21,205
4				17,664	13,600	31,264	59,500	28,236	.683	19,285
5				17,664	13,600	31,264	59,500	28,236	.620	17,506
6				17,664	13,600	31,264	59,500	28,236	.564	15,925
7				17,664	13,600	31,264	59,500	28,236	.513	14,485
8			16,000	17,664	13,600	47,264	59,500	12,236	.466	5,701
9				17,664	13,600	31,264	59,000	28,236	.424	11,972
10				17,664	13,660	31,264	59,500	28,236	.385	10,870
11				17,664	13,600	31,264	59,500	28,236	.350	9,882
12				17,664	13,600	31,264	59,000	28,236	.318	8,979
13				17,664	13,600	31,264	59,000	28,236	.289	8,160
14				17,664	13,660	31,264	59,000	28,236	.263	7,426
15			16,000	17,664	13,600	47,264	59,500	12,236	.239	2,924
16				17,664	13,600	31,264	59,500	28,236	.217	6,127
17				17,664	13,600	31,264	59,500	28,236	.197	5,562
18				17,664	13,600	31,264	59,500	28,236	.179	5,054
19				17,664	13,600	31,264	59,500	28,236	.163	4,602
20				17,664	13,600	31,264	59,500	28,236	.148	4,178
										188,382

1. O & M costs = operations and maintenance costs

be a high risk due to seasonal variations in rainfall. A significant expansion in such production would be needed to have a major impact on Sudan's food situation. In 1985, for example, Sudan received US$ 300 million in food aid, of which US$ 200 million went to Kordofan and Darfur provinces. The land area under mechanized farming would have to be doubled to produce the equivalent value of food, and almost quadrupled to generate sufficient income to purchase it as imports.

Implicit in the preceding analysis is the need for environmentally sensitive farming techniques such as the use of shelter belts and fallowing to maintain output over time. In practice, this has not always been the case.

Various land conservation techniques are available, including fallowing, planting gum arabic trees on exhausted lands, growing leguminous crops to restore nitrogen levels, and using improved crop varieties and cultivation methods. One problem is that the low annual rent does not encourage land users to consider land as an investment. Improvements in productivity are costly, and it is easier for land operators to move into new areas once existing areas have been heavily farmed.

Even this does not present the whole picture. The analysis could be improved, and its usefulness to policymakers increased by taking a society-wide perspective. This would consider the benefits and costs to society relative to the do-nothing baseline case. Costs would include infrastructure investment (roads, communication), loss of wood supply for fuel and construction, loss of gum arabic production, and costs of forgone agricultural yields, especially those accruing to nomadic and settled farmers who operated the land before mechanized farming.

Benefits may include employment generation, particularly where farming is introduced to marginal lands with otherwise unused labour resources, and environmental protection benefits if sound land conservation measures are simultaneously introduced.

Equity considerations could also be important. Mechanized farming has proved highly profitable for a number of operators, but the unequal distribution of income between traditional and modern agricultural sectors has widened. Adverse equity effects could be offset by facilitating involvement of small farmers in co-operatives running mechanized farms.

References

Ibrahim, F.N. (1978),
    The Problem of Desertification in the Republic of Sudan with Special Reference

to the Northern Darfur Province, University of Bayreuth, Bayreuth, West Germany.

ILO (International Labour Organization), (1976),
Growth, Employment and Equity: A Comprehensive Strategy for Sudan (Geneva: ILO).

8
Benefit-Cost Analysis of the Farm Improvement With Soil Conservation (FISC) Project in Maphutseng, Mohale's Hoek District, Lesotho

Jan Bojö

Précis

This study presents economic and financial analyses, corresponding to macro and micro views of the Farm Improvement with Soil Conservation (FISC) Project in Maphutseng, Lesotho. The economic analysis showed a negative net present value, primarily because of large capital investments and employment of skilled personnel. However, from the farmer's viewpoint, continued use of the inputs introduced by the project would yield very high rates of return, even if purchased at regular market prices. Making the farmers aware of the profitability is the important first step, but high rates of adoption cannot be expected until the farmers' problems of risk and lack of credit are overcome.

Introduction

The FISC Project was initiated in 1981 and first implemented in 1985 by the Swedish International Development Authority (SIDA) to encourage rehabilitation and construction of terraces, waterways, and drainage systems in Mohale's Hoek District in Lesotho. Farmers working on physical conservation structures on their own land are given incentive payments in the form of improved seed and fertilizer, and people working on communal land are given cash payments. The project also encourages controlled grazing schemes, afforestation, and fruit and vegetable cultivation.

The project's first three-year budget is only 2 million maloti (US$1 million), but it is considered to be very significant as the pilot phase of a new nationwide effort to combat erosion. The FISC Project uses simple, labour-intensive technologies and – unlike earlier conservation projects in Lesotho – emphasizes popular participation and training to ensure that practices are continued and structures maintained even when external funding is withdrawn. The project has encouraged the establishment of a Village Conservation Committee (VCC) in Maphutseng, and it is hoped that the VCC will assume a leading role in maintaining conservation works.

The FISC Project is active in several areas of Mohale's Hoek District, but this case study focuses only on the Maphutseng area where implementation first began. It includes both an economic and a financial analysis of the project's costs and benefits. The study is part of on-going monitoring and evaluation of the project, and the database is still too limited for conclusive statements about the project's worth, but some preliminary indications are given and a framework for future specialized data collection is established.

The economic analysis

The aim of the economic analysis is to estimate what surplus (if any) society could be expected to gain over the lifetime of the project's impact. The main criterion is the net present value (NPV).

A time horizon of 20 years and a discount rate of 5% are used in the base case of the analysis.

Table 8.1: Financial project costs (current Maloti)

	1985	1986	1987	1988	1989	1990
Buildings	168,034	1,803	11,000	5,000	0	0
Vehicles	66,591	6,640	50,000	50,000	0	0
Skilled pers.	93,109	138,507	151,250	155,050	134,000	138,000
Semi-sk. pers.	8,195	21,208	75,300	79,000	83,000	87,100
Unsk. pers.	29,583	62,633	57,000	60,000	60,000	50,000
Incentives	21,972	51,492	52,000	57,200	63,900	45,000
Equipment	7,562	25,585	0	32,000	0	0
Nursery	124,048	213,821	179,250	175,050	154,000	158,000
Other	66,332	102,315	56,000	50,000	50,000	30,000
Total	585,426	624,004	631,800	663,300	544,900	508,100

Sources: FISC monthly reports and Swedforest Lesotho Office. Figures for 1985 and 1986 are actual expenditures; the remaining periods show budget estimates.

Quantification of costs
Project costs shown in Table 8.1 were taken from project accounts and complemented by data from Swedforest, the consulting company managing the project, for costs paid by SIDA. To convert

from financial to economic costs, the following adjustments were made:

- Costs related to the fruit and vegetable nursery are eliminated. This component of the project has a very long gestation period, and no significant distribution of seedlings has taken place to date.
- It is assumed that 70% of total project costs in 1985 fell on the Maphutseng area, and that this percentage will decrease as emphasis is shifted to other areas. Corresponding figures for 1986 and 1987 – 90 are 40% and 20%, respectively (FISC Team Leader, personal communication).
- Buildings were depreciated at 3% per year and vehicles at 33.3% per year. This corresponds to rates used by the Central Bank of Lesotho (Mellander 1987). Farm equipment has been written off at 20% per year. This results in a residual value of buildings to be credited to the Maphutseng project in 1991.
- Imported components were adjusted by a factor of 0.80 to account for duty rebates from the Southern African Customs Union.
- Cash payments to unskilled personnel were shadow priced at zero due to lack of alternative employment opportunities. In-kind payments to unskilled labour were costed at their opportunity cost.
- An inflation factor of 18% for 1985-86 and 15% thereafter was used to convert to constant 1986 prices.
- Fertilizer prices were increased by 30% to compensate for government subsidies.

The adjusted economic costs are shown in Table 8.2.

Quantification of benefits
Crop benefits. Random crop samples taken in 1985 – 86 (Bojö *et al*. 1987) showed a relative increase in yield of 81% for maize and 95% for sorghum in "with-project" areas. We assume an initial increase of this magnitude and constant yields thereafter. In the "without-project" scenario, yields are expected to decline at 2% per year due to erosion, poor management, and continuous monocropping. Figure 8.1 illustrates maize yields under these assumptions.

However, it cannot be assumed that the entire difference in yield between the "with-" and "without-project" scenarios was caused by the project. For the base case, we have chosen to attribute only 50% of the use of fertilizer and improved seed to the FISC project. Since it is fairly certain that no physical conservation works would be undertaken without the project's presence, all conservation benefits can be attributed to the project (i.e., prevention of a 2% annual decline in yields).

Table 8.2: Adjusted economic project costs for the Maphutseng area (Maloti)

	1985	*1986*	*1987*	*1988*	*1989*	*1990*
Capital costs	53,487	2,027	12,200	11,000	0	0
Recurrent costs	132,725	125,409	66,910	68,250	66,180	60,020
Less duty	12,698	4,507	4,432	4,448	2,556	1,800
TOTAL	173,514	122,929	74,678	74,802	63,624	58,220
Inflation factor	1.18	1.0	0.87	0.76	0.66	0.57
TOTAL (in constant prices)	204,747	122,929	64,970	56,850	41,992	33,185

Data from extensive field interviews in 1987 show that the total "with-project" area in Maphutseng was 254 ha in 1986 and 244 ha in 1987, and it is assumed to remain the same from 1987 onward. Of the cultivated area, approximately 68% is planted to maize and 32% to sorghum.

Table 8.3 shows how the gross benefits from increased maize yields are calculated. "Q(WO)" represents the expected maize yield without the project, based on average historical yield in the district and a 2% annual decline from the base year 1986. "Q(W)" is the with-project level, average yield (694) times relative increase (1.81) = 1,256. The next column, "dQ," is the difference between the with- and without-project yields.

"Area" is the hectarage under improved maize management. The figures were derived by multiplying the area planted to maize (i.e., 68% of 244 ha, or 166 ha, from 1987 on) by 50%, the assumed degree of project impact. "TdQ" is the total resulting increased yield per year in tons. (The 1985 harvest was not affected by the project.)

The economic value of maize is the import cost saved. This is M380 per ton in 1986 prices (IFAD 1986). However, maize has undergone an average real price decrease of about 2.3% per year for the last 25 years, and a continued downward trend of 2% per year is assumed. Total increased yield was multiplied by the price to arrive at gross annual benefit for maize.

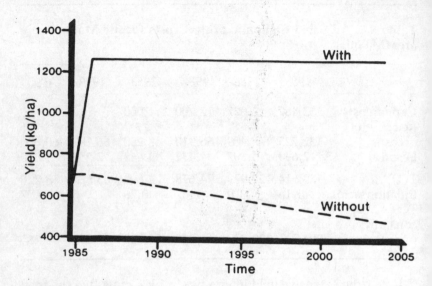

Figure 8.1: Projected maize yield, with and without FISC Project

Similar calculations were done for sorghum, using the average historical yield of 816 kg/ha; a yield increase of 95% in the "with-project" area; and a price of M370/t, which decreases at 2% per year.

Note that increased variable costs still have to be deducted from gross benefits to arrive at net benefits.

Fodder benefits. The area for fodder (Eragrostis) production in 1986 was only 6 ha. However, it is assumed that this area will expand at 3 ha/yr until it reaches a maximum of 24 ha in 1994. The average yield is estimated to be 2 t/ha.

Whereas increased maize and sorghum production in Maphut-seng ultimately replaces imports, increased fodder is only used in the limited local market. Fodder prices have been obtained from the project management: M4.50 per 20-kg bag for Eragrostis. Con-ant real prices will be assumed throughout for this commodity.

Table 8.3: Differential crop yield and gross crop benefits (maize)

Year	Q(WO) (kg/ha)	Q(W) (kg/ha)	dQ (kg/ha)	Area (ha)	TdQ (t)	Price (M/t)	Gross Ben.(M)
1985	694	694	0	0	0	388	0
1986	694	1,256	562	86	48	380	18,366
1987	680	1,256	576	83	48	372	17,800
1988	667	1,256	589	83	49	365	17,856
1989	653	1,256	603	83	50	358	17,895
1990	640	1,256	616	83	51	350	17,917
1991	627	1,256	629	83	52	343	17,923
1992	615	1,256	641	83	53	337	17,915
1993	602	1,256	654	83	54	330	17,894
1994	590	1,256	666	83	55	323	17,859
1995	579	1,256	677	83	56	317	17,813
1996	567	1,256	689	83	57	310	17,755
1997	556	1,256	700	83	58	304	17,686
1998	545	1,256	711	83	59	298	17,607
1999	534	1,256	722	83	60	292	17,519
2000	523	1,256	733	83	61	286	17,423
2001	513	1,256	743	83	62	281	17,318
2002	502	1,256	754	83	63	275	17,206
2003	492	1,256	764	83	63	270	17,086
2004	482	1,256	774	83	64	264	16,960

Note: Slight discrepancies due to rounding.

There is an opportunity cost to the fodder growing, as cropland will then diminish. Since the land used for fodder production is presumably of relatively poor quality, it is estimated to yield only about 75% of the average crop yield for the area (Shone, personal communication). This corresponds to a forgone yield of about 521 kg/ha if maize production is the crop that would have been grown. This opportunity cost is charged against the income from growing fodder.

Afforestation benefits. It is estimated that 4,000 of the 9,000 pine seedlings planted in 1986 will survive to the cutting age of 12 years. At that time they are expected to have an average volume of 0.15 m³ each. The total harvestable volume is therefore 600 m³ (May, personal communication).

It is assumed that locally produced fuelwood will to some extent replace alternative sources of energy such as brushwood, dung and crop residues; there is not much replacement of imported coal and fuelwood in this particular area. The Central Planning and Development Office (CPDO) has recently produced estimates of substitution values for fuelwood based on consumption shares, energy equivalents, and economic costs of substitutes (CPDO 1987). The value of 1 m^3 of fuelwood was calculated to be M28.71, and this price is assumed to remain constant. Thus, the 600 m^3 harvestable in 1998 are valued at M17,400.

Table 8.4: Benefit summary (1986 Maloti)

Year	Maize	Sorghum	Fodder	Fuel	Resid.*	Cons M*	Cons S*	Sum
1985	0	0	0	0	0	0	0	0
1986	18,366	11,757	2,700	0	0	821	483	34,127
1987	17,800	11,190	4,050	0	0	1,537	891	35,469
1988	17,856	11,188	5,400	0	0	2,237	1,297	37,978
1989	17,895	11,177	6,750	0	0	2,894	1,677	40,394
1990	17,917	11,158	8,100	0	0	3,511	2,035	42,720
1991	17,923	11,131	9,450	0	23,006	4,088	2,369	67,968
1992	17,915	11,097	10,800	0	0	4,628	2,682	47,123
1993	17,894	11,056	10,800	0	0	5,132	2,974	47,857
1994	17,859	11,009	10,800	0	0	5,603	3,247	48,519
1995	17,813	10,956	10,800	0	0	6,042	3,501	49,112
1996	17,755	10,897	10,800	0	0	6,450	3,738	49,640
1997	17,686	10,834	10,800	0	0	6,829	3,958	50,106
1998	17,607	10,765	10,800	17,400	0	7,180	4,161	67,914
1999	17,519	10,692	10,800	0	0	7,505	4,350	50,866
2000	17,423	10,614	10,800	0	0	7,805	4,523	51,165
2001	17,318	10,533	10,800	0	0	8,081	4,683	51,415
2002	17,206	10,448	10,800	0	0	8,335	4,830	51,619
2003	17,086	10,360	10,800	0	0	8,566	4,965	51,778
2004	16,960	10,269	10,800	0	0	8,778	5,087	51,895

*Notes: Resid. = residual value of buildings
Cons M = conservation benefits for maize
Cons S = conservation benefits for sorghum

The opportunity cost of lost grazing areas because of afforestation is insignificant in this case. Villagers can cut and carry grass while trees mature, and when the trees are large enough to be safe from livestock, animals will be allowed to graze in the area. The spacing of the trees is very wide to minimize interference with range productivity.

Table 8.4 summarizes all the quantified project benefits.

Other potential benefits. Intangible and unquantified benefits of the project include the following:

- training received by the Extension Agent, Conservation Assistant, lead farmers, and members of village committees involved in project-related activities;
- potential spin-off effects from the introduction of improved communal management for areas not directly involved in the project;
- extension of the useful lifetime of small dams because of less siltation;
- improved income distribution, both among regions and individuals;
- the "option value" of preventing irreversible losses of production capacity for the future;
- potential for irrigation and communal gardens;
- improved water quality (an aesthetic value, but will not significantly affect washing facilities or drinking water);
- secondary community benefits (multiplier effects) of increased income and consumption, which are not included because the bulk of these benefits will probably go to South Africa;
- increased crop residues suitable for animal feed;
- conservation benefits from up-slope tree planting.

Results

Table 8.5 summarizes the quantified costs and benefits and shows the yearly net benefits. Overall, the net present value (NPV) of the project – when a 5% discount rate is applied – is minus M125,000. This corresponds to an internal rate of return (IRR) of approximately 1%.

It appears that the project will become economically more attractive when the expatriate personnel are supplemented by more domestic assistance and the project area increases, "diluting" the high costs of skilled personnel.

Uncertainty and sensitivity analyses

Major assumptions were tested with sensitivity analysis: yield patterns, FISC Project impact, price trends, discount rate and the appropriate time horizon. Resulting changes in the IRR and NPV are as follows.

Table 8.5: Benefit-cost summary (1986 Maloti)

Year	FISC	Inputs	Crop L.	Cost Sum	Ben. Sum	Net Ben.
1985	204,747	0	0	204,747	0	−204,747
1986	122,929	1,920	1,164	126,013	34,127	−91,887
1987	64,970	16,157	1,677	82,804	35,469	−47,336
1988	56,850	16,157	2,147	75,155	37,978	−37,177
1989	41,992	16,157	2,578	60,728	40,394	−20,334
1990	33,185	16,157	2,971	52,314	42,720	−9,593
1991	0	16,157	3,329	19,487	67,968	48,481
1992	0	16,157	3,654	19,811	47,123	27,311
1993	0	16,157	3,509	19,667	47,857	28,190
1994	0	16,157	3,370	19,528	48,519	28,991
1995	0	16,157	3,237	19,394	49,112	29,718
1996	0	16,157	3,109	19,266	49,640	30,374
1997	0	16,157	2,986	19,143	50,106	30,963
1998	0	16,157	2,867	19,025	67,914	48,889
1999	0	16,157	2,754	18,911	50,866	31,954
2000	0	16,157	2,645	18,802	51,165	32,363
2001	0	16,157	2,540	18,697	51,415	32,718
2002	0	16,157	2,439	18,597	51,619	33,022
2003	0	16,157	2,343	18,500	51,778	33,277
2004	0	16,157	2,250	18,408	51,895	33,487

Note: The FISC column shows economically adjusted project costs. The next column shows economic input costs for the farmers, in order to sustain the higher yields. The Crop L. column shows crops lost because of expanded fodder production. The next column is the sum of all the previous columns. The cost sum minus the benefit sum is the undiscounted net benefit (last column).

Yield patterns. In the base case, the assumption was made that yields in the "without-project" situation would decline by 2% per year as a result of continuous erosion. This assumption was tested by assuming a decline of only 0.5% per year and, at the other extreme, a 5% annual decline. The results are shown in Table 8.6. Even at the higher level of yield decline in the "without-project" scenario, the net discounted benefits from the project are less than zero.

Table 8.6: Sensitivity for yield patterns

Decline (%yr)	IRR (%)	NPV (M) at 5% discount
0.5	–3.2	–225,811
2.0	1.2	–124,615
5.0	4.5	–18,454

FISC Project impact. In the base case, it was assumed that 50% of the use of fertilizer and improved seed are a direct result of the project. This assumption is tested using 0% as a minimum and 100% as a maximum (Table 8.7). The project NPV is still less than zero even at the 100% rate.

Table 8.7: Sensitivity for FISC Project impact

Impact factor	IRR (%)	NPV (M) at 5% discount
0%	–4.2	–282,374
50%	1.2	–124,615
100%	3.1	–56,696

Price trends. The assumption that maize and sorghum prices would continue their decline of about 2% per year was changed to (a) constant real prices and (b) a price *increase* of 2% per year. The resulting changes in IRR and NPV are shown in Table 8.8. Note that at a price increase of 2% per year, the project shows a positive NPV.

Table 8.8: Sensitivity for price trends

Price Change (%/yr)	IRR (%)	NPV (M) at 5% discount
–2%	1.2	–124,615
0%	3.6	–53,151
+2%	5.9	36,025

Discount rates. In the base case a discount rate of 5% was used to calculate the NPV of the project. This assumption is changed to (a) 0% and (b) 10%. The results are shown in Table 8.9. Note that at a 0% discount rate the NPV is positive. (Of course, since the project has an IRR of 1%, this result is not surprising.)

Table 8.9: Sensitivity to discount rates

Rate (%)	NPV (M)
0	58,665
5	−124,615
10	−200,858

Time horizon. In the base case, a 20-year time horizon was incorporated into the analysis. It could be argued that the probable lack of maintenance of structures and withdrawn institutional support from the project will result in a shorter time horizon, say, 10 years. On the other hand, it could be argued that successful demonstrations and solid institution building will make the project last for 50 years. The resulting changes in IRR and NPV are shown in Table 8.10. Longer time horizons yield higher IRRs and NPVs since most costs occur in the initial years. If project benefits last for 50 years, the NPV would be positive.

Table 8.10: Sensitivity to time horizon

Time horizon (yrs)	IRR (%)	NPV (M)
10	−16.7	−283,998
20	1.8	−124,615
50	6.1	79,302

Summary of sensitivity analysis. Based on the sensitivity analysis, the discouraging results about the project's economic desirability appear rather robust. To make a strong case against the main thrust of our previous results, one would have to assume fairly unlikely developments.

The financial analysis

The farmer's viewpoint
In order to evaluate the impact of adopting the project's suggestions on the farmer, we must calculate the net return/ha for an
average farmer and discuss the incentives for him/her to join and
continue with the project.

Actual crop yields/ha in Maphutseng for 1986 are taken from
random crop samples (Bojö *et al.* 1987). The correct price to use
in the financial calculation is the price the farmer receives, or the
price he or she would have paid for the crops (replacement cost).
Project management has made the judgement that the local price
is a few Maloti above the official price; we will therefore use the
economic prices (M380/t for maize and M370/t for sorghum) as a
minimum estimate of the financial price.

It is reasonable to assume that some extra labour days will be
needed, and marginal additional costs may be incurred for transport of inputs and crops. On the other hand, stover yield will
increase with the use of the project input package. There is no
empirical data from Maphutseng on these points and they will not
be included here.

Table 8.11 shows the "with-" and "without-project" costs and
benefits of growing 1 ha of maize, from a farmer's perspective.
A net benefit in the "with-project" case of M470 is expected for
maize on an investment of M154, plus labour costs. The farmer
is likely to look at this situation as one of investing an additional
M126 (154 – 28) in costs in order to obtain an additional gross benefit
of M279 (624 – 345). This represents a rate of return of 121%, which
should be attractive enough. For sorghum, the corresponding
financial figures are an increase in gross benefits of M370 for an
additional investment of M105. This represents a 252% rate of
return (less additional unaccounted costs as mentioned above).

However, crop yields for Maphutseng in 1985–86 were ex-
ceptionally high. Normally farmers in Lesotho cannot hope
to receive such yields and rates of return, and their decision to
adopt the programme would probably be based on longer term
expectations of net benefits. A more appropriate calculation for
the farmer's expected marginal net benefit might therefore be:

$$E(NB) = (Y \times dY \times P) - dvC$$

where Y = 13-year average yield in the district
  dY = relative increase in yield obtained in 1986 (%)
  P = market price of crop
  dvC = (absolute) increase in variable input costs.

E(NB)   = Expected marginal net benefit.
For maize, the calculation becomes
    E(NB)   = (694 × 0.81 × 0.38) − 126 = 214 − 126 = 88
For sorghum, the corresponding figures are:
    E(NB)   = (816 × 0.95 × 0.37) − 105 = 287 − 105 = 182

Table 8.11: A farmer's comparison of 1 ha of maize "with" vs. "without" FISC Project (1985/86)

	Without	With
Yield (kg/ha)	909	1,642
Unit price	0.38	0.38
Gross benefit	345	624
Fertilizer cost	0	63
Bags	18	33
Seeds	8	48
Interest foregone	2	10
TOTAL COSTS	28	154
Net benefit	317	470

Sources: Yield figures, Bojö *et al.* (1987); prices, FISC Project management and Co-op Lesotho; interest rate, Central Bank of Lesotho.

The farmer's marginal returns on investments now become 70% (88/126) for maize and 173% (182/105) for sorghum. Assuming that after the initial investment in conservation structures labour requirements are 75 days/ha with or without the project (IFAD 1986), average returns per person-day increase from M4.23 to M6.27, or by 48%. These returns appear convincing enough, but there are a couple of important constraints: risk and credit.

The problem of risk. Crop yields are very unreliable in Lesotho. The farmers are quite aware of this and will (informally) calculate the chances of losing the little money they have available for investment. To calculate the breakeven point, one must also make an assumption about the implicit labour cost, i.e., what the farmer demands in return for effort. Assume that he or she demands M2 per day (as recruitment at M2.5 has not been a problem). With the assumption that the farmer works 75 days/ha, the imputed labour cost is M150. This value is added to the total input costs and compared to the yield that would be needed to have crop revenue (yield × price) just equal to the total of labour and input costs. For maize, this is 800 kg (800 × 0.38 − 150 − 154 = 0); for sorghum it is 759 kg (759 × 0.37 − 150 − 131 = 0).

Available data show that maize yields have been less than the breakeven amount in 7 of the last 13 years (54%). The corresponding figure for sorghum is 8 out of 13 years (62%). Thus, in over half of the years, yields would not meet the break-even criterion.

Utilizing the project's input package certainly raises the mean yield above historical levels, but by how much is uncertain. The standard deviation of expected returns is still very large. It is certainly rational for farmers to adopt a cautious approach in the face of these risks.

The problem of credit. If the farmer could rely on a perfect credit market, risks might be taken care of. Good years could outweigh bad years, and expected average yield within the personal time horizon would be the guiding variable. Real interest rates are low (4 to 5%), but in the Maphutseng area there is no facility that extends credit to smallholder farmers. Apparently the potential demand is too small to be of interest to credit institutions, and there may be a problem with collateral.

Policy implications

The indication that the project is a financially attractive but economically doubtful package of measures suggests that this is a case of "over-subsidization". If farmers could be made aware of the financial benefits for themselves, they should be willing to invest out of self-interest. The main obstacles, however, are risk and credit.

The project may be able to extend assistance in these areas and thereby increase the chances for long-term survival of its ideas. These problems could also be addressed by government assistance through insurance and credit schemes.

Note
The complete study appears as an appendix to *The Economics of Dryland Management*, by Dixon, James and Sherman (London: Earthscan Publications, 1989). This shortened version was abstracted by Regina Gregory.

References

Bojö, J., K. Pettersson, and G. Shone (1987),
  "Crop sampling in the Maphutseng and Brakfontein areas", mimeo, report no. 6 from the SADCC Coordination Unit for Soil and Water Conservation and Land Utilization, Maseru.
Central Planning and Development Office (1987),
  "Fuelwood and poles forestry sub-project: economic analysis", mimeo (Maseru: CPDO).
Farm Improvement with Soil Conservation Project
  Monthly Reports, mimeo (Mohale's Hoek FISC Project).
IFAD (International Fund for Agricultural Development) (1986),
  Appraisal Report: Lesotho Local Initiatives Support Project, report no. 0026-LE, vols 1 and 2.
Mellander, A. (1987),
  "Cost-benefit analysis and soil and water conservation projects, a minor field study" (Stockholm: Stockholm School of Economics).
SIDA (Swedish International Development Authority), (1983),
  "Insatspromemoria (terms of reference)", mimeo, 83 10 11 (Stockholm: SIDA).

List of persons contacted in Lesotho

Ms A. Bratt, FISC Project Horticulturist
Ms A. Dahlberg, Consultant, Social Anthropologist
Mr J. Eklof, Bureau of Statistics
Mr E. Karlsson, Governor of the Central Bank of Lesotho
Mr M. Masilo, Director of Conservation & Forestry
Mr M. May, Forester, Lesotho Woodlot Project
Mr E. Modise, Chief Crops Officer
Mr M. Phakoe, Marketing Manager, Co-op Lesotho
Mr Pomela, Agronomist, Agricultural Research Division
Mr B. Rydgren, Physical Geographer, Institute of Land Use Planning
Mr G. Shone, FISC Team Leader
Ms Takalimane, Price Office, Co-op Lesotho
Mr H. White, Central Planning & Development Office
Mr E. Yaxley, Senior Land Use Planner, Institute of Land Use Planning

III

Rangeland Management

Rangelands are among the most degraded of the world's drylands. About 80% are suffering from serious or moderate degradation with mismanagement of grazing activities a leading cause.

Grazing systems are a potentially renewable resource. If the stocking rate is not too high, a long-term sustained yield of products can be obtained. The correct balance between sustainability and exploitation is determined by both economic and environmental factors.

Range condition is an important element – with appropriate land conservation and grazing management strategies, the sustainable yield can be increased. Conversely, if the resource is abused or allowed to degrade, the yield will correspondingly fall. A goal of long-term sustainability may require short-term flexibility in stocking rates and resource use to respond to environmental conditions.

To establish economically and environmentally sound grazing practices, a full understanding is needed of the biological properties of rangeland systems. Simple steady-state models indicate that the same sustained yield may be obtained with a large or small stock of animals. This has implications for the average costs of production, in that a sustained yield of a given quantity may be accompanied by either high or low cost conditions.

One of the aims of rangeland rehabilitation is to raise the productivity of the resource, so that average costs can be lowered and net returns increased. This is the theme of the study by Wilcox and Thomas (Chapter 9), which deals with grazing management in the Kimberley region of Australia. The underlying theoretical model is explained in an appendix to the Wilcox and Thomas study, as well as in the companion book, *The Economics of Dryland Management*.

Land use rights often affect grazing practices and their effects on land condition. Arntzen presents an interesting case study from Botswana, showing how uncontrolled grazing can adversely affect both range condition and agricultural activity. In some areas, wildlife exacerbates the problem. Botswana is experimenting with systems of communal fencing to regulate cattle movement. Private fencing is also used. The results, assessed in a benefit-cost framework, indicate that agricultural yields and grazing output can achieve significant improvements. The economic assessments required to demonstrate these effects are relatively straightforward.

The ecological dynamics of rangeland systems can be explored through analytical mathematical models of varying complexity. Differential equations and optimal control models are often used by economic theorists for such purposes. For an operational approach to rangeland management, however, computer simulation models are more widely used. One of the important tasks of rangeland managers is to identify the general ecological properties and dynamic behaviour of rangeland systems. Of particular importance is the system's response to stochastic variables such as rainfall.

The risks of alternative management strategies can be

assessed by simulating their effects on the performance of the system. Because of the usual rich diversity of possible outcomes, resource economists must determine how the system can be best managed from an economic viewpoint. The case study by Braat and Opschoor shows how computer simulation techniques can be used to study grazing systems. The setting is Botswana, where grazing is an important dryland activity. Economic variables can easily be incorporated in such models. Methods are also available to handle economic risks and uncertainty, as explained in *The Economics of Dryland Management*.

9
The Fitzroy Valley Regeneration Project in Western Australia

D.G. Wilcox and J.F. Thomas

Précis

This case study examines land degradation in the Fitzroy Valley in Western Australia. The main land use activity is grazing. An explanation is provided of the causes of land degradation. The main technical and institutional mechanisms required to restore range condition and improve land management are described. An economic analysis is conducted of the consequences of degradation and the benefits of rehabilitation. A theoretical model of grazing management is presented in an appendix.

Background

Almost all rangelands in Australia have deteriorated following the introduction of large numbers of European, hard-hoofed domestic animals. Prior to this, pastures were only lightly stocked by fluctuating numbers of soft-footed marsupials.

This case study discusses land degradation in the Fitzroy Valley of the Kimberley region in Western Australia. It describes the extent and nature of land degradation, the technical and institutional mechanisms set up to overcome it, and the economics of degradation and remedial measures.

The Fitzroy Valley lies between south latitudes 17° and 19°, as shown in Figure 9.1. The area has an arid to semi-arid monsoonal climate with almost all rain falling during the summer (December to March). The average annual rainfall in the valley is about 500 mm, and the mean duration of pasture growth is about 15 weeks. Tussocky, perennial grasses under a scattered cover of low trees, characterize the vegetation. Temperatures are high throughout the year, with a mean of 20°C in July and 30°C in November. Additional background information on the region is found in Jennings *et al*. (1979, 1984).

Settlement with cattle (and sheep for a time) began in 1880. The land was rapidly colonized because the permanent waterholes along the river and the productive pastures of the lands marginal

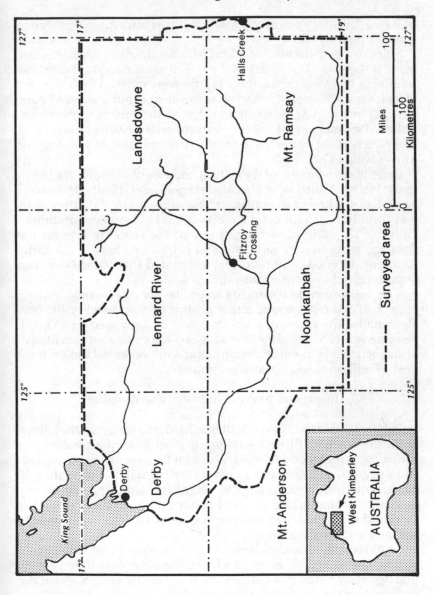

Figure 9.1: West Kimberley survey area, 1972 (showing 1:250,000 map sheets)

to it (the "frontage country") made the area attractive. Settlement was complete by 1887.

Stock were concentrated along the fertile river frontages for most of the year. The effects of the heavy, continuous grazing and trampling by many thousands of cattle were masked for a number of years since the country had some resilience, but a series of poor seasons in the 1920s soon demonstrated the effects of over-use. Bolton (1954) states that "all the pastures on the river frontages had completely disappeared, which was bare and almost nothing but a lot of scalded ground."

Quantitative reports of the nature and extent of the degradation in the Fitzroy Valley were also made (Speck *et al*. 1964). Of the total area of 32,486 km² of river plains ("frontage country"), 22% was in bad condition, 27% in good condition, and 51% in fair condition. Payne *et al*. (1979) have suggested that the stocking rate for the frontage rangeland in bad condition is between zero and 1 cattle unit/km². In good condition, they estimated that these lands can support about 10.5 cattle units/km².

The recommended carrying capacity for the whole project area is 84,500 cattle units, although the present level is 100,000. Potentially, the carrying capacity could be increased to 143,000. Assuming a 12% off-take rate each year, the estimated loss of revenue incurred by not realizing the land's full potential ranges from A$1.89 million to A$2.56 million annually.

The present pastoral industry and its value

All of the land in the Fitzroy Valley is held under terminating lease from the Crown, all leases falling due in 2015. Pastoralism, or ranching, is regarded as a residual use for these semi-arid lands and not a prime use. Leaseholders pay a small rental, not exceeding 30 cents/cattle unit area/yr, for the use of the land and are merely enjoined to place a minimum of water points and fences on the land and to stock it, in return for a guarantee of occupancy until the termination of the lease.

Until recently, leaseholders were not provided with advice that would encourage them to stock the land conservatively or to manage their herds in a sustainable manner. Ignorance about the potential of the land, the great variations in annual production, and the unrealistic expectations of a continuously high and stable productivity have caused degradation of the frontage lands – the most accessible, best watered, and productive lands in the West Kimberley (Western Australia Department of Agriculture 1981).

The perennial grasses on the frontage country have been

replaced by annual species in the degradation process. The frontage land can only be used opportunistically for about three months each year.

The cattle industry in the Fitzroy Valley is primitive (i.e. largely confined to the pursuit and capture of cattle annually and the segregation of saleable cattle from breeding and young stock). At the annual muster all cattle are branded and the males castrated. The annual off-take, about 12% of the total herd, is principally castrated male cattle with a lesser number of old cows.

Present management of the country calls for sale cattle to be grazed on the frontage for a short period to take advantage of the pasture available there. The value of output from the frontage country in its present condition is estimated to be A$296,000 a year. It is assumed that all of the potential male cattle turned off are grazed there for 90 days and that the live-weight gain is 0.5 kg/day. A price of A$1.40/kg is assumed for all carcass meat produced. About 9,500 male cattle would be fattened on the frontage country each year, assuming a 12% turnoff of which two-thirds is male. After land improvement, annual revenue from the frontage land could be increased to A$578,000. A different management strategy, assuming a turnoff rate of 22% and grazing for 12 months of the year, an average carcass weight of 185 kg and a meat price of A$1.23/kg could generate an annual revenue as high as A$784,000. The annual loss of revenue attributable to degradation of the frontage lands thus varies from A$282,000 to A$488,000 depending on the management strategy adopted.

Systems view of the Kimberley pastoral industry
The rehabilitation of eroded frontage country in the Fitzroy Valley forms part of an integrated programme for improving the Kimberley cattle industry (Hacker (ed.) 1982). A model of the production system was developed, including the major environmental influences on cattle production and biological and economic influences on the efficiency of converting forage to saleable product. Feedback loops were identified. The model was then used to generate proposals for productivity improvement. The model, which is illustrated in Figure 9.2, may be briefly summarized under two headings.

Environmental factors affecting forage quantity and quality. The environmental components are rainfall, temperature, solar energy and landform/vegetation characteristics. The short growing season in the Kimberley has a major effect on animal growth since it prolongs the length of time for which low quality, dry forage is the only food source. The high temperatures of the Kimberley, while promoting luxuriant plant growth in the wet season, also produce forage not easily digested with low concentrations of nutrients. The forage is therefore inferior from an animal production point of view.

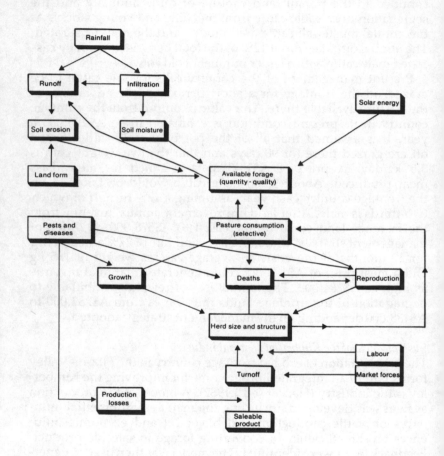

Figure 9.2: A conceptual model of the Kimberley cattle production system

Severe range degradation is largely restricted to the small core area (20% of the total) of high quality land. This area is critical to the overall productivity and economic well-being of the industry.

Efficiency of conversion from forage to saleable product. The main factors considered were selectivity of pasture consumption by animals; animal growth patterns; reproduction; deaths; pests and diseases that affect reproduction, growth, and hides; herd size and structure and its effect on turnoff; labour availability; and cattle handling before and during shipment.

Animal growth patterns are closely related to seasonal pasture availability, with up to 30% weight loss during the dry season. Cattle are generally turned off Kimberley stations as lean, aged animals suitable for manufacturing beef. Death rates of mature animals, particularly cows, are thought to be high due to the poor quality of dry-season pastures and lack of breeding management. Estimates of overall death rates in the Kimberley range from 13 to 20% – the highest of any cattle-producing area in Australia.

Because of the environmental limitations imposed on the basic processes of growth, reproduction and death, the West Kimberley herd contains relatively few breeding cows. Low growth rates, high death rates and poor reproductive performance result in generally low turnoff of cattle. Turnoff percentages have ranged from 8 to 20%.

Erosion treatment programme

Institutional arrangements
Legislative provisions such as the Soil and Land Conservation Act were just one of the factors that facilitated commencement of the erosion treatment programme. Financial assistance was made available by the Commonwealth (federal) government as well as the state (provincial) government.

Commonwealth government support. Following presentation of a report on Land Degradation (Anon 1982), the Commonwealth government of Australia undertook to provide funds to the states to assist with soil conservation and land reclamation programmes. The financial assistance is designed to serve as a catalyst to encourage all sectors of the community to practice soil conservation. These funds, provided under the National Soil Conservation Programme, are for programmes that satisfy a number of criteria including the following:

- land must be used within its capability, and programmes must be based on whole catchment or regional land management concepts;
- all land users and the State Government must meet their soil conservation responsibilities;
- effective co-operation and co-ordination must exist between all sectors of the community involved with the use of the land; *and*

• the whole community should adopt a land conservation ethic.

These requirements indicate that the programmes must have a high level of community support. The Fitzroy Valley programme has achieved such support through the Soil Conservation District and District Committee, which is thus seen to be central to the project.

The funds provided by the Commonwealth government have been used by the Committee to purchase fencing for those areas requiring treatment. Although the funds provided only partially defray the cost of the project, the contribution has been sufficient to convince landholders that the government is prepared to share the cost and responsibilities of land reclamation.

The field programme
The fieldwork of reclamation in the Fitzroy Valley began concurrently with the formation of the Soil Conservation District. It has two distinct aspects: (a) involvement with contractual commitments from pastoralists, and (b) the fieldwork itself, including the research component with guidelines for adoption of procedures.

Contractual obligations. The conditions of Commonwealth support for the project require a commitment from individual landholders that they will contribute to the cost of the operation and will follow the prescriptive practices designed to meet their particular circumstances. These practices usually include the erection and maintenance of suitable fencing and the exclusion of cattle from degraded areas for a specified period. In return, fencing materials are supplied, and the state undertakes to cultivate and reseed the affected areas.

Contractual arrangements were entered into by 8 of the 13 properties in the project during the first two years.

Treatments applied. Because the project initially attempted to transfer techniques from one part of the Kimberley to another, the results were not encouraging. The research programme has attempted to address the nature of the reclamation problem, particularly in relation to soil types, their distribution, and the specific constraints they impose on successful revegetation. A special "ponding" technique was developed to accommodate the unique needs of Fitzroy Valley soils.

A wide range of indigenous and exotic grass, legume and shrub species has been assessed for suitability. Following treatment, several monitoring sites are installed and plant measurements are taken to provide a baseline upon which the rate of recovery may be judged.

Economic evaluation of range regeneration

Approach to evaluation
Changes in the economic welfare of the producers of rangeland commodities from the Kimberley region resulting from the regeneration project have been taken as the measure of relative benefits.

The term "producer" is used in its widest sense. Potentially, it includes not only the individuals and companies who hold pastoral leases, but also station and meatworks employees. Benefits to producers from regeneration are assessed as the net difference between their monetary receipts and the estimated opportunity costs of their participation in rangeland production, with and without regeneration. Here, opportunity cost refers to the potential output forgone in an alternative employment.

The Kimberley pastoral industry produces almost entirely for overseas manufacturing meat markets. The impact of range rehabilitation on Australian consumers of meat is sufficiently small to be ignored. Also, because of the specialized nature of the market, negative effects on meat producers in other Australian regions can be assumed to be negligible.

Modelling the effects of regeneration
The station (ranch) was adopted as an appropriate unit for the analysis. A simulation model was used to assess the effects of regeneration and improved grazing practices. The underlying conceptual model is described in the Appendix to this chapter.

Although rehabilitation is confined to specific land systems, it affects station operations as a whole through its effects on the average cost of production. Ideally the station model should have been applied to each of the 13 stations in the study area to reflect individual differences. However, for the purposes of this paper an average, or representative, station is analysed. Only those changes in station performance that depend on range condition in the treated areas are analysed. As mentioned previously, other components of the overall plan for the industry are not considered here. Basic statistics of the "average station" are given in Table 9.1.

A 20-year period was adopted for the analysis, since this length of time would be needed for completing treatment and subsequent adjustment of herd characteristics. Terminal-year discounted

Table 9.1: Representative station statistics

Gross area	2,498 km²
of which in – good range condition	676 km²
– fair range condition	1,280 km²
– eroded country (for treatment) in bad condition	97 km²
– other country in bad condition	445 km²
Estimated current carrying capacity	6,550 CU*
Estimated current stocking level	7,700 CU
Potential carrying capacity that would result from the integrated programme	11,000 CU
of which – treated country	1,000 CU
– other	10,000 CU
Predicted stocking level assuming correct management of treated country and current stocking level in remaining country	8,700 CU

* A cattle unit (CU) is an adult bullock with a live weight of 400 kg or more. The size of a herd of mixed age and sex is derived as Herd = (CU × 1.18).

values of continued production beyond the 20-year horizon were considered in sensitivity testing. From the simple station model, implications of improved range condition can be drawn for the economic prospects of the industry. Changes in range condition affect financial and economic outcomes by their effects on herd size and structure. Improved range condition leads to larger carrying capacity and higher turnoff ratios which, in turn, lowers the average cost of production. Improvements in animal condition and herd structure are also possible, leading to an improvement in the average price received. The station model has two submodels – a herd submodel and an economic submodel.

Herd submodel. The herd submodel provides a deterministic simulation of herd age-sex structure. Input data are the existing numbers of cattle in each age-sex group, age-sex specific mortality rates, net reproduction rate per mature cow, and rules for extracting turnoff of bullocks and cows. Normally in the Kimberley, bullocks are taken off at age four years, and cows at age eight or nine years. The herd submodel can be used to determine the age-sex distributed turnoff required to maintain a stable stocking rate.

The effect of a change in range condition is to change mortality rates and, by the size of the mature cow population, the overall reproduction rate. Likely changes in mortality rates were assessed based on comparison with those experienced in degraded and in better quality rangeland. It was then assumed that, for improved range condition, herd size should be constrained to the level of safe carrying capacity, and the model was used to generate the increased turnoff necessary to achieve this.

It was recognized that the economic or financial success of the range improvement programme would partly depend on the weather. This prospect opens up much scope for decision analysis using stochastic simulation techniques. However, the West Kimberley climate has been remarkably reliable. Therefore, in this study sensitivity analysis of climatic variation was not undertaken.

Economic submodel. The economic submodel takes projections of herd size and male and female turnoff each year from the herd model, and estimates the implication for station input costs and returns. The submodel is economic, rather than financial, in that such items as taxes, interest, and rents paid are not included as costs, since they are actually transfers of income from the pastoral enterprise. As far as possible the opportunity costs of inputs were entered, as distinct from market prices.

For most inputs, the opportunity costs were valued at market prices (e.g. helicopter hire and freight charges), but an indirect tax component of input costs was deducted. This represents an appropriation of the income of the pastoral enterprise by government. The indirect tax component was assessed as 3% of non-labour input costs. Two inputs for which market prices may not reflect opportunity costs are labour costs and land rental payments.

In the first case, wage rates in the Kimberley pastoral industry would appear to exceed market clearing rates. Many employees of pastoral enterprises have no alternative employment; thus, they receive an economic rent or surplus above the opportunity cost for working in the industry. This rent is as much a benefit to the employees as profit is to the station lessee.

In sensitivity testing, up to 25% of wages were considered as an economic rent to employees (i.e., the opportunity cost of labour was assumed to be 75% of the actual rates). Lease rental payments were treated as a transfer of income out of the industry, rather than as compensation to the landlord (the government) for alternative output forgone. This assumes that since there is no present alternative use for the land resources in question, there would be no opportunity cost associated with land use for pastoralism. Mining, recreation and tourism can proceed conjunctively with pastoral use and are usually focused on small areas. They are not an opportunity forgone by land use for pastoral purposes.

Annual input costs were divided into categories, according to their different relationships to herd size:

- labour (decreasing function of herd size);
- other costs which are a decreasing function of herd size;
- costs which are an increasing function of herd size;
- costs which are in fixed ratio to herd size; *and*
- absolutely fixed costs.

The cost functions, which were based on data in Jennings *et al.* (1979, 1984), with additional estimates, are as follows:

Labour costs $C1 = 8 - 0.0001$ per stock unit (A\$/beast)
Other decreasing costs $C2 = 13.4 - 0.00029$ per stock unit (A\$/beast)
Other increasing costs $C3 = 2.025 + 0.00002$ per stock unit (A\$/beast)
Fixed proportion costs $C4 = 0.5$ per stock unit (A\$/beast)
Fixed costs $C5 = 0.152$ (A\$/beast)

For example, for a herd size of 10,000 cattle, annual labour costs would be A\$7 per beast, or A\$70,000 in total. For 7,000 cattle they would be A\$7.3 per beast, or A\$51,100 in total. The cost functions reflect the theoretical discussion in the Appendix to the extent that increased stocking rates following improvement of range conditions will be associated with falling average cost.

Prices received were taken as A\$307 per four-year-old bullock and A\$150 per eight-year-old cow, which are the normal ages at turnoff in the Kimberley. The market appears to have the capacity to absorb all turnoff from the West Kimberley, and based on market forecasts, the assumption of constant real prices for cattle over the period to be analysed appears reasonable.

It was assumed that regeneration, including restocking, would take place within the normal working programme of each property and would be accomplished within 10 years. These were entered as year-specific cost items.

Land improvements (treatment) included ploughing and re-seeding, fencing, and water point installation. Ploughing was estimated to cost A\$48/ha. Only one-fifth of the land was to be ploughed; thus, the cost of treating the eroded area was A$9.6/ha (A$48/5 = 9.6). Fencing was estimated to cost A$1,000/km, and water points A$30,000 each. Each water point was expected to serve 750 cattle units. Costs for the average station to provide for fencing and water points were developed and entered into the analysis.

It was further assumed that stocking of the treated areas would be achieved at the cost of forgone sales of cows. A figure of A$150 per animal was used.

Results

Results are presented for a "base case" and a "treatment case". Before presenting the results, a summary of the assumptions made about each case is required.

Base case
In the base case, it was assumed that the current stocking rate of 7,700 cattle units in the untreated station would be maintained. The stocking rate is considered to exceed stable carrying capacity at present; but to preserve the link with the current situation, this degree of overstocking was assumed to be not deleterious. To achieve this, the herd model was run with a slightly improved calving rate as compared to best estimates of the current situation.

The assumed sales policy is to turn off cows at nine years of age and steers at four years, which is normal practice in the West Kimberley. Mortality rates were held constant at current levels. These assumptions yield a herd stable in size and generate a turnoff rate of approximately 15% with just under 10% being bullocks. This is somewhat better than the overall average at present, which is 12%. The range of turnoff of individual stations varies from zero to 25% in a given year. The integrated programme for the West Kimberley herd as a whole is aimed at raising the turnoff rate to more than 20% (Hacker (ed.) 1982).

Treatment case
It was assumed that stock will be introduced to the treated front-age areas over a 10-year period, starting in the third year. Mortality rates were assumed to be lower and calving rates higher on the treated frontage country than are experienced on the remainder of the station. Selling policy would be aimed at culling whenever the herd exceeded the carrying capacity of treated country. To achieve this, the herd was divided into two subherds: the "treated

frontage herd" and the "remainder herd". The result would be to increase the station herd from 7,700 cattle units in the base case to 8,700 cattle units by the end of the period, with the additional 1,000 cattle units being equal to the estimated carrying capacity of the treated country. Over the 20-year period, the herd size is predicted to increase from 9,076 to 10,276.

The selling policy for the "remainder herd" is assumed to lead to an equilibrium consistent with carrying capacity. Higher culling rates, in excess of the normal takeoff rates for four-year-old steers and nine-year-old cows, were simulated only for the the "treated frontage herd".

The result was a turnoff rate of some 22.3% for the frontage herd by the twentieth year, which raised the overall station turnoff from 14.9% in the base case to 15.9% in the treatment case in that year. Table 9.2 shows the simulated turnoff of bullocks and cows each year, for the "residual" herd (no land treatment), the "frontage" herd, and the overall station herd.

Table 9.2: Expected average station turnoff of male and female cattle each year with and without erosion treatment

Year	No erosion treatment		Treated frontage country		Total after erosion treatment	
	Male	*Female*	*Male*	*Female*	*Male*	*Female*
1	775	581	0	0	775	581
2	768	534	0	0	768	534
3	835	494	13	12	848	506
4	969	461	31	24	1,000	485
5	1,022	427	47	38	1,069	581
6	962	394	61	50	1,023	444
7	942	367	76	63	1,013	430
8	942	414	91	75	1,033	489
9	942	432	106	88	1,048	520
10	942	407	122	100	1,064	507
11	942	401	137	113	1,079	514
12–20	942	401	152	125	1,094	526

Net benefits of land treatment

Estimates of the net benefit from erosion treatment, for a 7% discount rate, are given in Table 9.3. The table shows that when the regeneration project is analysed over a 20-year period at the 7% discount rate, the net benefits to tax recipients and station lessees are close to zero. The internal rate of return (IRR) from regeneration is 6.4%.

Table 9.3: Summary of present value of net benefits to the average station from erosion treatment at 7% discount rate, evaluated over 20 years of operation of the project (A$ million at 1986 prices)

Item (all discounted over 20 years)	*Without erosion treatment*	*With erosion treatment*	*Difference*
Station revenue	3.68	4.07	0.39
Station operating costs	−2.38	−2.50	−0.12
Gross margin	1.30	1.57	0.27
Erosion treatment and stocking costs	0	−0.28	−0.28
Net margin	1.30	1.29	−0.01

Note: Unrecorded items include:
1. Further 20 years of net output from treated frontage country: discounted value of A$0.12 million.
2. Benefits to station employees (excess of wages over opportunity costs): no value was estimated.
3. Additional incomes in meat processing: no value estimated.
4. Loss of net income from existing limited use of degraded frontage country: discounted value of A$0.07 million (see text).

Although the present value of average station revenue is increased by erosion treatment from A$3.68 million to A$4.07 million, and operating costs increase by rather less – from A$2.38 million to A$2.49 million – the increase in discounted gross margin of A$0.27 million is not quite sufficient to offset the discounted costs of treatment and "purchase" of additional stock. A discount rate less than 6.45 is required to obtain positive net benefits. Such a rate is probably too low for Australia in its present economic condition. It has to be recognized, however, that the real rates of return of long-term investments in agriculture, mining, and manufacturing in Australia have historically been well within the 7% limit indicated for this erosion treatment project.

Further benefits not taken into account here include benefits to pastoral industry employees and to operators and employees of the Broome meatworks.

For station employees, there would be only a small increase in any economic rents from regeneration of the frontage country, because labour inputs tend to be relatively stable over the range of projected herd sizes. If the treatment programme were to employ otherwise unproductive labour, this could make a significant difference to the opportunity cost of the treatment and, in turn, it would increase the social internal rate of return of the project. However, skilled labour is required for the regeneration project and award rates may fully reflect opportunity costs for this group of employees.

These results correspond to the "with treatment" situation. In the "without treatment" situation, revenue would still be earned. If only the net gains of treatment are assessed, the IRR falls to around 3% instead of 6.4% for the 20-year analysis. If a longer term view is adopted, and the net benefits of a further 20 years of net output from the treated frontage country are taken into account, the IRR rises from 6.4% to 9.7%. Table 9.4 summarizes the estimated benefit-cost ratios for erosion treatment over a range of discount rates. By changing any benefit or cost estimate and reading off the new benefit-cost ratio, Table 9.4 can be used to estimate the effect on the IRR.

Table 9.4: Benefit-cost ratio as a function of discount rate from 1% to 13%

Discount rate (% per year)	Benefits (a) 20 Years	Benefits (b) Incl. resid.	Costs	Benefit-cost ratio (a)	Benefit-cost ratio (b)
1	0.55	1.17	0.39	1.41	3.00
3	0.43	0.78	0.35	1.23	2.23
5	0.34	0.54	0.31	1.10	1.74
7	0.27	0.38	0.28	0.96	1.36
9	0.21	0.28	0.25	0.84	1.12
11	0.18	0.22	0.23	0.78	0.96
13	0.15	0.18	0.21	0.71	0.86

Note: Benefits and costs are in A$ millions. The benefit-cost ratio compares benefit measures (a) and (b) to costs.

Conclusions

This study has outlined the evolution of the Fitzroy Valley Regeneration Project from the development of the problem of overgrazing and degradation to the formation of the Fitzroy Valley Soil Conservation Committee and government commitment to productivity improvement. The role of erosion treatment on the frontage country was described in the context of an integrated programme for productivity change in the industry. Pastoralists participate in the programme as contractual partners with government.

The model used in the study examined the economic situation of the pastoral industry in relation to range condition, and in particular, the relationship between costs of production and range condition under long-term steady-state conditions. The model suggested that rehabilitation of degraded rangeland is likely to have three economic effects: first, an increase in stable carrying capacity (and production capacity); second, a reduction in average production cost; and third, an improvement in product quality and price received.

The Fitzroy Valley Regeneration Project was evaluated by means of a conventional social benefit-cost analysis, using a representative station as the basic unit. It was concluded that the Regeneration Project would increase the carrying capacity of the study area from an estimated 100,000 cattle units at present to around 113,000 cattle units, assuming no changes in stocking rate in the untreated country. This would lead to a modest overall improvement in the turnoff ratio.

Revenues to study area stations were predicted to increase from around A$4.2 million/yr to A$4.6 million/yr without any treatment and eventually to A$5.4 million/yr following regeneration of frontage country. Average costs would be expected to fall, so total costs would rise more slowly than revenues. Thus, estimated gross margins of study area stations would increase from around A$1.3 million/yr at present to around A$2.2 million/year when the project's effects on herd size and structure had worked through.

The IRR from erosion treatment over 20 years of operation of the project was calculated as 6.4%. When 40 years of improved productivity were allowed for, the IRR rose to 9.7%.

The study did not consider the regeneration project from the viewpoint of the individual station lessee. This would require a financial model taking into account the complexities of tax deductibility for soil conservation works and company or individual income taxation, and also some knowledge of the financial circumstances of individual properties. The benefit-cost analysis does, however, provide an indication of the economic benefits and costs accruing to society from the project. The relative contributions of the government and the private sector are a matter for financial rather than economic negotiation.

Appendix: theoretical economic model of grazing management

A relatively simple model is developed here of the biological and economic dimensions that may clarify the nature of the problem faced and the economic factors that may be relevant to policy evaluation. Other models such as those in Harrington *et al.* (1984) discuss the relationship between economic productivity and stocking rate, but not in a way which makes the dynamics of change between stable range conditions and returns explicit. It is assumed that economically rational rangelands management will meet the objective of maximizing the net economic yield from the resource.

The analysis begins with the biology of grazing systems. In dealing with the relationship between stocking rates and rangeland condition, it is initially assumed that the ratio of offtake to stocking rate is fixed. Figure 9.3 shows a theoretical relationship between stocking rate and range condition, in terms of a set (or locus) of stable states which might be established for a rangeland with given initial vegetation characteristics.

The line MM' represents that stocking rate which cannot be exceeded while maintaining the rangeland in a stable condition. Nevertheless, offtake in excess of MM' is certainly possible and may be economically optimal in some situations. The curve RR' indicates the locus of possible stable states, in terms of range conditions, that can be achieved. Its shape suggests that stocking rates can approach the maximum stable level with little deterioration of originally good rangeland. However, where rangeland condition is poor, the stable stocking rate will be quite low. Any point that is not on RR' implies an unstable range condition: it may be either improving or deteriorating.

Any point to the right of RR' implies a deterioration in range condition, and any point to its left implies improving range condition. For example, if the system starts at $\Delta 1$, and stocking rate remains constant, range condition must improve along the trajectory $\Delta 1 \ldots \Delta n$ until the stable position Δn is reached. Conversely, with a stocking rate such as that at $\gamma 1$, range condition must deteriorate along some trajectory $\gamma 1 \ldots \gamma n$ where sooner or later

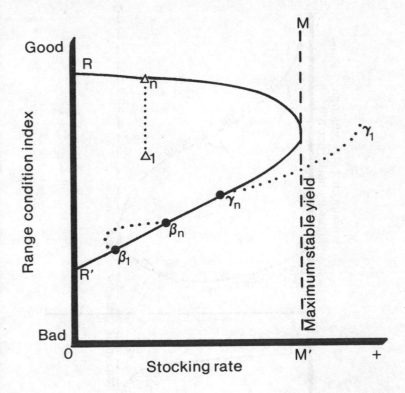

Figure 9.3: The relationship between stocking rate and range condition

a stable state is reached. In the worst case this will occur when the rangeland is so badly degraded that no stock can be carried, at R'. Finally, trajectory $\beta 1 \ldots \beta n$ illustrates that, under a strict interpretation of this model, improvement of degraded rangeland can only be initiated by a reduction in stocking rate. However, this assumption can legitimately be relaxed if there are rangeland management measures such as, for example, control of stock movement or reseeding that permit simultaneous improvement in both range condition and stocking rate, such as has been proposed in the Fitzroy Valley Regeneration Project.

The economic dimensions of the problem can now be addressed, retaining the assumption that offtake is proportional to the stocking rate. Consider the average cost of production. Figure 9.4 shows a locus of the average costs, AA' corresponding

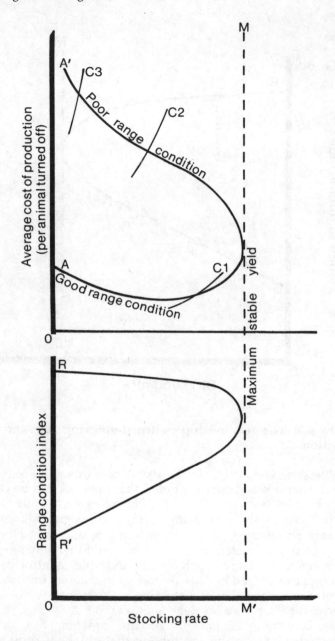

Figure 9.4: The relationship between stocking rate, range condition, and costs of operation

to the locus of stable states for range condition and stocking rate, RR'.

When range condition is good, average cost is low and falls as output (turnoff) is increased. When range condition has deteriorated, average cost increases; and if deterioration continues, the locus of average costs becomes backward-sloping. For any given stable state of range condition and stocking rate, the industry short-run average cost curve – such as C1, C2, and C3 – will pass through AA' and may be presumed to have positive slope.

Producers may elect to stock at levels beyond the maximum sustainable yield, MM'. By definition, this must lead to range deterioration; and if production technology is fixed, the producer will eventually experience backward shifting short-run average cost curves. This strategy may or may not be economically optimal. Also, it is clear that the maximum stable yield will be economically optimal only in a special case.

When range condition is good (e.g. at C1), the short-run average cost curve approximates to AA', which is also the long-run average cost curve. Producer decisions to increase or decrease stocking rate in response to changes in demand and prices move the rangeland to a new stable state and average cost of production, with minor change in range condition. By contrast, if the range is initially in a poor condition the short-run average cost curve will be relatively steeply sloping as at C2, reflecting the fact that while there may be some opportunities for increasing offtake, even from degraded rangeland, the scope for this is limited and short-lived. If herd size responds to any increase in demand, market equilibrium can be achieved only by erosion of producer incomes via higher costs, or by raised prices and reduced output – in either case with further range deterioration. In this situation, higher prices cannot act as an indicator of investment opportunities due to the trend in costs and producer incomes.

An important implication of the model is that when the rangeland is degraded, there are powerful economic incentives for producers to resist reductions in stocking rates. Their need to maintain income becomes paramount, and this implies that stocking rates will not be allowed to fall except as an enforced outcome of range deterioration. Producers find themselves in a low-income economic and biological trap that can only be escaped by means other than variation in stocking rate, at least initially. Thus, emphasis needs to be placed on such aspects as stock control, and possibly cultivation techniques, as only in these ways can producer incomes be maintained while range condition improves. Thus far, the model has assumed that the ratio of turnoff to herd size is constant for all range conditions. This assumption, however, may not hold in practice for two reasons.

First, in short-term unstable states of the herd, there is an inverse relationship between turnoff and herd size. Increased turnoff is the main means of reducing herd size. Where range condition is good and the stocking rate is below the maximum stable level, this mechanism implies no great departure from stability. For example, if prices fall and turnoff is reduced, herd size increases without serious range deterioration and there is a downwards adjustment of the turnoff:herd size (T:H) ratio.

This simply means that the constant T:H ratio assumed in the model has to be thought of as a long-run average. With poor range condition, there is potential for greater instability. A price fall followed by reduced turnoff and increased stocking rate takes the system off its stable position and leads to further range deterioration. The T:H ratio then returns to its original value at a lower stocking level and higher average cost. In conditions of extreme degradation, this effect may be modified, if the sum of turnoff plus deaths is constant (i.e., if reduced turnoff is exactly compensated by increased animal deaths).

The second cause of a variable T:H ratio results from long-term improvement in herd characteristics, which result from the transition from degraded to good range condition. Improved reproduction, reduced mortality, improved animal health, and improved herd structure are all dependent on improved range condition. (In the West Kimberley, T:H ratio varies from less than 10% in degraded areas more than 20% in areas where range condition is good. This trend poses very little difficulty for the model. Instead of a constant T:H ratio, it is merely necessary to assume some transformation of T:H as a function of range condition.)

The economic model can be used to identify more precisely the nature of the management alternatives considered in the Regeneration Project, to move from a purely theoretical to an empirical evaluation. At the outset of the study much of the rangeland in the Fitzroy was degraded, and offtake and stocking rate exceeded the sustainable level. The estimated stocking rate of 100,000 cattle units (CU) would be represented by a point to the right of RR' and in the lower segment representing poor range condition. It was further estimated that for the existing range condition in the Fitzroy, a stable state stocking rate would be 80,000 cattle units. This could broadly be interpreted as a point on RR', still in the lower segment. The regeneration project, plus other aspects of the integrated programme, was designed to lift stocking rate to 140,000 cattle units on a sustainable basis under good range condition. This would correspond to a position on RR' in the upper region with a larger stocking rate.

Thus, the time rate of change of stocking rate and its implication for turnoff were important aspects that had to be considered in the analysis. Moreover, according to the theoretical model the Regeneration Project should result not only in increased stocking rate and T:H ratio, but it should also be accompanied by a reduction in average cost per cattle unit sold.

References

Anon. (1982),
> *A Basis for Soil Conservation Policy in Australia* (Canberra: Department of Environment, Housing and Community Development, Australian Government Printing Service).

Bolton, G.C. (1954),
> "The Kimberley pastoral industry" in *Western Australian University Studies in History and Economics* (Perth: University of Western Australia Press).

Hacker, R.B. (ed.), (1982),
> *The Problems and Prospects of the Kimberley Pastoral Industry*, technical report no. 6, Division of Resource Management (Perth: Western Australia Department of Agriculture).

Harrington, G.N., A.D. Wilson, and M.D. Young (eds) (1984),
> *Management of Australia's Rangelands*, CSIRO Division of Wildlife and Rangelands Research (Melbourne: CSIRO).

Jennings, B.G., *et al.* (1979),
> *The Present and Future Pastoral Industry of Western Australia* (Perth: Western Australia Department of Lands and Surveys).

Jennings, B.G., *et al.* (1984),
> *Kimberley Pastoral Industry Inquiry. An Industry and Government Report on the Problems and Future of the Kimberley Pastoral Industry* (Perth: Western Australia Government Publishing Service).

Payne, A.L., A. Kubicki, D.G. Wilcox, and L.C. Short (1979),
> *A Report on Erosion and Range Condition in the West Kimberley Area of Western Australia*, technical bulletin no. 42 (Perth: Western Australia Department of Agriculture).

Speck, N.H., R.L. Wright, G.K. Rutherford, K. Fitzgerald, F. Thomas, J.M. Arnold, J.J. Basinski, E.A. Fitzpatrick, M. Lazarides, and R.A. Perry (1964),
> *General Report on Lands of the West Kimberley Area, Western Australia* (Melbourne: CSIRO).

Western Australia Department of Agriculture (1981),
> *Land degradation in the Fitzroy Valley of Western Australia*, technical report no. 7, Division of Resource Management (Perth: Western Australia Department of Agriculture).

10
A Framework for Economic Evaluation of Collective Fencing in Botswana

J. Arntzen

Précis

This case study deals with the problems of land degradation and diminishing crop productivity in Botswana. The benefits and costs of collective fencing from private and social perspectives are discussed. Insufficient data were available to actually estimate the present value of net benefits but the paper outlines the major benefit and cost categories and shows how a full economic evaluation would be carried out. The objective of studies such as this is to encourage greater use of economic assessment techniques within Botswana.

Introduction

Benefit-cost analysis (BCA) and other economic evaluation techniques are not widely used in Botswana. Possible explanations are the limited implementation capacity of the government, given the large number of projects to be undertaken, and the lack of data for such evaluations. Project records of expenditures and revenues, for example, are often incomplete. The recent Planning Officers' Manual provides a good basis for the more frequent use of BCA and other evaluation techniques in the future. Botswana has acknowledged the need to use BCAs in order to justify soil and water conservation projects (SADCC-SWCLUP 1986).

This case study describes how BCA might assist the allocation of government funds for development purposes. It addresses two specific problems of national significance: improving productivity in dryland cropping and grazing activity, and preventing of land degradation in agricultural areas. Collective fencing is the main land use practice examined. Data were not readily available from which to measure benefits and costs, but an appropriate framework of analysis, including the major items of benefits and costs, is presented here.

The land management problem

Land use pressure
Increased pressure on communal areas and increased spatial integration of livestock and crop production (so-called "mixed farming") have led to serious and widespread problems of crop damage by livestock and land degradation in mixed farming areas. Soil erosion is recognized as an important countrywide problem mostly associated with livestock, but theoretical calculations have shown it to be an important farmland problem also. Unfortunately, little is known about the exact extent of soil erosion. In order to reduce the level of dependence on imported food (at present 50 to 90%, depending on rainfall), these problems must be addressed. In the short run, less crop damage by livestock will reduce the dependence on food imports. In the long run, soil protection is essential to maintain the already limited productive potential of the land.

Alternative land use practices
Farmers have responded to soil erosion and crop damage problems by erecting fences, primarily around fields. The main objective appears to be reduction of crop damage, but fences also provide opportunities for better crop and soil management. Groups of farmers now frequently establish a collective fence, separating grazing and crop land during the rainy season.

This case study examines the case for collective (drift) fencing, erected by a group of farmers with government support. Such fencing consists of timber poles with wire. Government aid includes extension support (advice, design, location) and material support in the form of fencing wire and equipment to clear the land.

Collective fencing has been selected for a number of reasons. First, fencing is the most rapidly and widely adopted form of land management, and government support programmes are popularly accepted. Obviously, both individual farmers as well as government perceive net benefits from fencing; however, no systematic economic evaluation exists. Second, although fencing may not directly influence soil conservation, it facilitates the implementation of improved cultivation and grazing management practices, including soil conservation-oriented practices. It is not always a sufficient condition to trigger such responses. Third, some limited data are available to apply BCA.

Clear alternatives, apart from non-fencing, exist to separate grazing and arable land. One alternative to collective fencing is fencing of individual fields. Under the Arable Land Development

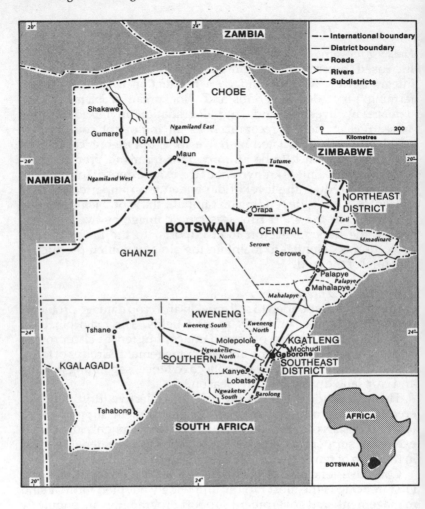

Figure 10.1: Location, districts and major settlements in Botswana

Programme, farmers may apply for government assistance covering 85% of fencing costs for a maximum of 10 ha. Individual fencing may be either bush fences or wire fences. The former are easier to construct but require more maintenance. The latter are more effective in keeping cattle out.

In practice, collective fencing sometimes coincides with individual fences, mostly erected prior to the establishment of the collective fence. In fact, continuation of individual fences has the advantage of providing extra security in case cattle fail to be kept outside the collective fence during the crop season.

Botswana's agricultural sector

Botswana is a landlocked, semi-arid country in southern Africa with a population of 1.1 million (see Figure 10.1). Most of the country's 586,000 km² is so-called *sandveld* with low and erratic rainfall. Around 80% of the population lives in the eastern *hardveld*, where livestock and crop production are concentrated due to better rainfall and soil conditions. Borehole technology (tubewells) has permitted livestock production to penetrate into western Botswana (Cooke 1985). There is also an area of farming in the Okavango Delta in the northwest. Natural conditions severely limit the productive potential of the eastern *hardveld* and crop failures are frequent. During the drought in 1987, the total crop production dropped to as low as 10,000 tonnes, or 5% of the estimated national requirement.

Rapid economic growth since Independence (1966) has boosted government revenues and the provision of public services, including agricultural support services such as vaccinations, extension services, and subsidized programmes. However, the rural economy has not drastically changed. The mining sector has limited linkages with rural areas. The livestock sector has been the dominant rural activity for some time. Environmental conditions (semi-aridity, soils) and, more recently, economic conditions, particularly access to high prices in European Economic Community markets, favour livestock production over crops.

Land use rights and public administration
Most land (71%) is held under communal tenure. Only 6% of the country is freehold, whereas 23% is state land. Most people rely on communal land for income generation to some extent. Important changes have occurred in the management of communal land.

First, the traditional management structure has gradually declined, leading, for example, to self-allocation of fields in areas previously used for grazing. The outcome has been a less clear distinction between grazing and cropland in so-called mixed farming areas, as well as the establishment of new institutions such as Land Boards in 1970 to allocate and manage the land resource. In practice, Land Boards have not yet filled the land management gap as anticipated under the Tribal Land Act.

Second, tribal land use has been restricted. Under the Tribal Grazing Land Policy, some 10% of tribal land has been designated for leasehold livestock ranching, mostly by individual ranch owners. Plans are well advanced to establish wildlife management areas where land use remains communal in principle, but wildlife use will receive priority over agriculture.

Third, land use pressure has rapidly increased. The human population has roughly doubled since 1966 and is estimated to grow annually by 3.3%. Similarly, livestock numbers had risen sharply until the start of the 1987 drought. The country now holds 2.4 head of cattle and 1.3 goats/sheep per person (Ministry of Agriculture 1985). Such increased pressure has led to widespread land degradation, including bush encroachment, soil erosion and localized desertification, and to an increase in conflicts between human activities, mostly livestock versus crops. In western Botswana, livestock competes with wildlife. The long-term productivity of the land and land-based human activities are consequently under threat. Legislation to curb some of the negative environmental effects exists but has, until now, hardly been used. For example, the Agriculture Resources Board has never used its prerogative under the Agricultural Resources Conservation Act to set stock limits for specific degraded areas.

Producer behaviour
Statistics on average returns to labour in different forms of production show that agricultural returns fluctuate considerably and that non-agricultural production is generally the most attractive, followed by livestock production and, finally, crop production.

Agriculture. The majority of crop producers adopt a low input and risk evasive strategy. Around 30% of crop farmers do not hold any cattle, whereas only 35% hold more than 20 head, responsible for 65% of the production (Ministry of Agriculture 1984). The most serious constraints are lack of draught power for those without enough cattle, lack of labour, and lack of implements and seeds (FAO 1974; Arntzen and Veenendaal 1986). Fields are large, up to 16 ha, but they are generally under-utilized.

Coincidence of general land pressure and under-utilization of arable land results from two factors. First, agriculture receives implicit priority over grazing. Consequently, despite a shortage of grazing areas, arable land is still allocated to agriculture even in grazing areas. The shortage of land is felt least in the agricultural sector. The second factor is the low input strategy of farmers, coupled with a lack of personal resources, and occasional droughts.

Fields are often only partly cleared (e.g., only 60% in Mmathubudukwane, east of Mochudi in Kgatleng district), and even less may be ploughed depending on rainfall conditions and the means of the individual farmer. The cultivated land per household is about 4.5 ha. Tillage practices have not changed since the 1930s (except for increased use of mechanized draught power). Little attention is paid to soil and water conservation.

Table 10.1: Arable land by district

District	Arable land[1] (ha)	% of district arable	% of national cultivation	1981[2] cultivated area (ha)	1981 % of district cultivated
Ngamiland	40,662	0.4	5.0	14,600	0.1
Chobe	2,839	0.1	0.4	800	0.0
Ghanzi	8,548	0.1	1.0	500	0.0
Central	325,065	2.2	39.9	108,500	0.7
North East	58,315	11.0	7.2	14,600	4.3
Kgalagadi	14,202	0.1	1.7	700	0.0
Kgatleng	52,494	6.9	6.4	19,800	2.6
Kweneng	137,965	3.6	16.9	34,000	0.9
Southern	152,426	5.7	18.7	63,100	2.3
South East	23,110	15.5	2.8	5,200	3.5
NATIONAL TOTAL	815,625	1.4%	100%	270,200	0.5%

Source: DHV (1980)
Notes
1. Situation in mid-1970s.
2. Last good rainfall year; excluding freehold cultivation and all fallow land.

Although 3 to 5% of the total land area of Botswana is suitable for crop production, cultivated land actually covers less than 1%. In some districts the proportion of arable land is as low as 0.1%; but in small districts such as North East and South East, this percentage is much higher – 11% and 15.5%

respectively (see Table 10.1).

Total production from arable land fluctuates considerably from year to year. Production variations closely reflect variations in planted area, which in turn depend on prevailing rainfall conditions (see Figure 10.2). The average productivity has remained stable at the very low level of approximately 250 kg/ha. Such productivity levels were reported as far back as the 1930s. Considerable variations in productivity exist, ranging from 167 kg/ha for the small farmers to 347 kg/ha for the larger farmers. Freehold farmers achieve productivity levels of 707 kg/ha (1981). These differences reflect mainly differences in available means and skills (cash and draught power) to adapt adequately to the adverse natural conditions.

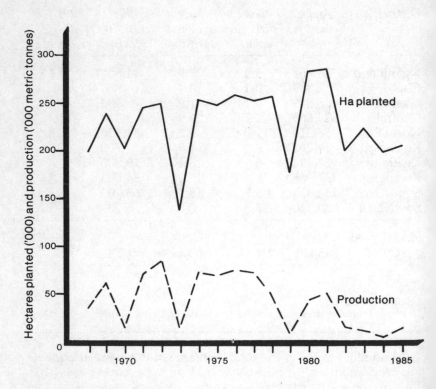

Figure 10.2: Area planted and production of grain crops

Table 10.2: Stocking rates and carrying capacity by location (ha/livestock unit)

District	Stocking rates		Potential carrying capacity
	1980	*1984*	
Barolong	4.2	6.6	12
Ngwaketse South	8.9	15.8	16–21
Ngwaketse North	12.9	10.0	16–21
South East	4.1	4.0	12
Kweneng South	12.9	21.6	12–16
Kweneng North	4.1	1.2	12–16
Kgatleng	8.3	9.0	12–16
Mahalapye	10.8	11.1	12–16
Palapye	5.5	6.0	16–21
Serowe	—	—	12–21
Mmadinare	6.9	7.9	12–21
Tutume	—	—	12–16
Tati	4.2	5.1	21
Ngamiland	—	—	12–16
Chobe	—	—	8
Ghanzi	—	—	16–27
Kgalagadi	7.0	13.5	21–27

Sources: Carl Brothers International (1982); Ministry of Agriculture (1985); and Arntzen and Veenendaal (1986).

Grazing. Most of the country is used as grazing by livestock and wildlife. Stocking rates of livestock exceed the calculated carrying capacity in most parts of the country (see Table 10.2). A decrease in stocking rates has occurred since the drought beginning in 1981, but this has probably been outweighed by a larger decrease in carrying capacity over the same period. Around 80% of the livestock is kept in eastern Botswana where most cultivation also takes place. Land pressure from population growth and increased livestock numbers has led to direct competition for land between agriculture and grazing (Odell 1980; Gulbrandsen 1984). Livestock is now kept in pure grazing areas, used by the larger livestock holders who can afford a borehole (Peters 1983), and in mixed farming areas.

Mixed farming areas are occupied mainly by small cattle holders and are more overcrowded than pure grazing areas. The Livestock Management Survey found average stocking rates of 13.9 ha/LSU in pure grazing areas as opposed to 7.5 ha/LSU in mixed farming areas (LSU = live stock unit). Smallholders are more or less forced to keep their cattle in such areas to spread their labour over livestock and crop production and to have access to cheaper water. As a result, they face worse grazing conditions and the likelihood of having to pay compensation for crop damage inflicted by their cattle. In Kgatleng, as many as 80% of the crop farmers face crop damage by livestock (Opschoor 1981). Affected farmers can bring the livestock owners involved to the "Kgotla" where the Chief decides on an appropriate level of compensation.

Economic evaluation

The three stages of economic evaluation consist of:

- identification of different categories of benefits and costs;
- quantification of effects leading to benefits and costs; *and*
- valuation of benefits and costs.

Table 10.3: Summary of potential benefits and costs of collective fencing

	Private	Social
Benefits		
Increased food production	X	X
Reduced labour needs for livestock	X	X
Improved grazing management	X	X
Improved agricultural practices	X	X
Group formation		X
Costs		
Construction of firebreak	X	X
Construction of fence	X	X
Maintenance	X	X
Management and operation of the fence	X	X
Adjustment of livestock watering points	X	X
Reallocation of fields	X	X

For this study, insufficient data were available to carry the analysis through to its final stage. It was possible, however, to identify the various categories of benefits and costs and to partially quantify the relevant effects. Methods of valuation are also suggested.

As usual, a distinction must be drawn between private and social benefits and costs. A general summary of benefits and costs from private and public perspectives is presented in Table 10.3.

Estimation of benefits
One benefit is higher food production due to a reduction in crop damage by livestock. This leads to higher incomes, either cash or in kind, for the project participants (private perspective) and to a decrease in food imports (social perspective). Possible indirect benefits arising from higher incomes should be incorporated if they are significant.

Available data do not allow comprehensive assessment of the increase in food production. Crop damage avoided depends on the number of affected farmers or fields, the extent of crop damage per farmer or field, and the efficiency of the collective fence in keeping livestock out during the growing season. In Central District, 48% of the farmers experienced crop damage in 1981, mostly caused by cattle (Zufferey 1982). In Kgatleng, up to 80% experienced crop damage in recent years (Arntzen and Opschoor 1986). The ex-ante situation in Central District (Zufferey 1982) showed an average yield of 180 kg/ha (mostly sorghum), subdivided into 158 kg/ha for affected farms and 370 kg/ha for unaffected farms. However, the difference was statistically not significant. Other factors may also cause differences in productivity levels, and droughts may alter the picture substantially. The actual efficiency of collective fences in terms of decrease in crop damage needs to be established and will probably vary from case to case.

Increased food production can be privately valued at the savings from reduced food purchases and the value of sales in case of a production surplus. Less than 10% of crop farmers are self-sufficient. From a social perspective, valuation according to import prices is suggested. Although foreign exchange at present is not a constraint to development, the government holds the view that the mineral boom has caused an overvaluation of the local currency and that a shadow price needs to be used.

Reduced labour requirements for herding livestock is another result: livestock can no longer stray far and cause crop damage. This is a mixed social benefit as less herding could in fact lead to poorer livestock management, but the released labour can be deployed elsewhere such as in crop production or education.

According to the Farm Management Survey of 1984, holders of herds of less than 20 cattle spent on average 114 days tending their livestock, mostly herding and watering. Farmers' response to collective fences in terms of labour reduction is not documented and will require in-depth research. The private benefit of reduced labour input in livestock herding can be valued according to the opportunity cost approach (e.g., labour returns in crop production).

Benefits may be derived from improved grazing management involving rotational grazing. Grass in the cultivation zone can be used only after harvesting. Agricultural research in Botswana has not been conclusive in demonstrating the benefits from rotational grazing on livestock performance. Ex-ante information exists on the grazing situation (quality and quantity) in four villages east of Palapye in Central District (Zufferey 1982). Any new comparison should allow for the impacts of drought. Valuation based on average meat price and average body weight is one possible approach.

Facilitation of improved practices and better management of land and water resources may yield further benefits. Such benefits are difficult to quantify as they are not a necessary outcome of collective fencing alone. Other factors such as education, extension and increased incomes may also be responsible. Improved farming practices aimed at higher production can be valued according to reduced purchases or higher sales. Those aimed at improved land and water management can be valued according to long-term production increases or costs to achieve similar resource improvement.

Potential benefits may also accrue from the formation of farmers' groups, which could also address other issues relevant to production and conservation, such as management of water points and soil conservation. Despite strong government support, formation of such groups has been very limited in most areas. Benefits cannot be easily quantified unless obvious spin-off effects occur in the case study area, nor can they be easily valued.

Estimation of costs

Data exist to estimate material and labour requirements for the construction and maintenance of collective fences. Collective fences are made from wooden poles and wire. Wire, gates, and cattle grids are usually supplied by the government. Poles are obtained from trees, and labour is supplied by participants.

Costs are also incurred in constructing a 20-m firebreak to guard against bush-fire damage to the fence. Equipment is mostly provided by the government and labour by the participating farmers.

Maintenance of the firebreak and fence is the responsibility of participants, who pay a membership fee. During the 1987 drought, the government drought-relief programmes paid subsidies to assist in the maintenance of collective fences.

An essential element in the management and operation of the fence is the decision as to when to move livestock out of or back into cultivated areas; enforcement of this decision determines the magnitude of reduction in crop damage. The functions of the management committee may lead to some operational costs, which will be paid from membership contributions.

Costs may also be incurred in changing the system of livestock watering. Livestock uses a variety of surface and groundwater sources during the year and move around accordingly. The collective fence may cut off access to some of these sources during the growing season, which therefore need replacement.

Depending on the position of the fence, some fields may have to be resurveyed and reformed, thereby creating additional costs. The proportion of cultivated and grazing land may also be changed by the fence.

In valuing all cost components, special attention must be paid to the shadow price of labour. Labour costs are low, both privately and socially. Construction activities usually take place during winter when alternative forms of employment are virtually absent. The national economy is characterized by a high level of un- and underemployment (25% and 7%, respectively), particularly among low and unskilled labour. The government estimates that the shadow price of unskilled labor is generally 50% of the minimum wage. In practice, case studies show shadow costs of labour locally to be as low as zero. In the particular case of collective fencing, one may argue that labour should be valued at the government contribution rate, as this is adequate to induce required labour. It is probably impossible to value leisure and the status of employment (Bojö 1986).

Material costs can be privately valued at the actual costs to the participants. In order to evaluate the impact of government subsidies, private costs could be calculated both inclusive and exclusive of government subsidies.

The social opportunity cost of capital is comparatively low due to excess liquidity in the country. The Ministry of Finance and Development Planning assumes an opportunity cost of capital in the range of 6 to 8%.

Wood can be valued according to its opportunity cost. In

some areas firewood is still free, whereas in others, charges vary between 2 and 10 thebe/kg (1 thebe = US$0.0058).

Distribution of benefits and costs

Distributional aspects can be included by distinguishing categories of farmers according to herd size as a proxy for wealth (e.g., no cattle, less than 20, 21 to 40, and over 40 cattle). Poor farmers usually own few or no cattle, and a reduction of crop damage is more valuable to them than to richer farmers who are less dependent on crop revenues. Reduced crop damage among the poorest farmers may be valued more highly from the social perspective, as social equity is one of the key objectives of development planning. Another consideration is that the benefits of improved grazing management accrue mainly to livestock holders. It seems unnecessary to make an additional distinction between project participants and non-participants. In practice, eventually all livestock holders join the fencing group, leaving out mainly people without livestock.

Benefits and costs are likely to differ regionally. Benefits such as reduced crop damage and improvement of agricultural practices depend to a large extent on the attitude of farmers. A recent survey in Mogapi, a village in Central District northeast of Palapye, illustrates this point. Around 65% of farmers with fields inside the drift fence continue to complain about crop damage by cattle, and the same percentage for damage by goats. Management of the collective fence can be improved in this case. Less than 30% of the farmers had an individual fence although this greatly reduced the incidence of damage by cattle. Individual fences were, however, less effective against goats.

Uncertainties in the analysis

A time horizon of 15 to 20 years is recommended for the economic analysis, as indirect effects may materialize only after some time, and recurrent droughts may affect the impact of fencing on food production. Sensitivity analyses are needed to deal with uncertainties about the accuracy of data and/or assumptions made. In this case study, this would apply, among other things, to the:

- extent of the reduction in crop damage;
- extent of reduction in herding labour;
- application of improved agricultural practices, including land management; *and*
- discount rate and time horizon.

As benefit-cost analyses are uncommon in Botswana, no generally accepted discount rate has been set by government. The Ministry of Finance and Development Planning considers the real opportunity costs of capital to be 6 to 8%. In practice, it may be best to use a range of rates (e.g., from 2 to 12%) in a sensitivity analysis (Bojö 1986).

Conclusions

The previous discussion suggests it should be possible to use economic analytical techniques to evaluate the advantages and disadvantages of collective fencing in Botswana. This would be useful in assessing the impact of collective fencing on food production as well as improved land management. The practice deserves considerable attention in view of the country's widespread land degradation and large food imports.

A full analysis of individual fencing, either alone or in conjunction with collective fencing, is also warranted to obtain a comprehensive assessment of the benefits and costs to individual farmers and to the community in general.

The approach suggested in this study would be helpful in evaluating the significant government support that is currently provided for both collective and individual fencing.

Acknowledgments

This paper has benefited from comments by Mr. N. Hunter, Mrs. B. Kgare, Mrs. B. Machacha, and Mr. Mpathi in Botswana; by Mr. J. Bojö, SADCC Soil and Water Conservation Unit, Lesotho; and by Messrs J. Dixon and P. Sherman, East–West Center, Hawaii.

References

Arntzen, J.W., and J.B. Opschoor (1986),
"Environmental pressure and land use change in Eastern Communal Botswana: the case of Kgatleng" in *Land Policy and Agricultural Production in Eastern and Southern Africa* (Tokyo: United Nations University).
Arntzen, J.W., and E.M. Veenendaal (1986),
A Profile of Environment and Development in Botswana. National Institute of Development, Research and Documentation, University of Botswana/Institute for Environmental Studies, Free University, Amsterdam, The Netherlands.

Bojö, J. (1986),
  An Introduction to Cost-Benefit Analysis of Soil and Water Conservation Project, report no. 6 (Lesotho: Coordination Unit, SADCC Soil and Water Conservation and Land Utilisation Programme).
Carl Brothers International (1982),
  An Evaluation of Livestock Management and Production in Botswana with Special Reference to Communal Areas, vols 1 – 3 (Gaborone: Ministry of Agriculture).
Cooke, J.H. (1985),
  "The Kalahari today: a case of conflict over resource use," *The Geographical Journal*, no.151, pp.75–85.
DHV (Department of Animal Husbandry and Veterinary Medicine), (1980),
  Cultivated Land Survey (Gaborone: Ministry of Agriculture).
FAO (Food and Agriculture Organization)/Government of Botswana (1974),
  A Study of Constraints on Agricultural Development of Botswana, Rome/Gaborone.
Gulbrandsen, Q. (1984),
  Access to Agricultural Land and Communal Land Management in Eastern Botswana (Gaborone: Applied Research Unit, Ministry of Local Government and Lands).
Ministry of Agriculture (1984, 1985),
  Agricultural Statistics, Gaborone.
Odell, M.A. (1980),
  Planning for Agriculture in Botswana (Gaborone: Institute for Development Management/Ministry of Agriculture).
Opschoor, J.B. (1981),
  Environmental Resources Utilisation in Eastern Botswana: The Case of Kgatleng. NIR Working Paper 38, University of Botswana.
Peters, P. (1983),
  Cattlemen Borehole Syndicates and Privatisation in Kgatleng, PhD thesis, Boston University.
SADCC-SWCLUP (Southern African Development Co-ordinating Conference – Soil and Water Conservation and Land Utilization Programme), (1986),
  Cost Benefit Analysis of Soil and Water Conservation Projects, report no. 4, (Lesotho: Coordination Unit).
Zufferey, F. (1982),
  Impact of Communal Fencing in Three Communities of Central District: Baseline Data (Gaborone: Rural Sociology Unit, Ministry of Agriculture).

11
Risks in the Botswana Range-Cattle System

L.C. Braat and J.B. Opschoor

Précis

This paper presents a study of range-cattle interactions. A generic computer simulation model[1] is used to explore the risks of traditional cattle farming in Botswana.

Some risks such as drought are of environmental origin while others such as overstocking are of human origin. The essential management problem in attaining a sustainable range-cattle system is to match the highly variable grazing capacity of the range with cattle stocking rates. The situation is complicated by erratic rainfall, lack of accurate carrying capacity estimates, and a mix of cultural and economic factors.

The simulation experiments indicate that if the present offtake rate (8% per year) is maintained, cattle numbers will reach a long-term average of 2.3 million, but with a 10 to 20% loss in drought periods. In addition, the range will be under continuous severe stress, which implies poor condition of the cattle. A fixed higher offtake rate (15% per year) lessens the stress on the range but reduces total offtake as compared with the 8% offtake rate. A policy that involves high offtake with low rainfall and lower offtake rates with high rainfall appears hardly more rewarding.

Extending the grazing area by developing additional boreholes does allow for a larger sustainable herd. However, that part of the herd on the additional land will be relatively small as the potential carrying capacity (PCC) of this added land will be lower than the PCC of the present grazing land.

Introduction

Botswana is a landlocked country in semi-arid southern Africa (see Figure 11.1). In developing their economy, the people of Botswana have always been confronted with a number of tightly linked ecological and socio-economic problems. Great progress in coping with these problems has been achieved in the 20 years since independence, but not all development problems

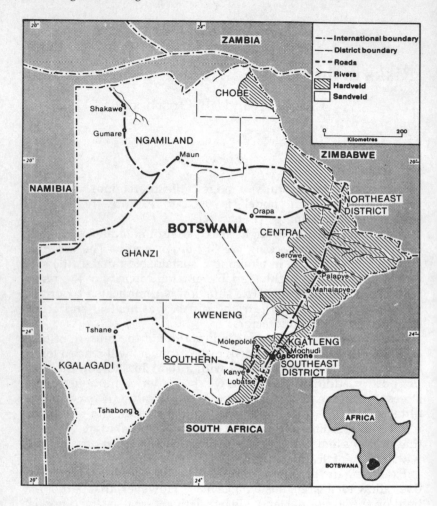

Figure 11.1: The Republic of Botswana

have yet been solved. The economic and ecological problems of cattle farming, which the country is expected to face in the near future, require an intensive additional effort in integrated resource management.

Historically, livestock farming has been the major source of rural income. Because of this tradition and the lack of economic alternatives, and because of the expected rates of increase of the human population which vary between 2.75 and 3.75% per year (Ministry of Finance and Development Planning 1985), livestock farming is expected to continue to play this role in the near future.

This paper presents a dynamic ecological simulation model, which is used to obtain insight in the structure, risks and long-term impacts of range and livestock management problems, and to present preliminary and tentative overview assessments of the feasibility of alternative management strategies.

The study concentrates on the relationships between rainfall, range area, grazing capacity, and cattle herd development. Other factors such as competitive browsing by small stock (sheep, goats), competition between wildlife and cattle, and alternative investment opportunities may well be relevant in evaluating the uncertainties, risks, and effectiveness of management strategies. Their exclusion from the present analysis follows only from the limited scope of the study.

The management problem

The key management problem in the range-cattle system is to match cattle stocking rates with the grazing capacity of the range. The majority of cattle (and small stock) grazes under a traditional farming regime on the open, unfenced range. Essentially, food and water availability can limit herd expansion in a given area. Historically, water supply has been the limiting factor as cattle had to rely on rainfed pools and *dongas*. Since the 1930s, and particularly since the mid-1950s, diesel-driven boreholes (wells) have penetrated the eastern part of Botswana and by now much of the western part. Currently, forage supply is the limiting factor.

Hay stocking has never been part of the traditional system, so livestock survival and quality depend on the immediate availability of forage on the range. Control over range quality and thus indirectly over livestock quality is rather limited. Overgrazing can in fact be observed in many areas, particularly in the eastern districts but also around the boreholes in the west. In other parts, deterioration may not be visible yet but is expected to approach threshold levels eventually. At the same time, the growing herd has led to an increasing stress on water and wildlife resources.

Range grazing capacity varies continuously in time and widely in space. To some extent this variation still functions as a natural regulatory mechanism for cattle herd development. The management situation, however, is complicated by ecological uncertainties such as multi-year dry spells and food alternatives for cattle such as browsing and crop residues, and by socio-economic uncertainties such as commercial offtake incentives (such as beef prices and quotas) and decisions on home slaughter during droughts.

Long-term average yearly rainfall, soil quality, slope, and exposition are instrumental in determining the potential carrying capacity of the range. The actual grazing capacity in a given year generally differs from the potential levels as a combined result of the actual rainfall and stocking rate over the past two or three years. We shall briefly discuss the characteristics of these factors with respect to the management problem.

Table 11.1: Potential carrying capacity (PCC) in ten districts (ha/LSU)

District	PCC(1)	PCC(2)
1. Kgalagadi	13–46	40
2. Ghanzi	5–34	21
3. Southern	5–100	14
4. Kweneng	9–26	12
5. Ngamiland	2–26	10
6. Central	5–46	16
7. Northeast	21–34	24
8. Kgatleng	9–20	12
9. Southeast	5–12	10
10. Chobe	2–16	8

PCC(1): Theoretical approach (Field 1977, 1978); from Arntzen and Veenendaal (1986 p.37). PCC(2) figures calculated as district average: (Σ area per PCC value * PCC value from Field (1978))/total area per district.

Potential carrying capacity
Rainfall and soil quality are the two most important factors in the estimates of potential carrying capacity (PCC) for rangeland in

Botswana. Estimates run from 100 ha required to feed one live-stock unit (LSU) in parts of the southwest (Kgalagadi District) to 1 ha/LSU in some parts of the Chobe District in the northeast.

The grazing capacity of the range can be calculated in two ways. One method requires data on grass primary production, measured in tonnes per hectare per year. Given the average need of 2,550 kg/LSU/yr, the grazing capacity in terms of hectares needed per LSU can be calculated. The second method starts with the PCC as determined by Field (1977, 1978), based on average rainfall, slope, and soil type. The average PCC of each district can then be calculated (Table 11.1). In constructing the model, a national average PCC of 11.5 ha/LSU has been estimated.

Table 11.2: Rainfall in Botswana

District	Annual mean (mm)	Annual variation (%)
1. Kgalagadi	286	45
2. Ghanzi	362	37
3. Southern	377	35
4. Kweneng	423	35
5. Ngamiland	459	35
6. Central	470	32
7. Northeast	485	40
8. Kgatleng	497	32
9. Southeast	562	30
10. Chobe	640	35

Source: After Ministry of Finance and Development Planning (1985).

Rainfall

Rainfall is a necessary requirement for grass biomass production. Average annual rainfall is low in the southwest and high in the northeast, and highly variable in time (see Table 11.2).

Rainfall data are available from 1910 onward. Analysis of temporal dynamics has generated hypotheses about a cyclical pattern, with an estimated period of 16 to 20 years (Vossen 1986; Tyson 1980). In our model we generate future rainfall data through a set of equations that combine a 17-year cycle with deviations from the long-term mean for the country.

Stocking rate

The stocking rate is defined as the number of hectares available per head of cattle. To determine the stocking rate, the available grazing area and the herd size must be known.

Table 11.3: Grazing area (km^2)

District	Theoretical grazing area	Present borehole-based area	Additional grazing area by borehole development
1. Kgalagadi	42,500	7,040	700
2. Ghanzi	20,700	2,560	4,600
3. Southern	25,100	25,100	—
4. Kweneng	31,000	22,120	8,900
5. Ngamiland	51,350	17,350	17,000
6. Central	100,000	62,400	26,320
7. Northeast	2,300	2,300	—
8. Kgatleng	7,400	7,400	—
9. Southeast	475	475	—
10. Chobe	4,750	3,520	—
NATIONAL	285,575	150,165	57,520

Grazing area. Grazing land can be defined in two ways. From a theoretical point of view, all the land not in use as urban area (housing, industry and transportation), cropland, National Park, Game and Forest Reserve, or Wildlife Management Area is available for grazing. In practice, however, grassland is useable only if water supplies are available to the animals within roaming distance. The second method to estimate the available grazing area is therefore based on the number of boreholes and hand-dug wells. One borehole can "open up" about 6,400 ha of grazing land. Table 11.3 lists both the theoretical and borehole-based grazing areas. The difference is remarkable, especially in the western districts, and has consequences for management options, as will be indicated later. In this model the borehole-based grazing area has been used. (Grazing area will also expand by making greater use of hand-dug wells. The present estimates of hand-dug well grazing area development may be too low.)

Based on expected quality of deep groundwater, the authors have made rough estimates of potential additions to the total grazing area by borehole development. These estimates are indicated in the last column of Table 11.3.

Cattle numbers. Cattle herd data are available from several sources (see Arntzen and Veenendaal 1986). In 1966, the total national herd in the traditional farming system numbered around 1,060,000 livestock units. A steady growth, only slightly slowed by the mid-1960s drought, has brought the total to a peak value of more than 2,500,000 units in 1982, after which the early 1980s drought began to show effects.

The district stocking rates. Since early times, the eastern *hardveld* (see map in Figure 11.1) has been more densely inhabited than the western *sandveld* (an area of low and erratic rainfall). Most of the herd used to be held close to the settlements and water sources because of factors such as rainfall, proximity of rivers, and soil fertility. In colonial times all road and railway development also took place in the eastern part of the country.

Table 11.4: Cattle numbers and stocking rates in 1980

| | | Stocking rates (ha/LSU) | |
Districts	*Cattle*	*Method 1(*)*	*Method 2(**)*
1. Kgalagadi	59,000	72.0	11.9
2. Ghanzi	43,000	48.1	6.0
3. Southern	333,000	7.5	7.5
4. Kweneng	252,000	12.3	8.8
5. Ngamiland	255,000	20.1	6.8
6. Central	1,174,000	8.5	5.3
7. Northeast	141,000	1.6	1.6
8. Kgatleng	110,000	6.7	6.7
9. Southeast	23,000	2.1	2.1
10. Chobe	5,000	95.0	70.4

* Calculated with theoretical grazing area
** Calculated with borehole-based grazing area (used in the model)

This has led to stocking rates that far surpassed the carrying capacity of the eastern range. The stocking rates listed in column 4 (and, to a lesser extent, column 3) of Table 11.4 illustrate this clearly when compared with the PCC values in Table 11.1. In some areas in the east, there is no grass cover left at all. These areas generally still support bush and tree growth, some of which provide food for cattle through browsing. Browsing and crop residues and the density of water points (rivers, boreholes, and ponds) in the eastern districts have made continuous high stocking rates possible. In the western *sandveld*, the overall density of the cattle is relatively low; but around the water points and villages, stocking rates have already reached critical levels. Because of uncertainties in grazing area and cattle herd estimates, the stocking rate is not an easily determined variable. Estimates differ with the method chosen, which complicates management activities.

Actual grazing capacity
With estimates for potential carrying capacity, rainfall, and stocking rates, the actual grazing capacity per year can be calculated. The actual grazing capacity in an area (GRACAP in the model) may differ (yearly) from the PCC of that area because of rainfall and stocking rates. This is calculated as:

$$GRACAP = [(Rainfall\text{-}factor*PCC) + (Stocking\text{-}rate\ factor*PCC)]/2$$

The rainfall factor (RF factor), expressing the deviation from the PCC caused by the annual rainfall, may be estimated using the potential carrying capacity at national long-term mean rainfall (set at 450 mm), 2.5 times the PCC at the minimum rainfall (200 mm) and 67% of the PCC at maximum rainfall (700 mm) (see DHV 1980). The rainfall factor (RF factor) in the model therefore ranges from .67 to 2.5.

The stocking-rate factor (Stfact) has been estimated with a similar functional relationship. At low intensities of grazing, grass production is stimulated. In theory, there is a balance between grazing and grass production at the stocking rate that matches the potential carrying capacity of the area; and where the stocking rate exceeds the actual grazing capacity, the latter is expected to decrease. This may be because grass seedlings are being trampled, because the top soil has been compacted or eroded, and because the seed stock has disappeared.

Cattle herd dynamics
The cattle herd development equations in the simulation model have been based on Agricultural Statistics (Ministry of Agriculture 1980–84) and National Development Plans data. Births and natural deaths (including home slaughter) are affected by the condition of the range. Data for estimating the functional relationships between the condition of the range (the actual grazing capacity,

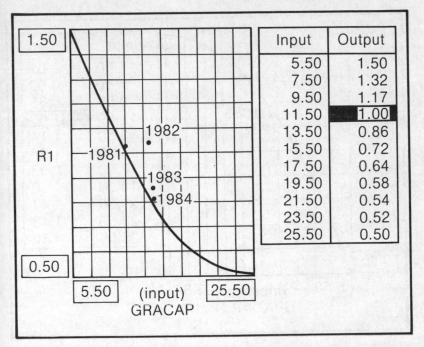

Figure 11.2: Impact of changes in grazing capacity (GRACAP) on birth rate influencing factor (R1)

GRACAP) and birth rate and death rate, respectively, were derived from agricultural statistics, using data from 1980 and 1981 as normal years and 1982, 1983, and 1984 as drought years (see Table 11.5).

Table 11.5: National cattle herd dynamics (× 1,000) (traditional farms only)

Year	Cattle	Births	Deaths	Offtake	Purchase
1980	2,455	582	404	190	40
1981	2,495	586	359	194	32
1982	2,504	604	450	205	53
1983	2,407	521	455	205	37
1984	2,306	502	484	169	31

Source: Ministry of Agriculture (1980–84)

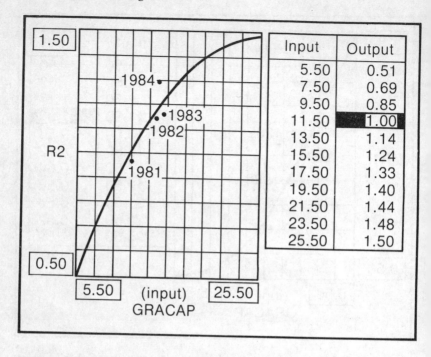

Input	Output
5.50	0.51
7.50	0.69
9.50	0.85
11.50	1.00
13.50	1.14
15.50	1.24
17.50	1.33
19.50	1.40
21.50	1.44
23.50	1.48
25.50	1.50

Figure 11.3: Impact of changes in grazing capacity (GRACAP) on death rate influencing factor (R2)

In Figure 11.2, the birth rate influencing factor (R1) is 1.0 if GRACAP equals the PCC of 11.5 ha/LSU. If the grazing capacity is extremely good (only 8 ha required per LSU), the birth rate is multiplied by 1.5. If the GRACAP is smaller than the PCC, the birth rate may drop to 50% of the equilibrium value. The reverse holds for the death rate influencing factor, R2 (see Figure 11.3).

The simulation model

Model structure
A diagram of the range-cattle model developed in this study is presented in Figure 11.4. The diagram shows the range submodel with grazing area (RANGE-AREA), the stocking rate (ST-rate),

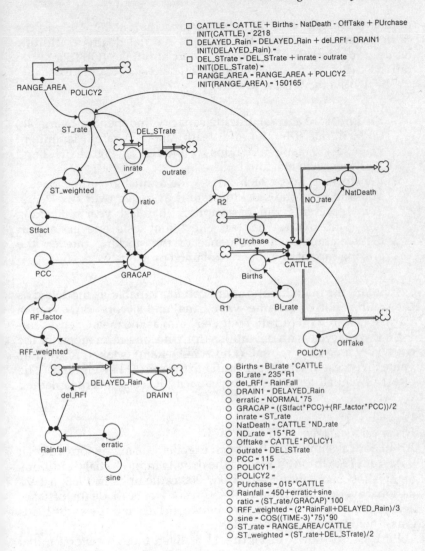

□ CATTLE = CATTLE + Births - NatDeath - OffTake + PUrchase
INIT(CATTLE) = 2218
□ DELAYED_Rain = DELAYED_Rain + del_RFf - DRAIN1
INIT(DELAYED_Rain) =
□ DEL_STrate = DEL_STrate + inrate - outrate
INIT(DEL_STrate) =
□ RANGE_AREA = RANGE_AREA + POLICY2
INIT(RANGE_AREA) = 150165

○ Births = BI_rate *CATTLE
○ BI_rate = 235*R1
○ del_RFf = RainFall
○ DRAIN1 = DELAYED_Rain
○ erratic = NORMAL*75
○ GRACAP = ((Stfact*PCC)+(RF_factor*PCC))/2
○ inrate = ST_rate
○ NatDeath = CATTLE *ND_rate
○ ND_rate = 15*R2
○ Offtake = CATTLE*POLICY1
○ outrate = DEL_STrate
○ PCC = 115
○ POLICY1 =
○ POLICY2 =
○ PUrchase = 015*CATTLE
○ Rainfall = 450+erratic+sine
○ ratio = (ST_rate/GRACAP)*100
○ RFF_weighted = (2*RainFall+DELAYED_Rain)/3
○ sine = COS((TIME-3)*75)*90
○ ST_rate = RANGE_AREA/CATTLE
○ ST_weighted = (ST_rate+DEL_STrate)/2

Figure 11.4: Structure of the model

rainfall (RainFall), and the grazing capacity (GRACAP); and the cattle submodel, with births (Births), natural deaths (including home slaughter) (NatDeath), commercial offtake (OffTake), and purchase (PUrchase) determining total herd size (CATTLE).

The two submodels are linked by:

1. the impact of annual grazing capacity (independent variable) on birth rate (BI–rate) and death rate (ND–rate) (dependent variables) via table functions R1 and R2 (see Figures 11.2 and 11.3), respectively, and by
2. the stocking rate which affects the annual grazing capacity. The impact of the stocking rate is averaged over two years. This represents the assumption that last year's stocking rate (DEL–STrate) has an effect that lasts one extra year (ST–weighted). The influence of the stocking rate on the grazing capacity has been explained previously.

Rainfall, the main independent driving variable, is modelled as the combination of the sine wave (sine) and a yearly draw from a normal distribution (erratic) with 450 mm as the mean, representing a 17-year cycle with deviations from the long-term mean for the country. Last year's rainfall (DELAYED–Rain) is taken for half its value to represent a moisture buffer in the soil (RFF–weighted). The effect of rainfall on the grazing capacity has also been explained earlier.

Historical simulation

An historical simulation has been executed, using historic rainfall data from 1966 through 1986 as the driving input. Initial conditions for this test simulation were 1,060,000 cattle units in 1966, a 1977 national average PCC, and 1980–81 values for birth, death, offtake, and purchase rates. Range area between 1966 and the early 1980s is assumed to be understocked.

Results are shown in Figure 11.5. Even though several initial conditions are not known and the rainfall table function can only generate historical data every other year, the simulated herd development follows historical cattle data rather closely.

Simulation for risk management

Risks in the future

Figure 11.5 shows the rapid development of the cattle herd during

| | SIMULATED DATA | | FIELD DATA | |
Time	RainFall	CATTLE	RainFall	CATTLE
1966	600	1,060	600	1,060
1967	505	1,241	392	
1968	410	1,434	415	
1969	423	1,501	369	
1970	435	1,541	438	
1971	344	1,594	577	1,650
1972	253	1,590	254	
1973	428	1,513	693	
1974	603	1,506	600	
1975	591	1,728	554	2,162
1976	580	2,008	577	
1977	464	2,288	600	
1978	348	2,401	323	
1979	449	2,361	485	
1980	550	2,344	554	2,455
1981	478	2,450	300	2,495
1982	405	2,533	406	2,504
1983	356	2,519	360	2,407
1984	308	2,455	309	2,306
1985	291	2,346		
1986	275	2,218		

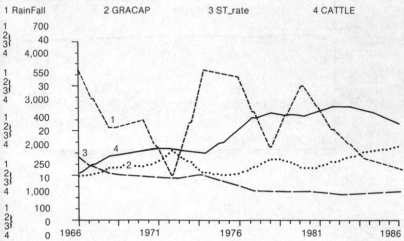

Figure 11.5: Historical simulation (1966–86)

the past 20 years. Questions such as "What will be the long-term future impact of drought periods on range and cattle?" and "What is the long-term sustainable cattle herd size?" have been asked by farmers, planners and resource managers.

The model that has been used to mimic the history of the range-cattle system has been applied to explore its future as well. The only difference is the way in which the annual rainfall is calculated. With data from the past and the assumption that the overall pattern will remain the same, future rainfall data are generated by the computer model.

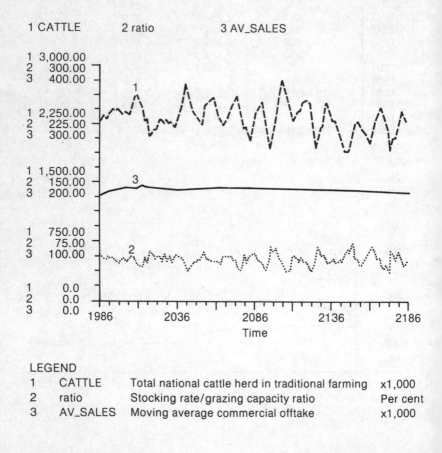

LEGEND

1	CATTLE	Total national cattle herd in traditional farming	x1,000
2	ratio	Stocking rate/grazing capacity ratio	Per cent
3	AV_SALES	Moving average commercial offtake	x1,000

Figure 11.6: Cattle and range development 1986–2186 with 8% commercial offtake per year

Figure 11.6 shows the results of simulating the range-cattle system from 1986 to 2186. The graphs suggest that after the drought of the early to mid-1980s, in which some of the herd was lost, the herd will resume its growth though not indefinitely. With the commercial offtake rate held constant at 8% per year, the herd size will oscillate around an average of 2.3 million livestock units, reaching peaks of 2.8 million and lows of 1.8 million units.

The oscillations driven by the assumed 17-year rainfall periodicity imply an average decrease of the total herd in 8.5 years of around 450,000 livestock units, which constitutes about 20% of the total herd. The constant 8% commercial offtake leads to a 100-year average offtake of 185,000 cattle per year, with a minimum of 145,000 and a peak value of 200,000.

An indication of the stress on the range and consequently the condition of the cattle is given by the stocking rate/grazing capacity ratio. If they match, then the ratio equals 100%. If there are more cattle on the range than would be warranted by the grazing capacity, the ratio becomes less than 100, implying hungry cattle. If there are few cattle on a good quality range, the ratio goes over 100 and the cattle have plenty of forage. In the case of a fixed 8% offtake rate, the long-term average ratio value becomes 55%, implying a range under continuous heavy stress.

According to the model, these values represent the mean long-term carrying capacity of Botswana, given current livestock management systems and variation resulting from rainfall patterns and stocking rate impacts.

Management options

The future as generated by the simulations described in the previous section may not be easily acceptable to all cattle farmers in Botswana. Some farmers, especially those with small herds, may be interested in ways to minimize the risk of losing approximately 20% of their herd. In the EDL (Environment and Development Linkages) Project, a number of management options have been distinguished (Arntzen and Veenendaal 1986 pp.53 – 57). In this paper the implications of only two policies are explored.

Policy 1. Increased offtake rate. It has been suggested that an increase in commercial offtake rate may be an effective management action to achieve both a better range quality and more income for the farmers. The national average offtake rate has been about 8% over the last few years.

Assuming that a market will be available, we have explored the consequences of 10 and 15% offtake (the latter being approximately the rate used on commercial farms), fixed for the next 200 years

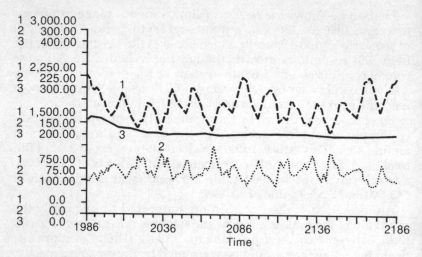

Figure 11.7: Cattle and range development 1986–2186 with 10% commercial offtake per year

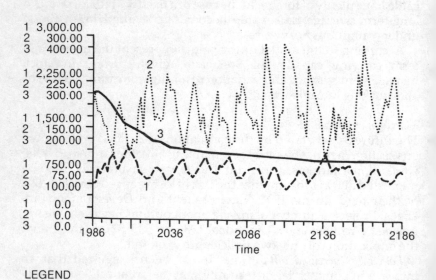

LEGEND

1	CATTLE	Total national cattle herd in traditional farming	x1,000
2	ratio	Stocking rate/grazing capacity ratio	Per cent
3	AV_SALES	Moving average commercial offtake	x1,000

Figure 11.8: Cattle and range development 1986–2186 with 15% commercial offtake per year

(Figures 11.7 and 11.8). The long-term average herd size drops to 1.75 and 1.00 million, respectively, which leads to 80 and 175% stocking rate/grazing capacity ratios. The long-term average yearly offtake drops in both cases.

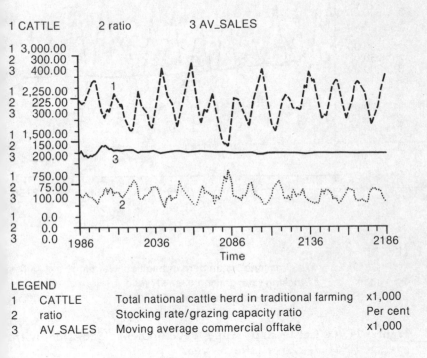

LEGEND

1	CATTLE	Total national cattle herd in traditional farming	x1,000
2	ratio	Stocking rate/grazing capacity ratio	Per cent
3	AV_SALES	Moving average commercial offtake	x1,000

Figure 11.9: Cattle and range development 1986–2186 with average 8% (+/– 2%) offtake per year

As an alternative to the fixed offtake rate, an "adaptive" offtake rate policy has been tested with the model. This policy is based on the assumption that by extra slaughter in low rainfall years and less than average slaughter in high rainfall years, the range is optimally exploited and total average offtake should be the same or better than with a fixed policy.

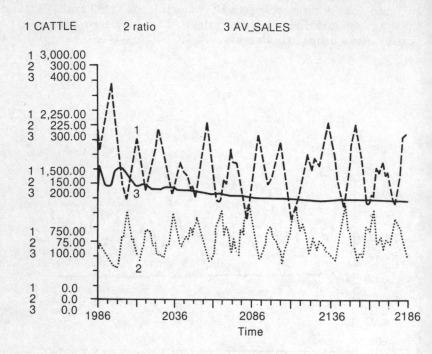

1 CATTLE   2 ratio   3 AV_SALES

LEGEND

1	CATTLE	Total national cattle herd in traditional farming	x1,000
2	ratio	Stocking rate/grazing capacity ratio	Per cent
3	AV_SALES	Moving average commercial offtake	x1,000

Figure 11.10: Cattle and range development 1986–2186 with average 10% (+/– 2%) offtake per year

In the simulation experiments, we have used the long-term national average annual rainfall (about 450 mm) as the threshold value. If rainfall is less than 450 mm, then the "high" offtake rate is applied; if rainfall is more than 450 mm, then the "low" offtake rate is applied. Figures 11.9 and 11.10 show the results of simulating with an 8% average and with a 10% average. The results are not much different from the fixed policy.

Policy 2. Adding grazing land by borehole development. An obvious option to decrease overall stocking rates and increase food supply per head of cattle is to enlarge the grazing area available to the

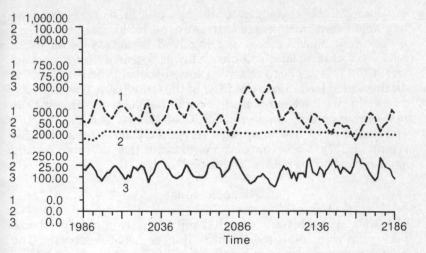

Figure 11.11: Cattle development 1986–2186 on 57,520 km² added grazing land with average potential carrying capacity of 12.5

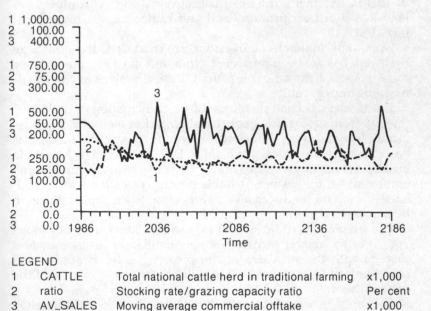

LEGEND

1	CATTLE	Total national cattle herd in traditional farming	x1,000
2	ratio	Stocking rate/grazing capacity ratio	Per cent
3	AV_SALES	Moving average commercial offtake	x1,000

Figure 11.12: Cattle development 1986–2186 on 57,520km² added grazing land with average potential carrying capacity of 13.5

cattle herd. Table 11.3 indicates the potential total extension of the borehole-based grazing area (currently 150,165 km²).

Assuming that the best grazing land is already being used, additional grazing land will have a lower potential carrying capacity (PCC). This implies a relatively low sustainable density of cattle on the added land. Since the PCC of the land that will be added is uncertain, we have simulated two alternative developments: the first one assuming an average PCC of 12.5 ha per LSU (Figure 11.11); the other assuming an average PCC of 13.5 ha per LSU (Figure 11.12). These simulations indicate that a proportionally smaller herd can be held on the added land.

Conclusions

The study provides an extended but basically simple predator-prey type simulation model including negative feedbacks. The model concentrates on the role of rainfall and stocking rate in determining the quality of the range and the role of range quality and quantity in determining cattle herd development. It does not fully represent the details of the range-cattle system. In fact, several factors that influence cattle survival such as competition, land loss by desertification, and substitutes for grazing are not included.

Since only numbers of livestock are modelled, the quality of the herd has to be interpreted from the stocking rate/grazing capacity ratio. If the ratio is less than 100%, the area is overstocked, meaning hungry cattle.

The model has been developed by a combination of deductive (mainly from ecological theory) and empirical methods. Data are incomplete and from different sources. Testing of the model has been limited to historical simulation. Still, the model is thought to include the major processes and control mechanisms functioning in the range-cattle system, is stable through realistic negative feedback loops, and produces a relatively close fit to empirical data in historical simulation.

The simulations indicate that (a) the regulatory feedback loops built into the model lead to a stable oscillatory behaviour, and that (b) with the structure of the present model, droughts will cause serious losses of cattle but will not lead to a collapse of the national herd.

The rapid growth of the cattle herd between 1966 and 1982 shall probably not be continued after the drought of the early 1980s. If present offtake rates are continued, then the herd will stabilize at about 2.3 million LSU. Trying to maintain such a herd does imply severe risks, especially for the small farmers. The range is calculated to be under heavy stress (overstocked), implying local soil degradation, little room for wildlife and poor quality of great numbers of cattle.

Varying offtake rates are a slight improvement in terms of higher sustainable offtake and less stress on the range if they vary between 8 and 12%. The other offtake options tested did not provide an improvement compared with fixed offtake policies. However, market dependencies and difficulties of profitably investing revenues from high offtake years in order to finance purchase in good rainfall years may cause risks for those who adopt adaptive policies.

The basic assumption of the second policy examined is that addition of grazing land will enlarge the basis for cattle herd development. The total offtake and other benefits should therefore be greater. However, lack of water of good quality and the suspected quality of that part of the range not yet in use as grazing land lead to less than proportional increases in herd size and offtake.

Note

1. The model presented here is one of a suite of models developed in the context of the Environment-Development Linkages Research Project sponsored by the Directorate-General for International Cooperation of the Dutch Government (see Arntzen and Veenendaal 1986, for the final report).

References

Arntzen, J.W., and E. Veenendaal (1986),
  A Profile of Environment and Development in Botswana (Amsterdam/ Gaborone: Institute for Environmental Studies/National Institute of Development Research and Documentation).
DHV (1980),
  Cultivated Land Survey Botswana. DHV/Ministry of Agriculture, Gaborone.
Field, D.I. (1977),
  Potential Carrying Capacity of Rangeland in Botswana (Gaborone: Land Utilization Division, Ministry of Agriculture).
Field, D.I. (1978),
  A Handbook for Basic Ecology for Range Management in Botswana (Gaborone: Land Utilization Division, Ministry of Agriculture).

Ministry of Agriculture (1969),
   Agricultural Statistics, Gaborone.
Ministry of Finance and Development Planning (1985),
   National Development Plan 1985 – 1991 (1985), Gaborone: Government
   Printer).
Tyson, P.D. (1980),
   "Southern African rainfall: past, present and future" in M.T. Hinchley
   (ed.), *Symposium on Drought in Botswana* (Gaborone: Botswana Society).
Vossen, P. (1986),
   Personal communication (Gaborone: Department of Meteorological
   Services).

IV
Improvement Programmes at the Village/Local Level

Dryland areas in developing countries often pose special problems to those attempting to combat dryland degradation. Entire villages or even large regions may already be far along in the cycle of degradation, leading to increased poverty, to increased degradation, to increased poverty, and so on. These areas often suffer from many of the problems discussed so far – declining crop yields, overgrazing and deforestation. In such areas, an integrated programme designed to deal with all these issues is necessary if any long-lasting solutions are to be implemented.

Extreme poverty is a common characteristic of such areas. Inhabitants live at subsistence level with little or no cushion against droughts and other vagaries of nature. Short-term survival is paramount, even at the cost of increased resource degradation in the future. Programmes with long-term benefits have little chance of success if they involve current sacrifice for future gains – residents feel unable to make even small sacrifices out of their current production. Combined with this obstacle is the strong aversion to risk in such areas.

Though poverty stricken areas such as these have the most to gain from change, they are often the most difficult areas in which to implement a project successfully. In addition to the constraints imposed by poverty and risk aversion, other social and cultural factors often make it difficult for outsiders to be accepted by the community. These areas require a "bottom-up" approach as compared with the "top-down" approach so often imposed by donor groups.

This section describes two successful programmes implemented by the Society for Promotion of Wastelands Development in India. The first study is an example of an integrated soil and water conservation programme including a small-scale irrigation development in north India. Working with the village council, the programme was able to improve both cropping and grazing practices and change village attitudes toward nearby protected forests, allowing increased production of fuelwood.

The second study describes a successful programme that focused on establishing informal educational centres and strengthening local institutions. These educational centres eventually led to a collective decision to implement a large-scale afforestation programme. Special attention was given to equity issues so that participants would benefit to the degree they participated in the project and benefits would not be usurped by a small group of powerful individuals.

12
Economic and Social Change in a Small Rural Community in the Degraded Lower Shivalik Hill Range in North India

Society for Promotion of Wastelands Development

Précis

This study discusses a programme designed to reverse the effects of degradation in a small rural village in India and improve the quality of life of its inhabitants. Spurred by a study of siltation in a nearby catchment, the project considered how a soil and water conservation programme could be established to benefit an entire village.

The system devised was comprised of a number of features including water harvesting and small-scale irrigation, improved agricultural and grazing practices, and encouraging the villagers themselves to take charge of many aspects of the programme. As the high benefit-cost ratios show, an integrated programme such as this can bring about profound improvements without unduly high capital costs.

Characteristics of the project area

Location
The Shivalik hill range is situated below the Himalayan Mountain range and above the Indo-Gangetic alluvial plains, extending into the Indian states of Punjab, Haryana, Himachal Pradesh, and Uttar Pradesh and covering more than 1.9 million ha. It is fairly densely populated, mostly with small rural communities. Sukhomajri is a small village in the Pinjore range of the Shivaliks, 30 km from Chandigarh. It has a population of about 450, all belonging to a caste called Gujjars. Figure 12.1 shows the location of the project area.

Climate
The average annual rainfall is 1,137 mm (952 mm is dependable at a 75% probability), of which 792 mm (82%) is received from June to September (568 mm is dependable at a 75% probability). The coefficient of variation is 24.7%. Monsoon rains start around the end of June and end by mid-September. Rainfall of long duration and high

intensity is a common feature of the area. Rainfall intensities as high as 135 mm/hr for a 15-minute period and 105 mm/hr for a 30-minute duration have been recorded.

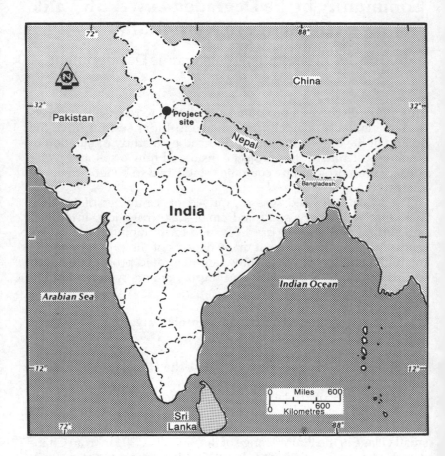

Figure 12.1: Location of Sukhomajri Project area

The mean maximum temperature is over 43°C during May and June, and the mean minimum temperature is recorded in January. The average annual pan evaporation is 2,300 mm. Average daily sunshine hours vary from 6.3 in July/August when the sky remains cloudy, to 9.6 in May. The average wind velocity varies from 3.5 to 9.6 km/hr.

Since groundwater is unavailable within a reasonable depth, there is no possibility of installing tubewells. No surface irrigation is available from any other area because of the terrain.

Soils
The soil in the agricultural watershed is generally sandy loam on the surface and loam in the lower layers. The soil in hilly forest watersheds is silty clay. In general the soils are very deep, but sloping lands near the foothills contain pebbles usually smaller than 4 cm at the surface with their quantity varying from 10 to 15% by volume. The slope of land varies from 1 to 3% on good arable lands and from 10 to 15% near the foothills.

The foothills are sparsely vegetated, sustain very poor crops, and are severely eroded. Soil erosion is severe in the formerly forested areas, which have become virtually devoid of vegetative cover, and moderate to severe in agricultural watersheds.

Land use
The principal land use in these semi-hilly areas is rainfed agriculture – maize followed by wheat in the valleys and forestry on slopes and hilltops. Maize suffers from moisture stress due to frequent dry spells and early withdrawal of monsoon rains and produces satisfactory harvests only once in five years. The lack of residual soil moisture after harvesting maize greatly depresses the yield of wheat. Agriculture is unable to provide even subsistence level needs of the rural community and therefore most of the population resorts to rearing livestock for manure, domestic fuel, and sale (to the plains) to ensure against crop failure.

The cattle population per capita is virtually double that in the plains. This large cattle population has led to overgrazing, leading to poor productivity in grass cultivation (resulting in severe erosion) and consequently to poor condition of livestock. Women have to spend a great deal of time collecting grasses for fodder and wood for fuel and often encroach on neighbouring reserved forests. Efforts by the Forestry Department to protect forests by fencing fail despite levying of fines and threats. Overgrazing of vegetative cover and felling of trees have led to severe soil erosion resulting in frequent landslides, formation of gullies, and flash floods.

Almost 50% of the average rainfall becomes runoff from hill slopes that have been rendered bare (supporting only sparse vegetation comprising scattered bushes of *Adhtoda vasica*, *Dodanea viscosa* and *Lantana camara*). The quantity of sediment washed off annually is estimated at 100 to 150 tonnes/ha of catchment.

Past attempts at rural development

Prior to 1976 a wide variety of strategies had been tried to improve the economic conditions. The Forestry Department attempted to raise plantations on the slopes and also fenced these plantations to protect vegetative and timber growth. But the shortage of fodder and fuel in Sukhomajri (and other villages in the area) was such that fences were repeatedly broken, and protected forest plantations were encroached upon so seriously by the village communities that this plantation development failed. Government extension agencies attempted to introduce controlled grazing and planting of fruit trees, but these efforts also failed to enthuse the village communities.

One of the most likely reasons that these programmes failed is that these efforts entailed a diversion of resources from current consumption of a poverty-stricken village community surviving at subsistence level. Since no immediate, direct visible benefits were perceived by the villagers, extension efforts continued to fail. Over-exploitation of natural resources continued.

Impetus for current project

Chandigarh was built in the 1950s as the capital of the Indian State of Punjab. The city has grown rapidly; its total population was 451,000 in 1981. A lake (Sukhna) was created in Chandigarh in 1958 to supply water to the city population. Within 18 years, more than 60% of this lake filled with silt, and its depth was reduced from 14 m to barely 4 m in 1976 despite increasingly heavy expenditures on desiltation. Each monsoon brought large quantities of silt into the lake.

The problem became so acute that surveys were undertaken to determine the viability of a number of alternatives to increase water storage for supply to the growing city. As part of these studies, the Central Soil and Water Conservation Research and Training Institute (CSWCRTI) of the Union Government Indian Council of Agricultural Research located in Chandigarh was asked to carry out a study of siltation. This Institute carried out a ground survey of the catchment area of the lake which revealed that 25% of the total catchment area located in the higher part of the region contributed 80 to 90% of the silt load.

The runoff of water and silt from Sukhomajri affects agricultural areas below the village although it does not contribute to the siltation of the Sukhna Lake in Chandigarh. However, the success in checking siltation in the Sukhna Lake from the lower Shivalik hills in neighbouring areas (by the construction of check dams along with plantations of Bhabbar grass, *Acacia catechu, Dalbargia sisso*) led the Institute to consider how similar water and soil conservation could be achieved in Sukhomajri for the benefit of the village community.

Table 12.1: Social and economic characteristics of Sukhomajri in 1976

Population

Total population	455
Male	263
Female	192
Number of families	59
Average size of family	8

Education

Graduate	Nil
Engineering Diploma	1
Matriculation	6
Industrial Training Institute Certificate	1
Middle School	26
People who can write	35
Illiterate	386

Employment

Teacher	1
Army Soldiers	5
Fitters	2
Constable	1
Drivers	2
Peons	7
Factory workers:	
Permanent workers	15
Casual workers	20
Daily wage earners	44

Land use

Total land area	120 ha
Agriculture land	100 ha
Residential land	4 ha
Waste land	16 ha
Area under double cropping	37.2 ha
Area under single cropping	62.8 ha

Land ownership

Land owned by individuals	52.3 ha
Panchayat (community) land being cultivated by individuals	47.7 ha
Panchayat (community) land used for grazing	16.0 ha

Land holding

Average holding per family	0.88 ha
Average holding per capita	0.11 ha
Families having marginal land holding (up to 1 ha unirrigated)	37
Families having small land holding (1 to 2 ha unirrigated)	20
Families having medium land holding (above 2 ha unirrigated)	2

Cattle population

Bullocks	79
Cows	14
Buffalos	129
Goats	144
Heifers	4
Buffalo calf	41
Total	411

Annual production in Quintals

Wheat	250
Maize	356
Fodder	960

Project description

After a detailed survey of both the social and environmental conditions of Sukhomajri (see Table 12.1), the Institute began to implement a variety of water and soil conservation measures. These included:

- shallow contour trenches to arrest sediment and harvest runoff;
- construction of stone check dams in gully bottoms to stabilize gullies and store runoff water;
- installation of an underground PVC pipe water conveyance system;
- planting of *Acacia catechu* on steep slopes;
- stall feeding of cattle and protection against grazing on vulnerable lands;
- protection against illicit felling of trees; *and*
- introduction of a variety of improved agricultural projects.

The main features of this programme are described in the following sections. Problems encountered during implementation are also discussed.

Storage dams
Areas similar to the project area with steep slopes, silty clay soil, low vegetative cover, and high drainage density generally release on average about 40 to 50% of precipitation as runoff. Taking the average yearly rainfall of 1,137 mm and the consequent siltation, evaporation, and seepage, it was calculated that 600 mm of water storage from each hectare of the catchment area would be possible. During 1976 – 79, three storage dams were constructed in the Sukhomajri village. This case study evaluates the economics of one of these structures, storage dam no. 2, since it is considered representative of the field conditions prevailing in the area.

After construction, conflicts arose as to who was entitled to the stored water. The large "revenue" village in the area claimed a large share, but this was resolved by recourse to land records that showed the dam storage area to be Sukhomajri community land.

The amount of water that could be stored was enough for two irrigation periods (1-15 November and 1-15 December) for wheat at 57.5 mm gross, or 37.5 mm net, irrigation requirement (assuming 65% irrigation efficiency). With this requirement, the mean available water supply from storage dam no. 2 can irrigate about 32 ha of the wheat crop (about 30% of the agricultural land area in the village). For effective utilization of scarce water, the whole of this area required proper levelling and grading. After water was available and land was levelled, improved seeds and fertilizers were introduced to the farmers to increase crop yields.

Water conveyance system
The water was conveyed to the fields by underground PVC pipes to minimize seepage loss. The main pipe was connected to a small tank from which water enters the underground pipelines. Four outlets were originally provided from the pipelines to release water at regular intervals, though this number was later increased to seven (see following section).

Institutional arrangements
Dam no. 2, together with underground pipelines for conveyance (with four outlet points), was completed in 1978. A member of the CSWCRTI staff was posted at the village to administer the distribution of water. Conflicts in the distribution of irrigation water arose when the largest landowner claimed a disproportionate share. For the next two years disputes in distribution of water continued to increase, together with allegations of misuse of power (by a few of the larger landowning families), though these were never expressed openly. These disputes were compounded by the fact that the pipeline could irrigate only 16 ha.

A characteristic of the Gujjar community is the important role women play in decision-making within the family. They are solely responsible for looking after livestock and working in the field. In addition, they make many of the decisions on agricultural operations (such as what crops to grow).

In a survey of women's attitudes on a variety of economic and social issues, including the development of the village carried out by an NGO, the women in the village expressed their views frankly about the serious deficiencies in the distribution of water and the performance of the staff appointed to distribute water. A further survey carried out by a water management expert revealed that the outlets provided were too few to enable equitable distribution and that it was feasible to extend the underground pipeline network as well as virtually double the number of outlets.

This expert, together with the NGO working in this village, held a number of discussions with the community and the *panchayat* (village council) and it was in these discussions that the concept of a water user's association (WUA) to manage and control the stored water was developed. After a series of further discussions, the WUA was established along with a system in which every member of the village was given an equal share of water regardless of the land he or she owned and freedom to sell that share to others. The staff from CSWCRTI was withdrawn, and the WUA appointed a person from the village who was then trained to carry out his functions (and to look after maintenance and operation). The pipeline system was extended to provide water to 32 ha, and the number of outlet points increased to seven (from four). Fish farming was subsequently introduced in the reservoir.

Grazing

Before the project started, there were 144 goats which formed about 35% of the total livestock population. Because of a reduction in open grazing and increased plantations in the hill slopes, the villagers changed the livestock composition. By the early 1980s, the number of goats declined to 11% of the total livestock population, and the share of buffalo in the total livestock population increased from 31 to 46%. This change not only prevented open grazing in the hilly areas but also increased milk production, thereby contributing to improved nutrition and income for the villagers.

Use of reserved forest

As part of the village development scheme, pressure was put on the Forestry Department to alter its practice of auctioning the right to harvest grass in the neighbouring 120-ha reserved forest area. Prior to 1982, the Forestry Department auctioned the rights to harvest grass to the highest bidders, generally contractors, who paid an average rate of Rs. 300/sickle/yr. The grass was then sold by the contractors to villagers at any price they were able to realize. In 1982, the Forestry Department offered the right to village women. Due to the progressively improving care demonstrated by village women in cutting grass without destroying the roots and removing only dried twigs, for example, the Forestry Department waived charges for grass cutting to village widows and women whose husbands are employed elsewhere and are unable to remit adequate funds to their support.

The villagers are now the protectors of the reserved forest area. The growth of both grass and timber has accelerated. With the increased availability of agricultural and animal materials (especially through stall feeding and change in livestock composition), the per capita fuelwood consumption has declined from about 4.6 quintals in the mid-1970s to about 2.5 quintals in the early 1980s.

Other effects
The change that has occurred in the agricultural and allied productive sectors is marked. While the total land area under agriculture remains more or less unaltered, the annual wheat output has increased by 300% and the annual maize output has been stabilized at a slightly higher level (about 550 quintals). There is a threefold increase in fodder output. Milk output has increased by about 200 litres/day (a 25% increase). The village, which previously purchased 50% of its foodgrain, has become self-sufficient.

Some families, generally owning little land, sell their shares of water to others for Rs. 10 to Rs. 14/hr while they pay the Association Rs. 8/hr. Several such families have also become sharecroppers of large landowning families; 12% of the agricultural land is now under sharecropping.

This overall improvement in the economic position has led the farmers of Sukhomajri to begin taking risks in planning their future economic activity. Many small farmers have now started to experiment with alternative crops and crop combinations that might be more remunerative. Fruit and timber trees are being planted in field bunds. Mud houses have been replaced by brick houses.

As a result of pressure from the villagers, a primary school has now been established in the village, and the number of children going to school has increased to 45, of which 25 are girls.

Many other characteristics have yet to change. An attempt to

Table 12.2: Total project capital costs (Rupees in 1982 prices)

Item	Year 0 (1977)	Year 1 (1978)
Basic construction work		
Earth work*	104,000	—
Foundation work	15,000	—
Watershed treatment	8,000	—
Land levelling	—	40,000
Water conveyance system	—	80,000
TOTAL	127,000	120,000

* including spillway

introduce improved woodstoves that will further reduce fuelwood consumption, as well as smoke, has yet to succeed. Women complain that cooking in this stove takes too long, and they cannot spare time from looking after livestock and other chores.

Project costs and benefits

Capital costs
The construction of the reservoir and treatment of the catchment area was completed before the monsoon of 1977. The water conveyance system was installed in 1978. At the same time, the land was levelled partly by CSWCRTI and partly by the farmers to make it suitable for irrigation. The total costs are listed in Table 12.2.

Distribution of project cost by resource categories is shown in Table 12.3.

Table 12.3: Distribution of project capital costs (Rupees in 1982 prices)

Item	Domestic material	Skilled labour	Unskilled labour
Basic construction work			
Earth work	15,000	5,000	84,000
Foundation work	10,200	1,200	3,600
Watershed treatment	4,000	—	4,000
Land levelling	8,000	—	32,000
Water conveyance system	60,000	4,000	16,000
TOTAL	97,200	10,200	139,600

Annual operating costs
Additional cost of wheat cultivation. Availability of irrigation requires more intensive labour and additional fertilizer inputs. Additional labour and fertilizer increased from year 2 to year 4, and thereafter remained at this level. It is assumed to remain constant throughout the life of the project (though further improvement in agricultural practices is expected).

Cost of irrigation. A supervisor (from the village) was hired and paid Rs. 2/hr of irrigation for 750 hours per year. In addition, he is also given Rs. 4/hr for maintenance of pipelines, fuel, and other matters. The full irrigation potential was realized in year 4. It increased from 250 hours in year 2 to 500 hours in year 3, reaching 750 hours in year 4 and is assumed to remain constant thereafter.

Cost of increased milk yield. Milk yield increased because of the availability of better fodder and change in the composition of the livestock population. The costs were (a) foregoing the right of open grazing of animals in the catchment area; and (b) use of the fodder available from the catchment area which, as an alternative, the villagers could have sold in the market. First-year increases in yield were mainly a result of the increased availability of fodder, and in the second, third, and fourth years because of change in livestock composition and improvement in breeds. Estimated increase was 20,000 litres in the second year, 40,000 in the third year, and 60,000 in the fourth year, remaining at that level thereafter. The price of milk is Rs 1/litre.

Table 12.4: Annual operating costs (Rupees in 1982 prices)

Item	1	2	3	Year 4	5	6-29	30
Additional cost of wheat cultivation							
Fertilizer	—	2,080	4,160	6,240	6,240	6,240	6,240
Labour	—	1,040	2,080	3,120	3,120	3,120	3,120
Cost of irrigation	—	1,500	3,000	4,500	4,500	4,500	4,500
Cost of increased milk yield	—	1,500	1,500	1,500	1,500	1,500	1,500
Maintenance of reservoir	240	200	160	120	120	120	120
TOTAL	240	6,320	10,900	15,480	15,480	15,480	15,480

Maintenance of reservoir. The reservoir (dam no. 2) requires desiltation every year in the summer. The cost in the first year, estimated at 30 person-days, was incurred by CSWCRTI. With the improvement in the vegetative cover in the catchment area, siltation has gradually been reduced and the cost declined to 25 person-days in the second year, 20 in the third year, and 15 in the fourth year. Although it is expected to decline somewhat in subsequent years, it has been assumed to remain constant at 15 person-days per year.

Annual operating costs are shown in Table 12.4.

Other costs
In addition to the annual operating costs in the construction year and the subsequent three years, the director of CSWCRTI and four other scientists devoted their time to this project and used the facilities of CSWCRTI. The estimated cost of their time and the use of their facilities (office premises, camp set-up at village, vehicles) are shown in Table 12.5.

Table 12.5: Cost of CSWCRTI staff and infrastructure (Rupees, 1982 prices)

| | Year | | | |
Item	0	1	2	3
Staff cost of CSWCRTI	48,000	48,000	48,000	48,000
Infrastructure	48,000	48,000	48,000	48,000
TOTAL	96,000	96,000	96,000	96,000

Direct benefits (consumption)
The project resulted in additional wheat output (5, 10 and 15 quintals/ha in the second, third, and fourth and subsequent years), fodder grass (at 15 t/ha from 6 ha of catchment area), timber output (from 4,680 trees in the catchment area), a net increase in the value of fish in the reservoir (500 kg/yr from the fifth year onward), and milk from buffalos and cows. The net increase in the value of fish and milk has been calculated by deducting the additional cost from the additional output. The cost of the fishery includes the cost of and feed for fingerlings, and maintenance. The cost of additional milk from changing the livestock composition in favour of stall-fed buffalo with assured fodder supply at the expense of open-grazed goats includes the cost of additional buffalo, additional cost of feed, and the income forgone from goats.

Indirect benefits (environmental)
The main indirect benefit arises from reduced soil erosion. The treatment of the catchment area by tree planting and grass cover and the construction of the reservoir has prevented the loss of topsoil estimated at 100 t/yr/ha from the sixth year onward. (In

the first five years, the reduction in erosion is estimated at 0, 20, 40, 60, and 80 t/yr/ha, respectively.)

While the benefits directly accruing to farmers can be calculated at market prices, the indirect benefits pose problems in estimation. Washing away of topsoil meant loss of nutrients from the area, where now trees and grasses have been planted. Though the actual replacement cost of topsoil has not been calculated, the market value of the replacement cost of nutrients has been estimated and taken as the benefit. (It can be argued that the continuing soil erosion would have become so acute that the community would have had to be resettled elsewhere or other occupations, such as industry or services, arranged. This would have entailed very large financing by government.) The major direct and indirect benefits from the project are calculated in Table 12.6.

Table 12.6: Project benefits (Rupees in 1982 prices)

Item	Years					
	1	2	3	4	5-29	30
1. Additional wheat output	—	20,280	40,560	60,840	60,840	60,840
2. Additional grass output	—	1,500	1,500	1,500	1,500	1,500
3. Timber output	—	—	—	—	—	491,400
4. Fish output	—	—	—	—	2,500	2,500
5. Increased milk yield	—	20,000	40,000	60,000	60,000	60,000
6. Reduced soil erosion	36,960	73,920	110,880	147,840	184,800	184,800

Other benefits
Apart from the preceding direct and indirect benefits, other benefits have accrued to the inhabitants of Sukhomajri which are not taken into account in this study. Prior to the erection of check dams, the erosion from gullies was adversely affecting downstream agricultural crop yields. There is a distinct improvement in the crop yield in downstream landholdings resulting from this project in Sukhomajri. The farmers in Sukhomajri are now

experimenting with various timber trees (*Eucalyptus*) and fruit trees (*Papaya*) in the field bunds.

Apart from these two benefits, which can be quantified, there are also several other qualitative benefits such as increased food security, improved nutrition and living conditions, reduced underemployment and poverty, and increasing community participation and social awareness.

Table 12.7: Benefit and cost flows (Rupees in 1982 prices)

				Year			
	1977	1978	1979	1980	1981		
Item	0	1	2	3	4	5-29	30
Benefits							
Add'l wheat output	—	—	20,280	40,560	60,840	60,840	60,840
Add'l grass output	—	1,500	1,500	1,500	1,500	1,500	1,500
Timber output	—	—	—	—	—	—	491,400
Fish output	—	—	—	—	—	2,500	2,500
Add'l milk yield	—	20,000	40,000	60,000	60,000	60,000	60,000
Reduced soil erosion	—	36,960	73,920	110,880	147,840	184,800	184,800
Costs							
Construction cost	119,000	—	—	—	—	—	—
Domestic material	25,200	—	—	—	—	—	—
Skilled labour	6,200	—	—	—	—	—	—
Hired unskilled labour	87,600	—	—	—	—	—	—
Watershed treatment	8,000	—	—	—	—	—	—
Domestic material	4,000	—	—	—	—	—	—
Hired unskilled labour	4,000	—	—	—	—	—	—
Land levelling	—	40,000	—	—	—	—	—
Domestic material	—	8,000	—	—	—	—	—
Family unskilled labour	—	32,000	—	—	—	—	—
Water conveyance system	—	80,000	—	—	—	—	—
Domestic material	—	60,000	—	—	—	—	—
Skilled labour	—	4,000	—	—	—	—	—
Hired unskilled labour	—	16,000	—	—	—	—	—
Operating cost	—	240	4,820	9,400	13,980	13,980	13,980
Fertilizer	—	—	2,080	4,160	6,240	6,240	6,240
Family unskilled labour	—	—	1,040	2,080	3,120	3,120	3,120
Hired unskilled labour	—	240	200	160	120	120	120
Skilled labour	—	—	500	1,000	1,500	1,500	1,500
Domestic material	—	—	1,000	2,000	3,000	3,000	3,000
CSWCRTI cost	96,000	96,000	96,000	96,000	—	—	—
Domestic material	48,000	48,000	48,000	48,000	—	—	—
Skilled labour	48,000	48,000	48,000	48,000	—	—	—
Fodder income forgone	—	1,500	1,500	1,500	1,500	1,500	1,500

Data on the distribution of benefits to different income classes are not yet available (though with equal shares of water allotted to all farmers that can be used or sold, plus the additional income to small landowners from sharecropping, it is likely that the benefits are not skewed in favour of richer farmers).

Table 12.7 provides a comprehensive summary of all the benefits and costs of the project considered in this study. Various elements are further subdivided wherever possible according to the share appropriate to each of the resource category.

Economic analysis

The economic analysis of the Sukhomajri project has been carried out from the point of view of Indian society. Inputs and outputs have been valued at both market prices and shadow prices.

Financial analysis
Consumption benefits of the project consist of the net addition to the value of output after the project, including increased crop (wheat) yield, grass output, and milk output after the project, as well as the total output of timber and fish resulting from the project. The total direct cost represents the actual construction cost in the first two years and the annual operating cost including the opportunity costs of forgone income from fodder.

Table 12.8: Present value of direct financial benefits and costs (Rupees) for a 30-year period

| | Discount Rate | |
Item	12%	15%
Present value of benefits	861,671	673,566
Present value of costs	323,619	301,292
Net present value	538,052	372,294
Benefit-cost ratio	2.66	2.24

Table 12.8 presents the present values of direct consumption benefits (items 1, 2, 3, 4, and 5 in Table 12.7) and direct costs (items 7, 8, 9, 10, and 11 in Table 12.7) at two discount rates, 12 and 15%, for a 30-year period.

Table 12.9: Present financial values of total benefits (direct and indirect) and total costs (direct and indirect) (Rupees) for a 30-year period

Item	Discount Rate	
	12%	15%
Present value of benefits	2,053,811	1,626,039
Present value of costs	662,228	623,457
Net present value	1,391,583	1,002,582
Benefit-cost ratio	3.10	2.61

In Table 12.9 we have attempted to show the present values when indirect benefits and costs are included.

Tables 12.8 and 12.9 indicate high financial benefit-cost ratios for the Sukhomajri project, even at a 15% discount rate.

Social benefit-cost analysis
We have adopted the accounting ratios shown in Table 12.10 developed by the Planning Commission for estimating social costs and social benefits.

Table 12.11 shows the results of the analysis using the accounting ratios shown in Table 12.10. These can be compared with the data presented in Table 12.9. The social benefit-cost ratios are higher than the financial benefit-cost ratios, indicating the enhanced desirability of the project from the social viewpoint.

The environmental benefit that accrues to society from reduced erosion is in itself sufficient to justify investment in this project: at a 15% discount rate, the net present value from reduced erosion comes to about Rs. 952,000, which is much higher than the entire social cost of the project of about Rs. 469,000.

In the Sukhomajri village, investment in the storage of water and prevention of siltation (which was found feasible) has led to rapid acceptance of improved techniques in agricultural practices, livestock practices and supplemental activities in fish farming. Just as important and possibly of great significance for the future is the reduction in risk aversion among the villagers, leading them to experiment with relatively new ideas such as new crops and new crop rotation, and planting of fruit and timber trees on field bunds.

There has also been a reduction in illiteracy (though so far not very substantial) and significant increases in the number of children attending high school. The success in Sukhomajri has also led neighbouring villages to adopt similar systems.

It is also evident, however, that this change occurred in some-

Table 12.10: Accounting ratios* for various items

Labour

Rural hired unskilled labour (in Haryana)	0.94
Rural family labour (in Sukhomajri)	0.40
Rural skilled labour	1.00

Non-traded commodities

Construction (material & machinery)	0.52
Infrastructure (office machinery)	0.37

Traded commodities

Pipelines	1.00
Fertilizer	1.00
Wheat	1.00
Milk	1.00
Fish	1.00
Tree	1.00
Grass	1.00

* Accounting ratios $A_i = PS_i/PM_i$, where
     PS_i = Social price and PM_i = Market price

Note: The accounting ratios for items 1, 4, 5, 6, and 7 are developed by the Planning Commission and summarized in Lal (1980). The other accounting ratios are estimated based on the Planning Commission's methodology.

Table 12.11: Present social values of total benefits and costs (Rupees) for a 30-year period

	Discount Rate	
Item	*12%*	*15%*
Present value of social benefits	2,053,811	1,626,039
Present value of social costs	479,386	469,072
Net present values	1,556,425	1,156,967
Benefit-cost ratio	4.13	3.47

what fortuitous circumstances – investigations on how to check siltation in the reservoirs supplying water to the growing city of Chandigarh, 30 km from Sukhomajri, led to the initiation of this project. In addition, village co-operation was eased because Sukhomajri is a purely cohesive community (all Gujjars) with no significant landlessness problem.

A wide variety of measures previously introduced to improve economic and social conditions failed to enthuse the villagers, since they entailed diversion of resources from immediate consumption in a community surviving at subsistence level, although they could provide substantial benefits in the longer term. In these circumstances, the catalyst was in providing irrigation water through check dams that could be erected quickly and inexpensively. A disappointing feature was the relatively low contribution of the village inhabitants for farm labour (Rs. 36,000 out of a total cost of Rs. 139,600 for unskilled labour).

Can this success, limited though it is, be replicated readily in other degraded areas? The estimate of the amount of degraded land in India is 12.9 million ha of arid and semi-arid land, 7.2 million ha of saline and alkaline lands, and 74 million ha of water eroded area. There is also about 30 million ha of degraded forest area. Clearly the techniques of rehabilitation will be different for each type of land.

In virtually all these areas, however, the problem will be to devise a strategy that does not entail any immediate significant drain or diversion of resources from current consumption when large numbers of people live at bare subsistence levels. Another important factor is to avoid the need for injection of unduly large capital resources from elsewhere in a capital-short economy. In addition, community participation must be promoted by both government and voluntary organizations, and arrangements devised that will prevent conflict between different classes of beneficiaries.

Sources and references

Grewal, S.S., *et al*. (1983),
      "Economic development and rehabilitation of degraded areas through soil and water management: a case study", *Indian Journal of Soil Conservation* , vol.2, no.1.
Lal, Deepak (1980),
      Prices for Planning: Toward the Reform of Indian Planning (London: Heinemann).

Mishra, P.R., *et al.* (1980),
Operational Research Project on Watershed Development for Sediment, Drought and Flood Control, Sukhomajri (Chandigarh, India: Central Soil and Water Conservation Research and Training Institute).
Seckler, David, and Deep Joshi (1981),
A Rural Development Programme in India, Sukhomajri (New Delhi: Ford Foundation).
Society for Promotion of Wastelands Development (1984),
Hill Resources Development and Community Management – Case Studies of Sukhomajri and Dasholi Gram Swarajya Mandal (New Delhi: SPWD).

13
Dryland Management Options in Wastelands Development: Jawaja Block, Rajasthan

Society for Promotion of Wastelands Development

Précis

Like many other dryland areas, the land near the villages discussed in this study suffered from increasing degradation due to overgrazing and deforestation. Past development efforts had aided small groups within the area, but the benefits of these programmes tended to be usurped by a small group of powerful individuals.

This study describes a successful development programme that focused its efforts on establishing informal educational centres where villagers could come together to discuss potential solutions to the problems they faced. The result was a large-scale afforestation programme, adopted by consensus from the villagers, that included a variety of safeguards to ensure equitable distribution of benefits.

The high benefit-cost ratios of this programme show that social forestry schemes such as this can bring about substantial improvements in village life.

Introduction

The Aravalli Hills extend about 692 km from Palanpur in the Indian State of Gujarat to the State of Haryana and the Union Territory of Delhi in the northeast. This range bounds the main watershed of the Indian State of Rajasthan. At a few places, the hills are discontinuous with gaps. LANDSAT imagery has shown that in the absence of adequate afforestation, these gaps act as "windows" through which the desert sand drifts toward the fertile areas of Jaipur, Ajmer and Sikar districts of Rajasthan State.

The Aravallis divide Rajasthan into two parts – the arid lands to the west covering about two-thirds of the State and the semi-arid lands to the east. The Aravallis cover only about 20% of the State but influence the ecology of about two-thirds of its area.

More than half the area of Rajasthan (35 million ha) has already become wasteland, and the degradation of other areas continues.

Large-scale degradation of land has led to serious fuelwood short-ages, particularly affecting women and children, and fuel scar-city has become a much more serious danger than food scarcity. Decreased production due to erosion has affected the availability of fodder for cattle. The composition of the livestock population is becoming increasingly skewed in favour of hardy breeds like goats, threatening to further intensify degradation and expand the desertification process.

Decreasing productivity of land has led to expansion of agricul-ture to marginal areas. Cropping on such marginal lands is result-ing in extensive degradation and exacerbating the poverty of the area's inhabitants. The result of all these factors is the creation of what are known as "ecological refugees" and the existence of non-migrant communities who must face regular drought and floods.

Description of project area

This case study deals with the area administratively known as the Jawaja Block. This block is among the poorest in the Ajmer district in Rajasthan. It consists of 198 villages and hamlets with a population of about 100,000. Most of the villages fall between the two ridges of the Aravallis which converge just beyond the Jawaja village. The southern part of the Jawaja Block has undulating ter-rain and very little arable land.

The total area of the Jawaja Block is 58,500 ha, of which 24,800 ha are agricultural, some 24,000 ha are barren and uncultivable, 2,400 ha are non-agricultural, and 7,300 ha are owned and con-trolled by the Forestry Department. The large part of the block indicated as agricultural land gives a misleading picture of the agricultural conditions since much of the area is prone to either drought or floods. The undulating terrain is devoid of grasses and other vegetation and contributes to this situation.

The minimum temperature in winter months ranges from 1ºC to 3ºC, and the maximum temperature in summer months ranges from 43ºC to 46ºC. Average annual rainfall is 500 mm, and the variation in annual precipitation ranges from 150 to 1,001 mm. Average evaporation is usually higher than the rainfall.

In such circumstances, irrigation facilities normally would be able to contribute significantly to an improvement in the overall condition by increasing agricultural output, improving land use and checking erosion. However, what little irrigation exists is from tanks and open wells. When rains fail, which occurs frequently, 70 to 80% of these tanks and wells become dry. There is also a small number of electrical pump-sets for water lifting. As a result, even those lands that are classified as irrigated are subject to the vagaries of nature. The condition of unirrigated land is even worse: there have been at least two recent occasions – 1975 and 1981 – when the rains were so heavy that the entire area was flooded because of the "U" shape of the valley.

Extremes of temperature also adversely affect crops. The most recent example is severe frost, leading to a drastic reduction in the yield of wheat and near total failure of the gram (legume) crop. A number of nurseries were affected by severe heat in the absence of tree cover which normally provides protection against hot winds.

In addition to the harsh natural conditions of the area, a sizeable livestock population of poor quality adds to the pressure on degraded land. The total livestock population (including goats and sheep) exceeds 100,000. Few farmers are able to grow fodder in their fields to feed cattle, and the practice of open grazing is widespread.

With the steady increase in the cattle population, the effect on natural vegetation has been clearly disastrous. Most hills are now totally devoid of any vegetation, and the few surviving trees are heavily lopped or cut altogether to meet fodder and fuel needs. The cumulative effect on the soil, which is moderately alkaline and calcareous, is that the organic matter content is now negligible.

Urban-rural links

Beawar is the main city of the area with a population of about 60,000. It serves as the main market centre for inputs and outputs of the neighbouring villages including those in the Jawaja Block. Though it lies within the boundary of the Jawaja Block, it has its own municipality and is not under the administrative control of the Jawaja Block Committee. The city is the official administrative headquarters for three contiguous blocks (including the Jawaja Block).

The city and the surrounding rural areas are closely linked. The head (*Pradhan*) of the Jawaja Block is a member of several city committees which are concerned with market activities in Beawar. Villagers buy in Beawar what is not available at the village level – stock shortages at the village level of even essential commodities are not uncommon. Beawar also provides a place for villagers to sell their own produce.

The city attracts job seekers from the surrounding villages. It also acts as a major loading and unloading centre for road transport traffic on the Delhi-Ahmedabad-Bombay National Highway.

It has a large number of industrial enterprises, shops, and *mandis* (wholesale commodities merchandising centres).

As the administrative headquarters in the area, Beawar becomes the focal point for state and central governance for the judiciary, revenue, education, post and telegraphs and so on. Officials administering such schemes as the Drought Prone Area Programme are also located in Beawar.

There is a strong link between traders in the city and traders in the villages who also act as moneylenders. The moneylender in the village and the larger, more prosperous farmers have strong links with traders-cum-moneylenders in the city. These links are reinforced by itinerant agents who are often employees or semi-employees of the city traders-cum-moneylenders and who visit villages regularly. The Beawar city traders-cum-moneylenders have close links with merchants who control various commodities in larger cities (including metropolitan cities). This channel of commodity and money flows keeps the urban-rural terms of trade in the former's favour; especially adversely affected are small farmers, village craftspeople, and labourers.

Social organization
In the Jawaja Block, the Rawats, a relatively high caste community, are the largest landowning farming community. The Rawats also trade and lend money. All the heads of the village committees are large landowners, at least in a relative sense. They have landholdings between 4 and 10 ha, as compared to the average landholding in the area which is as low as 0.4 ha.

The political and economic leadership in the area is comprised of large farmers, large farmers-cum-moneylenders-cum-traders, and traders/merchants-cum-moneylenders. Such leaders derive power by direct or indirect control of finance and marketing of agricultural inputs, as well as agricultural produce and the manufactures of village artisans.

Control is exercised in several ways. Loans extended by moneylenders are linked to the purchase of products in advance or after the harvest. With respect to handlooms, loans are often in the form of raw materials linked to the collection of the finished products, with the handloom weaver being paid a low wage. The more independent handloom artisans attempt to sell their output directly to the villagers and, to the extent they are able to do so, get a better price. The village market is small, however, and the markets outside the villages are controlled by moneylenders who purchase and sell through linked traders in Beawar.

Co-operatives for marketing of essential commodities (such as fertilizers, kerosene, cloth) and also for providing credit have proved ineffective so far and have failed to modify the long-established network of political and economic linkages. To date, the governmental administrative system too has failed to make any significant progress in these relationships.

Development activities in the Block

The implementation of most government policies and programmes depends on Block administration. The organization at the Block level consists of the Block Development Officer (BDO) and his subordinates. The Block Development Officer is usually a member of the official state services and, in a sense, is on "loan" to the Block Committee (*Panchayat Samiti*) as the Chief Executive Officer for Block-level action. He acts as Secretary to the Block Committee (*Samiti*). The Block headquarters, which is located in the Jawaja village, has four or five extension officers working under the BDO to implement government schemes and projects in the Block and to supervise village-level workers, headmasters, and teachers in the primary schools.

The Block activities conducted by the Block Committee are limited by its small budget. Generally, major Block activities are those that are determined at the district level, and these invariably represent state or national schemes. Though in these cases the Block Committee has little say in determining policy, it attempts to exert its power through implementing these policies (which is the responsibility of the BDO and his staff) and by exercising control of organizations such as agricultural co-operatives.

The village head (*Sarpanch*) implements government schemes and strives to appear to be the decision-maker in the village. This role is particularly important with respect to low-cost housing for weaker sections, land redistribution, Drought Prone Area Programmes (DPAP) for the development of pastures, subsidy schemes and, more recently, the Integrated Rural Development Programme (IRDP) and the National Rural Employment Programme (NREP). The village head is anxious to demonstrate that he controls all beneficial inputs, irrespective of the supply source of the inputs (from government or non-government agencies).

The Block has set targets in relation to all the major government programmes, such as the quantity of fertilizers to be distributed, family planning, number of houses to be provided for specified weaker sections, and number of new animal husbandry units to be introduced. The Jawaja Block was initially classified as an animal husbandry area since agriculture was sparse and unreliable, but this animal husbandry effort was confined to a relatively ineffective artificial insemination programme for cows and the introduction of Russian Merino sheep for cross-breeding.

In 1975, however, the Ajmer district was included in a major agricultural scheme in this part of Rajasthan, and consequently Jawaja was reclassified as an agricultural area. All the extension officers, except one education extension officer, were then instructed to concentrate on agriculture, as were the village-level workers (VLWs). However, since their experience in the Jawaja Block in the previous 10 years was confined to animal husbandry, their knowledge of agricultural practices appropriate to the conditions of the Block was highly inadequate. This lack of knowledge, combined with budgetary constraints, was detrimental to effective supervision by Block officials and contributed to a decline in their influence, with a corresponding increase in the influence of the local economic-cum-political power structure.

In 1975, the Indian Institute of Management at Ahmedabad, with a research grant from the Indian Council of Social Science Research, decided to undertake an innovative experiment in the educational system to make it a vehicle of change in rural areas. Jawaja Block was selected for this experiment. The problems were approached by initiating activities to develop local skills and thereafter to use such activities to derive educational value for village schoolchildren. Three items that need specific mention are handlooms, leather and tomato products. All three were initiated by attempting to improve local skills with the assistance of scientists and technologists from national scientific and technological institutions. Modifications in technology, in transfer of technical product design, in marketing, and in credit systems were deliberately introduced.

In the early stages, extension work with the village community was initiated by independent volunteers from outside, but slowly and deliberately local village teachers were encouraged to participate and extend the work. Those teachers who showed a greater degree of initiative eventually formed a core group within the educational system, and have since come to be known as the Jawaja Project Group. The State Department of Education fully supported the approach of the Institute of Management and released two teachers from their routine duties to act as co-ordinators of this project.

Handloom weavers and leather workers became relatively organized over a period of time. However, the tomato growers failed to organize because tomato growing included many farmers spatially distributed over a wide geographical area, who could not hold their own against the market dominance of the city traders.

It also became evident, however, that the partial success achieved in handloom and leather activities did not have much impact on the rest of the Block residents. Direct outside intervention played a limited role in the widespread development of the area, and it became apparent that a much deeper understanding of the issues affecting the social and economic life of the people was essential. This then became the objective of the experimental area.

To attempt to have a broader impact on the community, informal educational centres were set up in which the teacher was to be elected by the villagers. Classes were not for imparting literacy but essentially for serving as a forum to discuss various issues that affect the day-to-day life of the village community. Acceptance of this concept took almost four years, and the teachers who formed the core group played a crucial role in finally gaining community acceptance. The informal educational centres (now 26) gradually led to collective decision-making by the communities.

Those decisions that were within the physical and monetary limits of the community were implemented immediately. This collective emphasis also put pressure on government functionaries, albeit gradually, to do their job more effectively. Discussions in informal educational centres soon focused on the shortage of fuelwood, fodder and food, and the causes of such scarcity. The villagers gradually realized that without a proper nurturing of the immediate environment, such shortages would continue indefinitely. Unless steps were taken to restore the ecology of the area, current residents and future generations would never be better off. In their own way the villagers began to understand that afforestation of hills, field boundaries, and common lands was the only way to restore the ecology of the area.

The SPWD project

Attempts were made to afforest homesteads, schools, and field boundaries by procuring seedlings from the Forestry Department. Two of the 26 village communities took the initiative in protecting their hills by completely banning tree felling. Children were encouraged to collect seeds from the remaining trees and dibble them on barren hillsides. Enthusiasm was high among the poorest, but the results on the ground were far too inadequate and scattered. At this stage, the Society for Promotion of Wastelands Development (SPWD), a non-profit making, non-governmental organization, joined with the Jawaja Project Group (JPG) in this task.

After a careful study of the history and socio-economic conditions of the area, SPWD and JPG decided to adopt the following strategy:

- to remove obstacles to afforestation activities in order to sustain a high level of enthusiasm;
- while the initiative and action at the village level would remain with the local informal educational centres, teachers and local people, the organizers would introduce more scientific methods;
- the development of the natural resource base would be accompanied by the development of a proper social management of resources to ensure equitable distribution of the programme benefits.

In their analysis of the rather slow progress of afforestation and reclamation activities, the Jawaja Project Group identified the main constraint to be the unavailability of seedlings of the preferred species at easily accessible locations. It was therefore decided to develop a network of decentralized nurseries, each of which would grow the saplings demanded by the people and would cover three or four surrounding villages to minimize transportation. Other elements of the SPWD-JPG programme were:

- encouraging communities to protect hills by banning tree fellings;
- organizing schoolchildren for collecting, sorting, treating, and dibbling of seeds on hills; *and*
- grafting of ber (*Zizyphus mauritania*) trees to obtain high yields of fruits and fodder.

Equity considerations

In developing these activities, SPWD and JPG were conscious of the all-too-familiar history of eventual usurpation of the gains from development by a few powerful persons. Therefore, a deliberate attempt was made from the outset to develop systems in which conflicting interests could be resolved in a way that ensured social and legal protection of the rights of the poor to common natural resources. This was achieved by adopting a work ethic, along with technological and educational intervention consisting of the following.

Direct wage benefits. Disadvantaged groups in activities such as nursery raising were given direct wage benefits. Since the wage benefits were only slightly higher than those otherwise available in the area and such employment did not alter the availability of labour in the region, no conflict arose.

In-kind incentives. Availability of free inputs (like saplings) was linked to contribution of manual labour. Only those persons who had dug pits for planting saplings received them. This kind of arrangement did not have much attraction for the richer villagers; when they did participate in the programme, the same terms applied to them as the rest of the community.

Species selection. Species were selected so that their produce (mostly fuelwood) was not individually marketable and did not require cash expenditure on fertilizers, irrigation and protection. Most individuals could plant only a certain number of trees on their private lands and the yield from these would be only slightly higher than their individual needs. The surplus would be too small to justify the cost of transportation to the nearest market since fuelwood is not traded in the villages. Therefore, the only alternatives were for all residents to pool and market their surplus or to grow just enough trees to fulfil their consumption needs.

Forest plantations. Development of plantations on common lands, however, did provide sufficient marketable surplus, and there were genuine fears that such plantations would ultimately help only the villagers well entrenched in the existing economic-political structure. Before plantations were raised on village common lands, a consensus was established within the community for equitable distribution for the use of the trees. Such consensus decisions were subsequently legitimized by the village councils. Therefore, both socially and legally, the disadvantaged groups were made to feel more secure.

Different systems emerged in different villages. In some villages, the entire community planted the village commons and agreed to share the produce equally among the households under the guidance of village councils, whereas other village councils appointed security guards to protect the plantations. In some villages the common land was equally distributed among the households, and the responsibility of planting, protecting and using the land rested with each household. In other villages, plantation on common lands was carried out by children, but village councils adopted resolutions for equal sharing of the produce.

Similar systems emerged for produce from protected hills. Grafted ber trees belonged to individuals, and therefore so did the benefits.

In villages where no consensus emerged, intensive education through formal and informal channels continues, and the actual work could be initiated only on private lands and not on common lands. Overall summary results are shown in Table 13.1.

Table 13.1: Summary results

Activity	1984	1985
	(Year 0)	(Year 1)
Number of nurseries	18	30
Saplings planted	200,000	300,000
Number of villages	75	125
Number of people involved in tree planting	2,023	5,797
Number of saplings that survived (estimated)	100,000	150,000
Area protected by community action (ha)	50	100
Area dibbled by seeds by schoolchildren (ha)	10	30
Number of grafted trees	—	2,000

Economic analysis

The programme is on-going. This paper evaluates the work done in 1984 and 1985 and the streams of costs and benefits expected to flow over 20 years.

Costs
Table 13.2 shows the benefit-cost flows in constant (1984) market prices. All the cost elements have been subdivided according to resource category: D, domestic good; I, imported good; L, unskilled labour; and S, skilled labour. Except for skilled labour, pesticides, and a substantial portion of domestic material, the cost items consist of non-cash goods and services. For cash goods and services, actual market prices have been taken into account; for non-cash goods and services, estimated market prices have been used.

Table 13.2: Benefit – cost flows in Rupees at constant (1984) market prices

Item	0	1	2	Year 3	4	5	6 to 20
Benefits							
A. Productivity gains							
1. Tree output	—	—	—	—	90,000	230,000	270,000
2. Fruit output	—	—	500	2,000	3,000	4,000	4,000
B. Cost-saving gains							
3. Unskilled family labour	—	—	—	—	262,160	670,490	699,500
4. Reduced soil erosion	—	11,760	44,520	77,280	110,040	142,800	163,800
Costs							
5. Training	425	1,990	—	—	—	—	—
D. Domestic material	400	1,590	—	—	—	—	—
S. Skilled labour	25	400	—	—	—	—	—
6. Nursery cost	57,200	102,396	—	—	—	—	—
D. Domestic material	12,090	24,906	—	—	—	—	—
I. Insecticide	460	590	—	—	—	—	—
S. Skilled labour	39,250	67,400	—	—	—	—	—
D. Non-cash domestic material	5,400	9,500	—	—	—	—	—
7. Plantation cost	106,470	153,045	—	—	—	—	—
I. Insecticide	400	545	—	—	—	—	—
L. Unskilled family labour	100,000	150,000	—	—	—	—	—
D. Domestic material	6,070	2,500	—	—	—	—	—
8. Seed Dibbling	3,000	16,500	—	—	—	—	—
D. Non-cash domestic material	2,000	11,000	—	—	—	—	—
L. Unskilled family labour	1,000	5,500	—	—	—	—	—
9. Grafting	—	182	—	—	—	—	—
S. Skilled labour	—	182	—	—	—	—	—
10. Extension cost	29,900	39,975	30,521	30,521	30,521	—	—
D. Domestic material	3,950	9,454	—	—	—	—	—
S. Skilled labour	20,950	17,521	17,521	17,521	17,521	—	—
S. Voluntary skilled labour	5,000	13,000	13,000	13,000	13,000	—	—
11. Annual operations cost	64,000	134,000	89,000	59,000	14,000	14,000	14,000
L. Unskilled family labour	60,000	122,000	77,000	47,000	2,000	2,000	2,000
T. Tree income forgone	4,000	12,000	12,000	12,000	12,000	12,000	12,000
12. Management cost	19,100	17,771	6,198	6,198	6,198	—	—
S. Skilled labour	12,000	13,090	4,363	4,363	4,363	—	—
D. Domestic material	7,100	4,681	1,835	1,835	1,835	—	—

Note:
D = domestic good
I = imported good
L = unskilled labour
S = skilled labour

The cost items 5 through 9 are based on the actual outflows incurred in the first two years. Cost items 10, 11, and 12 have been estimated for future years on the following basis.

Extension cost. This consists of the actual salary of a senior teacher who works as the project co-ordinator, plus the nominal cost of 18 teachers who are in charge of their respective informal educational centres. It is estimated that their services will be required until year 4 (i.e., until the first harvesting of the plantation). Costs under this heading also include the estimated salary of a forester who trained nursery growers for 10 days in the first year and 15 days in the second year. Estimated costs of office and other facilities for the first two years have been also taken into account.

Annual operating cost. This comprises cost of maintenance of plantations and grafted trees, as well as tree income forgone because of a ban on tree felling in protected areas. The surviving saplings need soil working and weeding, which is estimated to require three person-days of labour for every 100 plants until the first harvest (year 4). The maintenance of grafted trees requires more intensive labour and is estimated at 10 person-days per 100 grafts from year 2 onward.

It is estimated that in the present degraded condition, people could not have harvested more than 2 quintals of wood from 1 ha. This represents the income they have to forgo in the protected area.

Management cost. This consists of the cost of SPWD staff time and facilities for the first four years.

Benefits

Benefits listed in Table 13.2 are in two categories: direct benefits and indirect benefits.

Direct benefits. Direct benefits or productivity gains accrue in the following forms:

- fuelwood from plantations estimated at 2 kg/tree/yr from year 5 onward. Harvesting of the 100,000 surviving trees planted in year 0 will be done in year 4, and the additional 150,000 surviving trees from the planting in year 1 will be harvested from year 5 onward;
- fuelwood from the protected area estimated at 0.5 t/ha/yr (50 ha protected from year 0 will begin yielding fuelwood in year 4, and 100 ha protected from year 1 will begin yielding fuelwood in year 5);
- fuelwood from the area dibbled with seeds at 1 kg/tree

from year 6 onward (estimated surviving saplings 100,000); *and*
- fruit output from grafted ber trees estimated at 0.25 kg/tree in year 2, 1 kg/tree in year 3, 1.5 kg/tree in year 4, and 2 kg/tree from year 5 onward.

Indirect benefits or cost-saving gains. The availability of fuelwood at the doorsteps of the people from year 4 onward will result in saving family labour currently used for collecting firewood from distant areas. It is estimated that at present about seven person-days are spent to collect 60 kg of fuelwood. At this rate, the resultant saving in labour will be about 26,216 person-days in year 4, 67,049 person-days in year 5, and 69,950 person-days per year from year 6 onward.

Indirect benefits from reduced soil erosion are estimated assuming a 5% reduction in year 1; 10, 15, 20, and 25% in years 2, 3, 4, and 5, respectively; and a levelling off at 30% from year 6 onward. Before the project began, the soil erosion rate was estimated at 8 t/ha. The total area brought under tree cover because of the project is about 390 ha. Though the actual replacement cost of topsoil is difficult to calculate, the market value of the replacement cost of nutrients has been estimated as a cost-saving benefit.

Both a financial analysis and a social benefit-cost analysis of the Jawaja Project have been carried out. Inputs and outputs have been valued at market prices and, where necessary, at shadow prices in the SBCA.

Table 13.3: Present financial value of direct benefits and costs (in Rupees) for a 20-year period

Item	Discount Rate (%) 12	15
Present value of benefits	1,252,670	98,712
Present value of costs	683,548	666,452
Net present value	569,122	302,260
Benefit-cost ratio	1.83	1.45

Financial analysis
Total benefits and costs (direct and indirect) have been valued at constant market prices. Consumption benefits of the project represent the net addition to the value of output after the project; it consists of the fuelwood output from the plantation and fruit

output from the grafted ber trees. Total direct cost represents the actual opportunity and construction costs which occurred in the first two years and the annual operating cost. Table 13.3 presents the present values of direct benefits (items 1 and 2 in Table 13.2) and direct costs (items 6, 7, 8, 9, and 11 in Table 13.2) at two discount rates – 12 and 15%.

In Table 13.4, an attempt has been made to show the present values of total benefits (items 1 to 4 in Table 13.2) and total costs

---

Table 13.4: Present financial value of total (direct and indirect) benefits and costs for a 20-year period (in Rupees)

Item	Discount Rate (%)	
	12	15
Present value of benefits	5,388,216	4,193,308
Present value of costs	958,518	919,871
Net present value	4,429,698	3,273,437
Benefit-cost ratios	5.62	4.56

Table 13.5: Accounting ratios for various items

Item	Accounting ratio* (A_i)
Labour	
1. Skilled labour	1.00
2. Unskilled family labour	0.40
Non-traded commodities	
3. Non-cash domestic material	0.50
4. Infrastructure	0.37
Traded commodities	
5. Tree	1.00
6. Fruit	1.00
7. Domestic material (cash)	1.00
8. Insecticide	1.00

* Accounting ratios (A_i) = PS_i/PM_i, where PS_i = Social Price and PM_i = Market Price

(items 5 to 12 in Table 13.2). The data in Table 13.4 indicate high benefit-cost ratios for the Jawaja Project for the 20-year period, even at a 15% discount rate.

Social benefit-cost analysis
The accounting ratios shown in Table 13.5, developed by the Planning Commission for estimating of social costs and benefits, have been adopted in this SBCA to derive shadow prices.

Table 13.6: Present social value of total (direct and indirect) benefits and costs (in Rupees) for a 20-year period

	Discount Rate (%)	
Item	12	15
Present value of social benefit	3,437,898	2,681,771
Present value of social cost	642,122	601,438
Net present value	2,795,776	2,080,333
Benefit-cost ratio	5.35	4.45

Table 13.6 shows the present values of total benefits and costs, valued at the appropriate shadow prices, for a 20-year period. The results indicate the desirability of the project from a social viewpoint. It can be shown that the environmental benefit that accrues to society in reduced soil erosion is itself sufficient to justify investment in this project: at a 15% discount rate, the net present value from reduced erosion comes to about Rs. 707,000, which is higher than the entire social cost of the project of about Rs. 601,000.

In the foregoing analysis, benefits and costs were calculated in imputed monetary terms. In reality, there will probably be no transactions in the commodities resulting from this project. However, it ensures the availability of fuelwood and grasses at the doorsteps of the people, especially the poorer residents. The ecological regeneration, along with the increased quality of life and increased energy security, are further benefits.

Clearly the relative success that has been achieved originates largely from the strict control on distribution of meagre monetary inputs to those in greatest need, together with reconciling such a distribution system with the cultural ethos of the area. The development of consensus for distributing user rights from common resources was and continues to be crucial. Although provisions for the supply of inputs exist in current government schemes, many aspects of the scheme have to be worked out in the community. The Jawaja experience indicates that this community participation in promoting development strategy is crucial for rehabilitation projects.

V
Environmental Management at the Regional Level

Perhaps the most important characteristic of dryland degradation is that it typically occurs on a large geographic scale. The damage inflicted by each individual land operator may, in itself, appear to be minor, but collectively such impacts may have a devastating effect on the natural resource base. A broad approach to resource management is thus required.

While it is important to understand the economic behaviour of individual land users, policy should be directed toward an integrated environmental management system. The "externalities" of individual producers should be "internalized", and the system managed as if it were the responsibility of a single owner or operator. In this way, the net socio-economic benefits of the integrated system can be maximized.

Incentives or other public assistance measures may be required to fulfil this objective. Funding agencies also need to be aware that feasibility studies for investments in land conservation or rehabilitation should extend beyond the boundaries of individual farms and tracts of land. Improvement programmes may have to be implemented on a regional scale to reap significant gains.

The two case studies presented in this section illustrate these general principles clearly. Both deal with problems that occur on a regional scale. The study by Dumsday and Oram is concerned with the effects of farming systems on dryland salinity. Climatic, geomorphic and hydrologic factors significantly affect the response of the natural resource system. The study by Thomas focuses on the catchment as the system to be managed and assesses land use options within the catchment in relation to river salinity.

The wide range of management alternatives and their environmental and economic effects are explored in both case studies by means of linear programming and simulation models. The Dumsday and Oram study uses these techniques to estimate the impact of salinity restrictions on farm income and to provide guidelines on public incentives to farmers. The Thomas study uses linear programming, combined with benefit-cost analysis, to optimize land use within the catchment. These techniques may be widely used by economic planners to jointly achieve economic development and environmental protection at the regional level. *The Economics of Dryland Management* gives a full description of the methods.

14
Economics of Dryland Salinity Control in the Murray River Basin, Northern Victoria (Australia)

R.G. Dumsday and D.A. Oram

Précis

This study addresses the problem of dryland salinity in Northern Victoria, Australia. Two areas were selected for the analysis: Axe Creek, used mainly for grazing; and Kamarooka, used primarily for cropping. The study gives a detailed explanation of the causes and processes of dryland salinity. Climate, geomorphology and land use are important factors. The problem should be addressed on a regional scale. The focus of this study is an on-farm analysis of the relationships between land use practices, farm income and salinity control. The technique used in the study is simulation modelling, combined with linear programming.

The results indicate that salinity can be reduced at little cost or even with some gain to farmers by modifying farming systems. Significant gains in farm income and reduction of salinity appear to be achievable, especially if forestry-based activities are introduced. Such practices would also yield important off-site benefits. Government assistance may, however, be required to encourage widespread adoption of forestry and agroforestry.

Introduction

About 35% of the total land area in Australia is affected by some form of soil degradation. It has been estimated that about 16,090 km^2 of land in the non-arid zone of Australia is affected by irrigation salting and 324,090 km^2 affected by natural and human-induced dryland salting. About 400 km^2 in Victoria suffer a significant loss in productivity from dryland salting, with at least an equal area believed to be affected by incipient salting.

Salinity represents a threat to agricultural productivity, the quality of water supplies, and to the natural environment. Analysis is required to determine the "best" strategies to control salinity, their costs and anticipated benefits.

This case study presents the findings of a farm-level study conducted as part of a joint project that examined local and regional implications of dryland salinity. The project was designed to provide insights into the private and social costs of soil and stream salinity emanating from dryland agriculture in that part of the Murray River Basin located in Victoria, and to evaluate the economic impact of alternative land management strategies designed to control the problem.

More specifically, the study is aimed at providing information on the trade-off between deep percolation of water and farm income through a model that simulates daily water balances for farming systems, in combination with linear programming models of representative farms. An additional function was to review the government policies available to promote environmental conservation and to recommend policy options. The options reviewed included direct controls, taxes and subsidies.

The problem of salinity

Salinity processes
The basic cause of dryland salting in this study is increased infiltration and percolation of rainwater, resulting from reduced evapotranspiration due to clearing of forests and their replacement with shallow-rooted pastures and crops. The extra water percolating through the soil profile after clearing, although only a small fraction of the annual rainfall, causes saline groundwater to rise. Where this groundwater emerges at low points, such as valley floors and gully drainage lines, vegetative cover is denuded and eventually soil salting occurs. Not only is the discharging groundwater saline, but it is further concentrated by evaporation, leaving highly saline bare patches that occur regularly across the landscape.

In many areas of Victoria the groundwater is highly saline, and this is exacerbated by the leaching of salts from the soil profile to the groundwater. The situation most often found in dryland areas of north central Victoria is vertical movement through soils of low permeability. Where impermeable layers are encountered, perched watertables may form, in many cases leading to hillside seepage salting. Watertables may also rise due to the indirect effects of increasing groundwater pressures, particularly the impedance of normal subsurface drainage through shallow aquifers.

Geological and geomorphic influences
The occurrence of dryland salting in Victoria, although widely dispersed, is related to specific geological and geomorphic situations

and climatic history. Geological effects include geological structure and the chemical nature of the soil-forming materials.

Geomorphic factors are controlled by soil structure and the processes of erosion and deposition. Three geomorphic regions are involved in soil salting in Victoria:

Region 1 – the central uplands of the Great Dividing Range, mainly pastoral;
Region 2 – the northern riverine plain, mainly cropping; *and*
Region 3 – the northwestern ridged plain, mainly cropping.

The uplands are the principal intake areas for the main aquifers beneath the plains and are therefore important in determining the occurrence and severity of salting in more than one region while also influencing the salinity of stream flows.

The transition zone between the uplands and the plains is particularly subject to salting, especially on the flats at the break of slope.

In the ridged, flat terrain of the Mallee (Region 3), salting occurrences are closely related to the geomorphic complexities of the area.

Climatic effects
Long-term changes in climate, operating over periods of geological time, have had a profound effect on groundwater regimes. Climatic fluctuations over the past 30 years do not appear to be the main factor in dryland salting in Victoria, although they would tend to modify the general upward trend of the groundwater level. The absence of salting in forests suggests that medium-term changes are ineffective in altering the hydrological balance sufficiently to produce salinity. In cleared areas, the effect of seasonal changes is more obvious. Abnormally wet years result in sudden expansion of salt-affected areas, but rarely do they contract in the intervening dry periods.

The Mediterranean-type climate of Victoria contributes to the volume of water percolating to the groundwater. In the cool, wet winters, potential evapotranspiration is less than rainfall, and water is stored in the soil for use in the hot, dry summer months. There is the potential in this situation for significant movement of water through the soil if an imbalance arises between the amount of water stored in winter and actual use throughout the year.

Land use
The specific land use conducted in a cleared area also plays an

important role in deep percolation of water and the incidence of dryland salting. The type of pasture, whether shallow-rooted annuals or more deeply rooted perennials, and the extent of grazing directly affect the accession of water and salt to the groundwater.

A comparison of adjacent catchments near Bendigo has shown a distinct trend toward increasing water storage at depth from forest to pasture and then to cropland. Compaction of the soil surface by grazing animals promotes runoff of water, thus restricting infiltration and producing lower soil moisture levels with a reduction in leaching of salts into the groundwater (Tunstall and Walker 1975). Cultivation procedures designed to limit excess runoff water and to increase soil moisture are also likely to increase groundwater recharge. Any action that promotes infiltration, such as deep contour ploughing and improvement of soil structure, may intensify this effect.

Options for salinity management

Salinity management is synonymous with water management, as it is a change in the hydrological balance. There are four categories of technical strategies for controlling salinity in irrigation and dryland systems: reforestation/agroforestry, agronomic, farm management and engineering.

Varying importance is placed on each category as a method of control, depending on whether irrigation or dryland salting is considered. For example, engineering works are important to the control of irrigation salinity but appear to have little potential in dryland areas.

A major obstacle to controlling dryland salinity is the lack of control over the source of water entering the system, namely rainfall.

However, since percentage of rainfall reaching the groundwater as recharge is less than 10%, possible alleviation strategies would only need to produce minor changes in the existing hydrological balance to be effective.

The removal of groundwater by pumping and subsurface drainage, which is an important method of control in irrigation areas, tends to be impractical for dryland salinity management. First, there is the high cost of implementation, particularly for tile drainage, due to the extensive nature of dryland farming. Second, soils are generally impermeable, which prevents the lateral movement of water necessary for the removal of large amounts of groundwater. Pumping of groundwater may be economical if high water-yielding aquifers are present (Shaw 1982), although this situation would still involve relatively high costs. Third, salting occurrences are widely scattered in dryland farming, often restricting the application of expensive engineering solutions to localized sites.

Regional recharge solutions
Recharge solutions can basically be considered as preventive measures and aim to reduce deep percolation to the groundwater over large areas of land by the increased and more efficient use of soil water supplied by rainfall. This tends to be more difficult to achieve under cropping rotations than for grazing systems due to the low salt tolerance of crops, particularly wheat, and the practice of fallowing that allows infiltration of water and encourages salt movement to the soil surface. The available recharge control mechanisms have been divided into the four categories listed previously.

Reforestation/agroforestry. Trees are considered an important control measure due to their high water use throughout the year, including summer when other plants die or are harvested (Morris *et al.* 1981). They are also important since tree removal is considered to be the basic cause of soil salting in the study area.

With regard to recharge control, measurements from catchments have shown that under total forest cover, recharge is negligible. The effectiveness of reforesting small areas (e.g., fencelines) or the forested areas needed for permanent control of salinity is uncertain, depending on the rate of water use by trees and the increase in groundwater recharge because of previous clearing (Morris *et al.* 1981). It has been estimated that 3 to 10% of total catchment area would need to be reforested, with the larger value corresponding to high rainfall areas. Other estimates range from 10% to 40% or higher. Williamson (1978) suggests that for a catchment with a rainfall of 1,200 mm/yr, 31% should remain forested.

Agronomic. The principal agronomic means of controlling recharge is the use of high water uptake plants. In cropping and grazing areas using shallow-rooted annual pasture, a satisfactory solution may be the introduction of perennial, deep-rooted plant species such as alfalfa (*Medicago sativa*), (Peck 1978; Shaw 1982). Plant breeding research may be necessary to develop plants with improved rooting depths and potential transpiration rates if currently available species are unable to control recharge effectively.

Farm management. Recharge control may be achieved through implementing appropriate crop or pasture management. According to Peck (1978), grazing of livestock should be regulated to maintain high transpiration rates; high stocking rates tend to restrict pasture growth and therefore limit transpiration.

For cropping systems, possible recharge control methods include introducing intensive or continuous cropping, reducing the number of cultivations and, more important, decreasing the length of fallow (Shaw 1982). Direct drilling largely, or completely, removes the need for fallowing and may provide a suitable avenue for recharge control.

Minimum tillage techniques offer cost savings from reduced machinery maintenance, labour requirements, and fuel and oil use, although there are added costs to consider for chemical weed control. More intensive cropping can create problems of declining soil fertility and greater soil acidity. Under continuous cropping rotations, complete reliance on herbicides could possibly lead to a spiral of resistant weeds, more persistent herbicides and, ultimately, residue problems in soils. More research is needed on such problems.

Engineering. Engineering control measures include surface water diversion, surface drainage, and interception banks to prevent water from reaching saline areas (Peck 1978; Shaw 1982). These measures may reduce the need for extensive reforestation or similar treatments that lower the economic productivity of recharge areas. Intercepted water tends to have lower salinity levels than water drained from salted land.

More exotic approaches such as pipelines to the sea, deep aquifer injection and solar distillation have been suggested, but they are not yet cost effective (Shaw 1982) and depend on the presence of high-yielding aquifers.

Local discharge strategies

These strategies are aimed at the direct treatment (reclamation) of saline areas and in the past have tended to be the main subjects of research into salinity control (Colclough 1973; Conacher and Murray 1973; Matheson 1968; Wagner 1957). Reclamation is generally restricted to surface treatment that reduces evaporation and encourages leaching by improved infiltration of rainwater (Morris *et al.* 1981), but these are only short-term measures and are unlikely to be successful without simultaneous implementation of recharge control strategies.

Treatment includes the establishment of vegetative cover, usually high salt uptake and salt-tolerant plants that assist in soil desalinization and in increasing productivity. Salt-tolerant plants that have proved successful include salt bushes (*Atriplex* spp.), saltwater couch (*Paspalum vaginatum*), tallwheat grass (*Agropyron elongatum*), and puccinellia (*Puccinellia ciliata*) , (Morris *et al*. 1981). These plants can be replaced with preferred species as soil salinity levels decline. Trees are normally established on the perimeter of the saline area, or upslope from it, to lower the water table in the immediate vicinity, facilitating treatment of the site.

The overall success of vegetative treatment depends on a number of factors including the depth of the water table, its salinity (since many plants, particularly trees, draw directly on groundwater), and whether movement of water to the discharge point is vertical or lateral. Management techniques that can assist in establishing plant cover include the use of soil conditioners (e.g., gypsum), deep ripping, fencing to control grazing, mulching and fertilization, and vermin control (Morris *et al*. 1981; Shaw 1982). Leaching of salts by applied water is generally uneconomic in dryland situations, as is artificial drainage that often only succeeds in transferring the problem elsewhere (Peck 1978).

A novel approach suggested by Oostenveld (1977) involves encouraging evaporation of saline water so that salt accumulation is confined to a small area, allowing the remaining salt patch to be revegetated.

Economic analysis of management options

Management systems for salinity control
A management system designed to control salinity needs to incorporate both recharge and discharge control. Discharge treatment alone is only a short-term, localized remedy. It has no influence on outbreaks of new saline areas and is unlikely to succeed if the cause of salting – recharge of groundwater – is not simultaneously treated.

The actual choice of a land management system requires an economic evaluation of the available options. Solutions to the salinity problem should involve regional land use changes, with the objective of partly restoring the original water balance, and treatment of affected sites. Long-term reclamation measures aim to increase water use on a catchment basis. It is also important to know the impact on income at the individual farm level of alternate strategies aimed at increasing water use to control the salinity problem.

It appears that reforestation and agroforestry are two of the most effective measures for permanent salinity control, but their implementation would require the planting of trees on land that is not already salinized. In many cases this would involve highly productive agricultural land, and the returns from forestry are often less than those from extensive agriculture. Returns from reforestation could be greatly improved if high-value tree crops such as "jojoba" were used.

Entire catchment reforestation might achieve total control of recharge with flow-on benefits by preventing future salinization and the gradual reclamation of currently salted land, but it is by no means clear that complete removal of the salinity problem is economically desirable or physically possible. Furthermore, the magnitude of groundwater recharge involved in the dryland salinity problem appears to be only a small fraction of annual rainfall, suggesting that major alteration of the present hydrological balance, as might be achieved under reforestation, may not be necessary.

Changes might include tree planting in less productive areas (e.g., fencelines, high recharge ridges), modified cultivation procedures and the introduction of deeper rooted plant species that could maintain or even improve upon present agricultural production and economic returns while achieving a satisfactory level of salinity control.

A framework for analysis

A useful framework for the economic analysis of salinity management options is a simulation model combined with linear programming. The simulation model used in this study is an extension of the model developed by Dumsday (1973) for cropping systems in northern New South Wales and southern Queensland. The model has been modified to incorporate the rotational characteristics of Victorian wheat production, including annual and perennial pasture, and alfalfa.

It was not possible to quantify the effects of different farming systems for spatial and temporal incidence of dryland salting and its effect on productivity and stream water quality. It is suggested, however, that because deep percolation of water beyond the root zone is the main factor contributing to groundwater recharge, quantification of relationships between farming systems and deep percolation provides a useful surrogate measure of the costs and benefits of controlling salting.

After including physical information (e.g., soil characteristics, climate and management strategies) on the selected areas, the simulation model estimates the amount of water percolating through the soil to the groundwater and the productivity of the systems (i.e., crop yield, pasture yield and stocking rates).

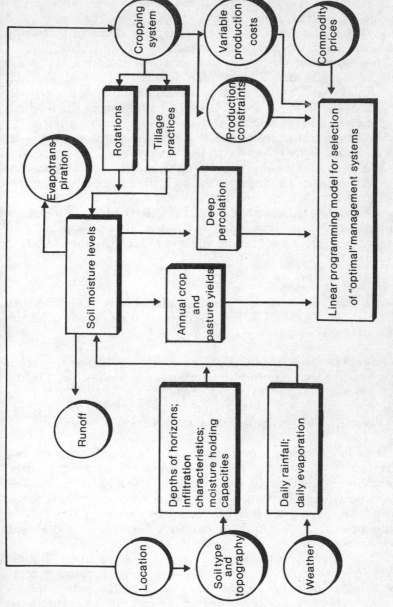

Figure 14.1: Summary of model relationships

Although the water use and profitability of farm management practices are already important in reality, there is a strong need to evaluate alternative practices principally aimed at increasing water use and restricting deep percolation.

The results from the simulation model are incorporated in linear programming models to determine, within certain economic and physical constraints, the most profitable farm management strategy for a specific study area. Figure 14.1 summarizes the relationships between the simulation and linear programming models.

The amount of water percolating through to the groundwater for each farm activity is related to a deep percolation constraint. As the constraint is progressively tightened (i.e., as less water is allowed to percolate through the soil), those activities employing greater water use became more attractive than those that are geared toward water conservation, as is the case for many current farming systems. Such analysis enables quantification of the trade-off between farm income and reduction in accessions to the water table.

Selection of study areas

Two specific areas were chosen in the Murray River Basin of Victoria (see Figure 14.2), representing two classes of landform and farming system:

1. the Axe Creek area in the Campaspe catchment southeast of Bendigo, representing the upper slopes of the Great Divide, devoted primarily to grazing; *and*
2. the Kamarooka area in the Loddon catchment north of Bendigo, devoted primarily to cropping.

These areas were chosen for several reasons. First, there is a diversity of land use between them due to variation in environment. Second, both areas are severely affected by salting because of deforestation. Third, due to the salting situation in these areas, several studies have been conducted by the Soil Conservation Authority of Victoria and an extensive body of data has been collected and analysed.

A further reason for choosing Axe Creek for study is that the excess deep percolation causing the soil salting problem is probably largely due to the limited root growth of the pasture species present. This situation provides an opportunity to examine the effect of root depth on accessions to the water table and, therefore, soil salting and stream salinity.

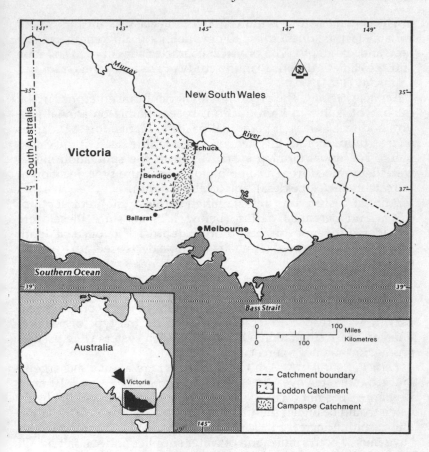

Figure 14.2: Study area, Murray River, Victoria

Axe Creek: grazing
Grazing, mainly by sheep, is the principal agricultural enterprise in this area. Less than 5% of the land is cropped.

Environment. The Axe Creek subcatchment has about 8,500 ha, primarily grassland and forest. It receives rainfall of about 500 mm/yr and has relatively shallow, slightly weathered soils. Three geomorphological classes were defined and examined: the upper slopes, lower slopes and valley floor.

The climatic regime is uniform over the classes; thus, the major variable factors, due to the geomorphological differences, are soil type and soil depth. The physical characteristics of each soil type and the climatic data used in the study are described in Oram and Dumsday (1984).

Farming systems. The predominant agricultural enterprise in the catchment is livestock production, based mainly on annual pasture and small areas of perennial pasture. Native forest occupies a large proportion of the steeper slopes at the head of the catchment. The initial farming systems run in the simulation model were determined from a combination of pasture type, location in the catchment (slope class), and total soil depth.

Annual pasture was not examined below a total root depth of 0.5 m and perennial pasture below 1.25 m, since these were considered the limits to their rooting depths. The total soil depth progressively increased for alfalfa as slope decreased, up to a limit of 2.0 m.

For each slope class, the base farming system in simulation analyses was annual pasture at a total root depth of 0.5 m. Other farming systems were treated as alternatives to the base system, varying with respect to total soil depth and the type of pasture. The important simulation outputs from each system were pasture production and deep percolation.

Impact of salting. At Axe Creek the average annual recharge to the groundwater over the entire catchment is around 10 mm. Recharge does not occur over the whole catchment, so the likely value would be higher than 10 mm for the actual areas of recharge. The resulting increase in salinity levels and rise in groundwater have caused both salinization of water supplies and soil salting. Of the 8,500 ha in the catchment, about 40 ha are already affected to some degree by soil salting. Stream drainage from the catchment is through Axe Creek, which flows into the Campaspe River. The annual salt discharge from Axe Creek is about 15,000 t/yr. Dams and storage wells in the catchment are also affected by rising saline groundwater.

Kamarooka: cropping

This area has mixed grazing and cropping, with 20 to 25% under crop.

Environment. Kamarooka is situated in the transition zone between the northern slopes of the Great Divide and the riverine plains. It lies in the subcatchment of Bendigo Creek, which forms part of the catchment of the Loddon River. The approximate area of Kamarooka is 2,100 ha.

Kamarooka has a rainfall of about 420 mm with deep, heavy red duplex soils that are more weathered than those at Axe Creek.

Geomorphically, the area consists of relatively uniform and gentle slopes. The general environment at Kamarooka is less variable than at Axe Creek, particularly soil depth where the heavier, deeper B horizons tend to average 1.5 m. As at Axe Creek, the A horizon is normally 0.1 m deep and, for simulation purposes, several subsoil horizons were combined into one B horizon. The physical characteristics of each horizon are described in Oram and Dumsday (1984).

Soil management. Consideration must be given to soil management at Kamarooka, as it has an important impact on wheat production and the control of recharge. Soil management for wheat production in Victoria has been referred to extensively (Rooney *et al.* 1966; Tuohey *et al.* 1972; Sims 1977), although research has primarily been directed toward the problem of soil erosion rather than soil salting (Adamson 1978; Garvin *et al.* 1979).

Several factors are important in a conventional wheat rotation system involving pasture (Storrier 1975; Clarke and Russell 1977; Sims 1977): the sequence of wheat and pasture phases; the number of wheat crops; the length and type of pasture phase; and cultivation practices, particularly the length of fallow. A pasture that contains legumes supplies nitrogen to the following wheat crop (Storrier 1969) and is responsible for rebuilding soil structure and generally improving soil condition. Pasture also assists crop production by interrupting the life cycle of cereal pests (e.g., cereal cyst nematode). This role may be fulfilled in some cases by grain legumes such as lupins (Gladstones 1975).

At Kamarooka the wheat crop following a pasture phase is normally preceded by almost a year of fallow in order to conserve moisture. Replacing part of the fallow phase with pasture may produce benefits through recharge control since more than 60% of rain falls between May and October. Benefits from increased grazing capacity may also be achieved (Cannell 1981).

Decreases in fallow length form the basis of conservation tillage systems. Conservation tillage was developed primarily for erosion control, although the practice is also suited to the control of soil water levels. The extreme case of conservation tillage involves direct drilling of crop seed, obviating the need for cultivation (McNeil 1982).

Farming systems. The main crop rotation at Kamarooka is a four-year rotation comprising wheat/wheat/annual pasture/annual pasture. The rotation is based on conventional tillage with a long fallow phase before the first wheat crop. For simulation purposes, cultivation was assumed to commence in August of the year preceding the first crop, and in April preceding the second crop. Crop sowing date is dictated by weather conditions and may range from May to July. The base sowing date was assumed to be June for both wheat crops in the rotation. A range of sowing dates was simulated, although they were not controlled by weather conditions as each sowing date was exposed to the same climatic environment. Observations were made of the influence of sowing date on simulated deep percolation and crop production.

Two important management strategies could be adopted to control salting while retaining the essential characteristics of the present (base) rotation system. These are a decrease in fallow length before the first wheat crop, and the introduction of deep-rooted perennial pasture species to replace the shallow-rooted annual pastures in the base system. In the simulation experiments, the fallow length preceding the first crop was reduced by eight months so that fallowing commenced in April, as for the second crop.

The alternative pasture species incorporated in the short fallow rotations were perennial pasture and alfalfa. Various combinations of fallow length, pasture types, and sowing dates were analysed in simulation experiments. Total soil depth was assumed to be constant at 1.5 m under all rotation systems. The effective rooting depth of each component in the rotations was assumed to be 0.5 m for annual pasture, 1.25 m for perennial pastures, 1.5 m for alfalfa, and 1.0 m for wheat.

Impact of salting. The average annual recharge at Kamarooka has been estimated to be in the order of 10 to 30 mm (Jenkins and Dyson 1983). Of the 2,100 ha, some 390 ha are severely affected by salt. Surface waters and groundwaters are also affected, with some dam supplies registering salinities as high as seawater. In the general area which includes Kamarooka, at least 10,000 ha have saline groundwater within 2 m of the soil surface.

Apart from the obvious loss of production from severe salting, wheat production in many areas has declined steadily over the years due to increased incipient salting. The effect of soil salting is to reduce farm income not only through the lost value of production, but also through increased operational costs resulting from the treatment of severe salting to prevent the potential secondary problem of soil erosion.

Geomorphological conditions are responsible for a closed aquifer recharge-discharge system operating at Kamarooka, controlled by groundwater movement through the bedrock from the ridges to the plains (Jenkin 1980). The closed system is caused by an impedance of subsurface drainage such that subsurface water movement is extremely slow (Jenkin and Dyson 1983) and by the absence of any surface drainage through creeks or channels. Consequently, most of the water infiltrating into the soil profile is either used by vegetation or, once reaching the groundwater, evaporates from salinized areas where the groundwater intersects the soil surface at discharge points.

Table 14.1: Marginal costs of reducing deep percolation in a grazing area (upper slopes of Axe Creek catchment)

*System**		*Area* (%)	*Average annual reduction* (mm)	*Marginal cost* (A$/mm)
A,a	Annual P. (BASE)	100	(27.1)**	
B,b	Annual P.	72	3.5	–1.13
C	Perennial P.	72	10.4	0.07
D	Perennial P.	33	13.3	1.75
	Alfalfa	55		
	Native vegn	12		
E	Perennial P.	9	16.5	2.35
	Alfalfa	63		
	Native vegn	28		
F	Alfafa	42	21.1	2.94
	Native vegn	58		
G	Perennial P.	12	24.2	5.46
	Alfalfa	5		
	Native vegn	83		
H	Native vegn	100	27.1	6.76
c	Agroforestry	71	22.7	–0.57
	Perennial P.	11		
	Alfalfa	18		
d	Agroforestry	83	24.2	0.50
	Perennial P.	12		
	Alfalfa	5		
e	Agroforestry	100	27.1	2.84

* Upper-case letters: selection from modified systems only
  Lower-case letters: forestry-based systems also available (discount rate = 10%)
** Annual deep percolation under base system

The closed system also constitutes a geomorphological contrast to Axe Creek, where an "open" system allows removal of water through both surface and subsurface drainage.

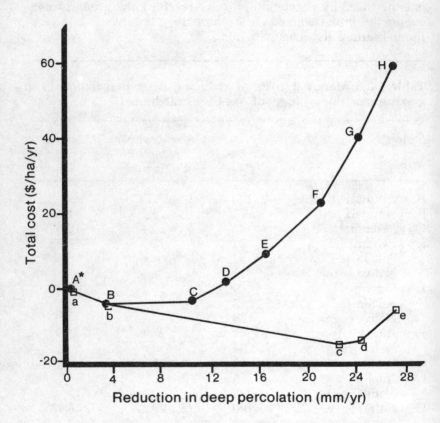

Figure 14.3: Total private costs of reducing deep percolation on grazing area (upper slopes of Axe Creek catchment)

Results of economic analysis

Results for the systems analysed in the grazing and cropping areas are summarized below. A more detailed discussion of earlier results is provided by Oram and Dumsday (1984) and Dumsday *et al*. (1985). The discussion first canvasses the existing possibilities for reducing salinity problems while maintaining, or increasing, private net benefits derived from agricultural production. The discussion then turns to consideration of the options that are available to governments for reducing salinity levels beyond those found to be profitable by farmers.

Results for Axe Creek
Results of simulations for various farming systems on the upper slopes of the Axe Creek catchment are shown in Table 14.1 and Figure 14.3. The farming systems consist of those excluding forestry and agroforestry (identified by upper case letters) and systems that include forestry-based activities (identified by lower case letters). A 10% discount rate is used for forestry activities.

Figure 14.3 plots the cost of salinity control, measured as a loss of farm income, against the reduction in deep percolation. The marginal costs of moving from one farming system to another, measured in A$ of forgone income per mm reduction in percolation per hectare per year, are shown in Table 14.1. These costs indicate the rate of tax or subsidy that would be needed to induce shifts in land use, either with or without forestry-based activities.

For the base case at point A, with all land used for annual pasture, average annual net benefits (farm income) are A$59/ha. The estimated annual deep percolation is 27 mm. By shifting to the farming system represented by point B, farm income can actually be increased while simultaneously reducing the level of deep percolation. The increase in farm income shows up in Table 14.1 and Figure 14.3 as a negative cost, hence "benefit" with respect to the base case at A. Without forestry and agroforestry, any further reductions in deep percolation result in a decrease in farm income. Beyond point C, the costs of reducing percolation escalate rapidly.

The introduction of forestry-based activities generally leads to an improvement in farm income and a reduction in deep percolation. The best result from a private perspective occurs at c, where 71% of the land area is allocated to agroforestry, 11% to perennial pasture, and 18% to alfalfa. Deep percolation is reduced by 22.7 mm. If system e were adopted, deep percolation could be stopped completely, accompanied by a 10% increase in farm income over point A. There should be no need to offer incentives to persuade farmers to move from System a (base system) to System c, the profit maximizing system. Of course, farmer decisions could be based on factors besides income, such as personal preferences and their attitude to risk. However, a tax (or subsidy) of at least A$2.84/mm deep percolation (reduction) per year would be required to persuade farmers to move from System c to System e.

Table 14.2: Marginal costs of reducing deep percolation in a cropping area (Kamarooka)

System*		Area (%)	Average annual reduction (mm)	Marginal cost (A$/mm)
A,a	WL/WS/A/A (BASE)	100	(18.7)**	
B,b	WS/WS/A/A/	39	14.0	–0.73
	WS/WS/L/L	61		
C,c	WS/WS/P/P	39	16.4	1.50
	WS/WS/L/L	61		
D,d	WS/WS/L/L	100	16.9	13.50
E	WS/WS/L/L	76	17.3	44.00
	Alfalfa	24		
F	WS/WS/L/L	35	18.1	46.70
	Alfalfa	65		
G	Alfalfa	100	18.7	49.70
e	WS/WS/L/L	62	17.6	32.35
	Agroforestry	38		
f	WS/WS/L/L	37	18.0	38.82
	Agroforestry	52		
	Alfalfa	11		
g	WS/WS/L/L	25	18.2	40.80
	Agroforestry	58		
	Alfalfa	17		
h	Agroforestry	65	18.7	41.00
	Alfalfa	35		

* Upper-case letters: selection from modified systems only
  Lower-case letters: forestry-based systems also available (discount rate = 10%)
  Rotations: WL – wheat, long fallow; WS – wheat, short fallow; A – annual pasture;
  P – perennial pasture; L – alfalfa
** Annual deep percolation under base system

The costs of reducing deep percolation were also estimated for the grazing systems on the lower slopes and valley floor of Axe Creek. On the lower slopes, the costs were similar to those on the upper slopes. Reduction of deep percolation by using only modified systems resulted in rapidly increasing costs to the operator. On the valley floor, modified systems were able to reduce deep percolation to almost zero while simultaneously increasing farm income, although systems employing agroforestry continued to maximize profits for reductions greater than 50%.

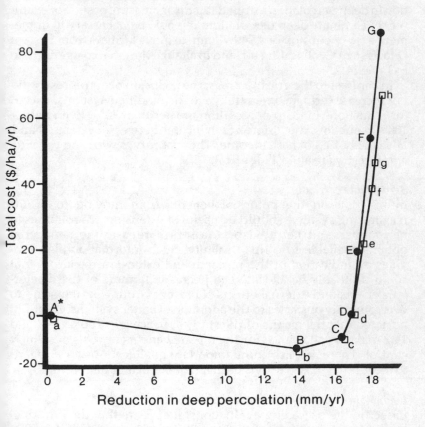

Figure 14.4: Total private costs of reducing deep percolation in a cropping area (Kamarooka)

Results for Kamarooka
Results for Kamarooka are given in Table 14.2 and Figure 14.4. The management systems are identified in Table 14.2. For the base

system in the cropping area, average net revenue was A$139/ha and average annual deep percolation was estimated to be 19 mm. A maximum increase in farm income of 7% was obtained by moving from System A to System B, resulting in a reduction in deep percolation of 14 mm (75%). The maximum possible reduction, without incurring increasing costs to the operator in comparison to the present system, was 16.9 mm or 90%, under System D. Further reduction in deep percolation implied rapidly increasing costs. For example, to eliminate deep percolation, it would be necessary to implement a tax or subsidy of A$49.70/mm to move farmers from System D to System G, allocating all land to alfalfa. Marginal costs are given in Table 14.2.

In contrast to the grazing areas, the inclusion of agroforestry did not increase farm income relative to the modified systems, except for reductions in deep percolation greater than 90%. Even with a 100% reduction, the difference in income between Systems G and h was only 13% of base income. The cost curves with and without agroforestry are almost identical.

Significance of results
Information on the potential benefits from moving to profit-maximizing systems should be useful in extension programmes to help farmers and their advisors to assess more easily the managerial options available to control salinity. Such information also provides an indication of the research and extension resources that could profitably be allocated to persuade farmers of the deleterious on-site and external effects of present farming systems and to overcome any obstacles to the adoption of better systems. It should be noted that the results of the study appearing in Tables 14.1 and 14.2 make no allowance for the off-site benefits or costs of salinity control. There are also some important qualifications with regard to the forestry-based activities that require further discussion.

Evaluation of forestry-based activities
Based on the preceding evaluations, it appears that the introduction of forestry and agroforestry to control dryland salinity offers greater economic incentives to private landowners than those obtained from modifying existing farming systems. In addition, greater social benefits are likely to be generated by forestry-based systems due to the ability of forestry (not necessarily agroforestry) to eliminate recharge to the groundwater. However, it is far from certain that forestry and agroforestry would return the equivalent incomes that is assumed in this study under field conditions, since gross margin estimates were based on a number of assumptions

that may not apply in the study area. For instance, the productivity estimates of the forestry-based systems used in this analysis were based on a study conducted near Ballarat in central Victoria, where average annual rainfall is 600 to 670 mm, so the actual returns from agroforestry in the grazing zone are likely to be markedly less than those assumed. In the cropping zone it is doubtful that the agroforestry system would be economically viable. Still, the method of analysis used in the study gives an indication of the minimum returns required by such systems, for them to compete profitably with traditional farming systems.

Table 14.3: Average public outlays (A\$/ha/yr) for subsidy based on reduction in deep percolation (DP)

	No Zoning[a]	Semi-zoning[b] (I)	(A)	Zoning[c]	Targeting[d]
Excluding forestry-based systems	51.0	0.95	30.7	16.1	8.1
Average annual DP reduced from 13.3mm to	3.1	8.20	3.1	3.1	3.1
Including forestry-based systems	9.0	4.9		4.3	3.5
Average annual DP reduced from 2.6mm to	0.8	0.8		0.8	0.8

[a]Uniform subsidy of A\$5/mm reduction in deep percolation

[b]Subsidy based on the marginal costs for Kamarooka and the representative locality in Axe Creek (lower slopes) that achieves the same reduction as the uniform subsidy (in these localities)

I = initial subsidy

A = Adjustment of the initial subsidy to achieve the same reduction as the uniform subsidy in all localities (when forestry-based systems are included, this adjustment is unnecessary)

[c]Subsidy based on the marginal costs at each of the 4 localities (3 Axe Creek zones and Kamarooka)

[d]Subsidy tailored to the schedule of the marginal costs of DP reduction at each locality

Even with the apparent superiority of the forestry-based systems, there is likely to be greater farmer opposition to their introduction which could largely be avoided if modified farming systems were employed. First, the introduction of forestry-based systems implies major changes to traditional forms of farming that have provided farmers with consistent income for many years. Second, associated with this factor is the considerable risk involved in establishing and maintaining a viable forestry system. Third, substantial capital expenditure is required to establish forestry. Fourth, the returns are not immediate and assumptions concerning discount rates are critical to the outcome of analyses.

For these reasons, added incentives might be required to persuade farmers to move from current practices to forestry-based systems. On the other hand, modifications to existing farming systems are capable of significantly reducing deep percolation while increasing income (up to a point), without requiring major managerial changes. The possibility of achieving salinity control by persuading farmers to employ modified systems is more promising than could be expected from forestry and agroforestry.

To encourage farmers to reduce salinity beyond profit-maximizing levels would require government intervention other than merely providing information and advice. Table 14.3 shows the public outlays required for several policy options based on subsidizing reductions in deep percolation. These options vary from a uniform subsidy offered to farmers in the study area (no zoning), to the targeting of funds by matching the subsidy to the marginal costs of deep percolation reduction for each location. The procedure for determining subsidies per mm of deep percolation reduction may be similarly applied to subsidies based on adoption of approved management practices, or to taxes imposed per mm of deep percolation remaining.

Conclusions and policy implications

The results from this study indicate that there is scope for significantly alleviating the problem of dryland salinity in both cropping and grazing regions through relatively minor changes in existing farming systems, involving modification of fallowing practices and introduction of deeper rooted perennial grasses and legumes.

At low real discount rates (less than 10%), reforestation and agroforestry appear to be more profitable approaches for controlling dryland salinity, but require drastic changes to current farming systems with a large capital investment and a higher level of risk. This suggests that additional incentives would be required to persuade farmers to move from current practices to forestry-based systems. The adoption of these systems may only be required in limited areas where existing productivity is low.

In situations where the introduction of modified systems leads to increased farm income and reduced salinity, society should benefit from efforts to improve the availability of knowledge and thereby increase the rate at which the improved systems are adopted by agricultural producers. This action is likely to be particularly effective where the causes and effects of dryland salinity are confined to land under the control of one individual or firm.

Because of the non-point nature of salinity, it is almost impossible to determine accurately the external damage caused by certain land use practices. Without this information, it may be argued on legal and equity grounds that a farmer should not be forced to incur the full costs of alleviating a problem that cannot be directly linked to his actions. This, combined with the likely resistance of farming groups to taxes, suggests that policies based on subsidizing appropriate land uses rather than taxing unsuitable practices may be politically more acceptable.

The suggestion that farmers are currently opting for a farming system that is sub-optimal in terms of their net income warrants closer examination. The authors believe that realistic assumptions have been made concerning price relationships and input-output coefficients, but the results are yet to be extensively tested under field conditions. Technical difficulties in establishing and managing the suggested farming systems may need to be overcome before widespread adoption can be expected.

The role of native vegetation in controlling dryland salinity was not directly examined in the modelling approach. However, where the introduction of modified farming systems over an entire catchment area is unable to achieve a desired level of deep percolation reduction, the model is capable of determining the area required to be left under native forest to satisfy the deep percolation constraint. Such information could be used to develop the suggestion by Hodge (1982) that governments impose transferable quotas on the extent to which operators are permitted to clear their land.

It is possible to extend the modelling approach to any location, including irrigation areas where salinity is a problem or is likely to develop, provided site-specific environmental and geographical data are available. The general relationships incorporated in the model, such as the daily water balance and the relationships between water use and production, should remain useful in most cases. The main requirement at this stage is to expand the model to enable a more diverse range of crops and pastures to be examined.

It is clear that discriminating between areas prone to salinity problems and the targeting of government funds may have substantial impacts on the private costs of adopting approved management practices and the public expenditure required to finance salinity control policies. The costs of administering these approaches have yet to be estimated. However, the analysis provides a useful guide to the public finances that could be profitably directed toward educating farmers on appropriate strategies, as well as establishing an effective zoning system on which to base policy initiatives.

References

Adamson, C.M. (1978),
   "Conventional tillage systems as they affect soil erosion", *Journal of the Soil Conservation Service* (New South Wales), vol.34, no.4, pp.199-202.
Cannell, R.Q. (1981),
   "Potentials and problems of simplified cultivation and conventional tillage", *Outlook in Agriculture*, vol.10, no.8, pp.379-84.
Clarke, A.L., and J.S. Russell (1977),
   "Crop sequential practices" in J.S. Russell and E.C. Greacen (eds), *Soil Factors in Crop Production in a Semi-arid Environment* (St. Lucia: University of Queensland Press).
Colclough, J.D. (1973),
   "Salt", *Tasmanian Journal of Agriculture*, vol.44, pp.171-80.
Conacher, A.J., and E.D. Murray (1973),
   "Implications and causes of salinity problems in the Western Australian Wheat Belt: The York-Mawson Area", *Australian Geography Studies*, vol.11, pp.40-61.
Dumsday, R.G. (1973),
   The Economics of Some Soil Conservation Practices in the Wheat Belt of Northern New South Wales and Southern Queensland – A Modelling Approach, Farm Management Bulletin no. 19, University of New England.
Dumsday, R.G., G.W. Edwards, S.E. Lumley, D.A. Oram, and W.A. Papst (1985),
   Economic Aspects of Dryland Salinity Control in the Murray River Basin of South-Eastern Australia, AWRC Research Project 80/137 (Canberra: Department of Resources and Energy).
Garvin, R.J., M.R. Knight, and T.J. Richmond (1979),
   Guidelines for Minimizing Soil Erosion and Sedimentation from Construction Sites in Victoria (Melbourne: Victoria Soil Conservation Authority).

Gladstones, J.S. (1975),
  "Legumes and Australian agriculture", *Journal of the Australian Institute of Agricultural Science*, vol.41, no.4, pp.227-40.
Hodge, I. (1982),
  "Rights to cleared land and the control of dryland-seepage salinity", *Australian Journal of Agricultural Economics*, vol.26, no.3, pp.185-201.
Jenkin, J.J. (1980),
  "Salting and vegetation", *Water Talk*, no.44, pp.13-16.
Jenkin, J.J., and P.R. Dyson (1983),
  Groundwater and Soil Salinisation near Bendigo, Victoria (Melbourne: Victoria Soil Conservation Authority).
Matheson, W.E. (1968),
  "When salt takes over", *Journal of Agriculture* (South Australia), vol.71, no.8, pp.26-72.
McNeil, A. (1982),
  "How to beat tillage costs – directly", *Australian Country*, vol.25, no.9, pp.71-8.
Morris, J.D., J.J. Jenkin, and K.O. Collett (1981),
  "Dryland salting and reforestation", *Aqua*, vol.23, no.2, pp.8-10.
Oostenveld, M. (1977),
  "Increasing evapotranspiration to reduce saline areas" in *Dryland Salinity and Seepage in Alberta* (Lethbridge, Alberta: Alberta Dryland Salinity Committee).
Oram, D.A. and R.G. Dumsday (1984),
  Modelling Cost Functions for the Control of Dryland Salinity, Occasional Paper no. 8 (Melbourne: La Trobe University, School of Agriculture).
Peck, A.J. (1978),
  "Salinization of non-irrigated soils and associated streams: a review", *Australian Journal of Soil Research*, vol.16, no.2, pp.157-68.
Rooney, D.R., A.J. Sims, and C.L. Tuohey (1966),
  "Cultivation trials in the Wimmera", *Journal of Agricultural Science, Victoria*, vol.33, no.3, pp.180-91.
Shaw, R.J. (1982),
  "Land management for the prevention, control and amelioration of soil and water salinity" in Australian Association of Agricultural Faculties, *Proceedings of the 23rd Annual Conference*, University of Queensland.
Sims, H.J. (1977),
  "Cultivation and fallowing pracitces" in J.S Russel and E.L. Greacen (eds), *Soil Factors in Crop Production in a Semi-arid Environment* (St. Lucia: University of Queensland Press).
Storrier, R.R. (1969)
  "Nitorgen fertilizer and wheat production in Southern New South Wales", *New South Wales Agricultural Gazette*, vol.80, no.2, pp.76-9.
Storrier, R.R. (1975)
  "Wheat nutrition" in A. Lazenby and E.M. Matheson (eds), *Australian Field Crops, Vol. 1: Wheat and Other Temperate Cereals* (Sydney: Angus and Robertson).

Tunstall, B.R. and J. Walker (1975),
"The effect of woodland disturbance on soil water", *Managing Terrestrial Ecosystems*, vol.4,pp.49-57.

Tuohey, C.L., A.D.Robson, and D.R. Rooney (1972),
"Moisture and nitrate conservation and responses to fallowing after medic ley in the Wimmera", *Australian Journal of Experimental Agriculture and Animal Husbandry*, vol.12,no.57,pp.414-19.

Wagner, R. (1957),
"Salt damage on soils of the Southern Tablelands", *Journal of the Soil Conservation Service* (New South Wales), vol.13,pp.33-9.

Williamson, D.R. (1978),
"Water is the villain in dryland salinity", *Victoria's Resources*, vol.20, no.4,pp.9-14.

15
Regional Land Use Planning: The Murray River Catchment of Western Australia

J.F. Thomas

Précis

This case study was conducted from 1973 to 1980 by a multidisciplinary team drawn from the Commonwealth Scientific and Industrial Research Organization (CSIRO), the Western Australia (WA) Forests Department and the WA Department of Agriculture.

The economic analysis that was performed in the study is reported here. The presentation begins with a brief description of relevant Australian and Western Australian salinity and conservation issues. Issues of multiple-use planning faced in the Murray River catchment, Western Australia, are described. The methodology of the case study is outlined, followed by a brief summary of results and sensitivity tests. The main technique used is linear programming combined with benefit-cost analysis. Following a discussion of the limitations of the work and its local impact, the paper concludes by drawing some comparisons between the thrust of the case study and recommendations made by the Advisory Committee on the Sahel.

Background

Australian context
In Australia, dryland farming is synonymous with the wheat-sheep zone, an area that normally receives between 300 and 700 mm of rainfall per year. Between 1950 and 1975, large areas of natural vegetation were cleared for dryland farming. Replacement of perennial native vegetation by cropping and by ley farming systems (i.e., used temporarily for hay and grazing) reduced the evapotranspirational demand for water and increased the recharge to regional groundwater systems. Saline aquifers were mobilized, and this in turn led to "secondary" salinization of land and streams.

A recent review (Peck *et al*. 1983) indicated that some 4,620 km^2 of dryland agriculture in Australia was affected by secondary salinization and in some areas streamflow was brackish or saline. It was estimated that damage and abatement costs associated with land and water salinity in Australia averaged some A\$93 million/yr (at 1982 prices) in the decade 1971 – 81.

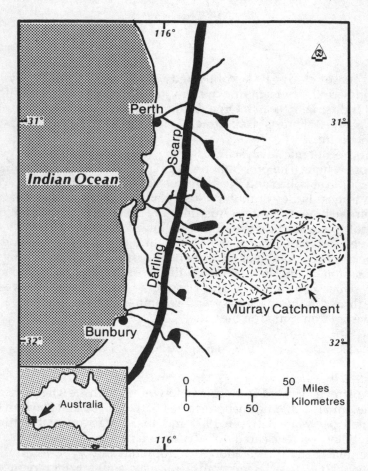

Figure 15.1: Location of Murray catchment, Western Australia

Concern has also been expressed over the planning of land use to allow preservation of indigenous ecosystems. In general, the Australian fauna is not well known and many species await description, particularly among the lower vertebrates and invertebrates. Leigh (1981) lists 2,206 species of Australian plants as being rare or threatened, with 46% occurring in Western Australia. Relatively little attention has so far been given to the working out of regional economic development plans that assess the alternatives for realizing conservation objectives. Leigh *et al.* (1983) suggest a series of co-ordinated strategies based on national parks and reserves. The implications of such a system of conservation for regional economic development have yet to be assessed.

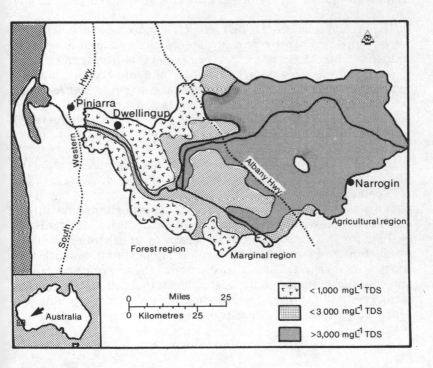

Figure 15.2: Stream salinity distribution

Case study setting
In Western Australia, clearing of perennial deep-rooted natural vegetation for dryland agriculture – mainly production of shallow-

rooted cereal crops and grazing land for sheep – has led to problems of waterlogging and salinization of agricultural land and has rendered some major rivers useless for urban water supply or irrigation.

A belt of uncleared eucalypt forest, some 350 km long and 30 km wide, runs parallel to the coast at the western edge of the plateau that rises 30 km east of the coast and stretches some 600 km inland. This area produces virtually all the region's fresh surface runoff. The forested area is ecologically adapted for survival through long rainless periods, fire and extremely low nutrient levels. In its natural state it is a resilient environment but once disturbed it becomes fragile, and not easily managed. It contains ecosystems that are unique to the region and provides numerous recreational amenities.

The upland soils of the forest are rich in bauxite, which has been mined since 1964 to provide raw material for an aluminum refining industry. Thus, there are many pressures that management and planning of the forested area have to take into account, including its use for bauxite mining, timber production, water resource protection, conservation needs and recreation.

The Murray River catchment south of Perth (see Figure 15.1) was selected for this study as a typical example of these inter-related resource management problems.

In considering water development options, the quality of Murray water is a serious concern, as is the potential for conflict between alternative uses of the catchment's resources. The most obvious conflict was between agricultural production in the upper catchment and water quality at favourable dam sites downstream (see Figure 15.2). Also, in the forested, lower catchment, timber production and bauxite mining could affect runoff, salinity and conservation values. The Murray is one of the few remaining wild and scenic rivers in the southwest of Western Australia. Canoeists, picnickers and campers are attracted to the river. Damming the Murray therefore could affect its use as a recreational resource.

Methodology

The analysis presented in this case study was conducted between 1973 and 1980 by a multidisciplinary team from the CSIRO (Commonwealth Scientific and Industrial Research Organization), together with the Western Australian Forests Department (now Conservation and Land Management) and the WA Department of Agriculture. Full documentation of the study is available in other published works (Bennett and Thomas 1982; Thomas *et al*. 1985).

As the issue of water resource development would have a strong bearing on the need for change in land use, the analysis began by identifying major options for water development. These were:

- no water development;
- development through two dams (an upper dam for diverting saline inflows from the agricultural areas and a lower dam to collect fresh run-off from the forested area);
- development through a single dam (if necessary with land use modifications to reduce salinity);
- single dam with desalting plants using the reverse-osmosis process; *and*
- limited development of fresh tributaries.

The next task was to identify the economically optimal pattern of land use for each water development option. Since the options differed in their costs and benefits, which are partly a function of land allocation, the problem was to select land uses that yielded a local optimum considering both the land use and the water development benefits and costs. Finally, discounted net benefits are compared for all water development options, including the option of no water development.

A mathematical economic model was designed to allocate land uses based on physical, biological and economic properties for the various scenarios of water planning. The catchment was divided into zones and all probable land use activities were considered for each zone. A computer program based on linear programming was written to account for all combinations of the activities in the zones. The task was to assess the economic value of each activity in each zone and to work out the most efficient mix of activities according to the various water development options.

Within each water development option, streamflow and salinity were allowed to vary as functions of the land use allocation. The economic value of the optimized solution was determined from the sum of the costs and benefits of the land use itself, and the effects the land use had on recreation, water quality and water quantity. In total the model considered 41 zones, 11 land use activities per zone, and 4 economic values per zone: recreation, water quality, water quantity, and land use values.

In applying the model, constraints were used to specify areas for certain activities (e.g., the conservation reserves), or the area of

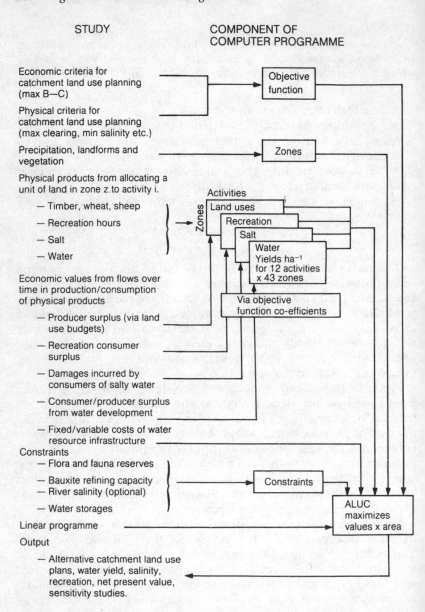

Source: Thomas, 1990.

Figure 15.3: Flow diagram of the model used

reservoir for a given water development scheme. In some applications, constraints such as the level of river salinity or the rate of bauxite mining as a function of refinery capacities, were also used to govern yields from land uses, recreation, water or salt. It was assumed that the physical quantity of output responds linearly to change in area allocated to an activity, and that the regional price of the output remains constant. A flow diagram for the model is shown in Figure 15.3.

Formally, the model may be expressed:

$$\text{Max } v = \Sigma_z \Sigma_i \Sigma_k b_{zik} a_{zi} - c$$

where v = net project benefits

b_{zik} = net discounted benefits, received in form k, of allocating one ha of land to activity i in zone z of the catchment

k = 1,...,4 indexes land use, recreation, water quantity, and salt flow, respectively

a_{zi} = area of land in zone z allocated to activity i,

c = fixed costs of water resource development

The sum of the net benefits thus involves the aggregation of the net land use benefits, the net water quantity benefits, the net water quality benefits, and the net recreation benefits, each of which is expressed as a net present value. The objective function is consistent with the criterion of economic efficiency, which seeks to maximize net project benefits, and then to choose between optimally designed projects. The sensitivity of solutions to changes in the discount rate was investigated, and different land assignments were obtained by varying either the objective function, constraints or values of coefficients. The following sections briefly describe how land within the catchment area was divided into zones, the land uses that were considered, and how estimates of physical and economic effects of each land use in each zone were determined.

Zonation

Geographical zones within the Murray catchment area were analysed based on variation in rainfall, topography, soil structure and current land use (McArthur *et al.* 1977). These factors combine to influence both the economic returns that can be earned from the land by its various possible uses, and the rate of discharge of salt and water into the streams. The zones divided the catchment into relatively homogeneous areas for mining, forestry, agriculture, recreational activities, and water and salt yields. For example, landform units divided the lateritic uplands, the only zone containing mineable bauxite, from the swampy uplands containing abundant flora and fauna, and from the slopes and valley floors that form productive agricultural lands.

Land uses
The land uses considered in the study were as follows:

- flora and fauna reserves;
- national parks;
- eucalyptus hardwood forestry;
- plantation forests (*Pinus pinaster* and *P. radiata*);
- bauxite mining (followed by forestry, agriculture or "roaded" subcatchments);
- agriculture;
- agroforestry (a combination of agriculture and forestry currently being investigated as a method of overcoming salt movement);
- plantations along streamlines (an alternative to agroforestry as a method of overcoming salt movement);
- water runoff enhancement (by sealing part of the land surface, i.e., "roading"),
- water storage (i.e., reservoirs are considered a land use as they involve the flooding of land); *and*
- desalination plants (which occupy a nominal area of land but have a cost-schedule and associated negative water and salt yields).

In running the model, the number of activities was varied from just the two currently dominant land uses (eucalypt forest and cereals/sheep farming) up to the preceding full list of activities. The plantations, agroforestry and streamline plantations were assumed to reduce salinity, although the extent to which they can do so on a sustained basis is still a matter of speculation. Nevertheless, research in the late 1970s indicated that plantations of eucalypts would achieve much higher rates of evaporation per unit land area than agricultural crops (Greenwood *et al*. 1985). More recent work has focused on new crops (e.g., grain lupins), which also produce favourable effects on regional groundwater recharge.

Water and salt yields
Water yields of the component geomorphological surfaces of the catchment were estimated by comparing measured water yields

in, or adjacent to, the Murray River. Graphs were then drawn relating water yield from similar surfaces to changes in rainfall. These estimates ranged from 4,000 m³/ha/yr for the wetter western valley surfaces to a negligible 20 m³/ha/yr for the dry eastern uplands. Variations in water yield from land use changes were then developed by comparing measured yields from forested and cleared land. Similar calculations were performed with respect to salt yields.

Valuation of costs and benefits
In determining the economic value of each activity in each zone, four separate effects were considered:

- the producer surpluses of the activities in each zone (i.e., the net benefits to entrepreneurs in profits and to employees in wages, calculated above an opportunity-cost baseline);
- the effect each activity had on recreational values in monetary terms (e.g., the effect bauxite mining would have on recreation in each zone can be valued by estimating visitor numbers at present and in the future and assigning economic value to these visits, using variants of the travel cost approach);
- the effect each activity had on overall water production and how much this would be worth in consumer's surplus aggregated over the life of the project; *and*
- the effect each activity had on salt flow from each zone (and hence the economic costs incurred by water consumers based on an estimate of the damage function for salinity).

Results

Land use and water quality
To illustrate the effect of land use on streamflow and salinity, the model was first run with just two land uses: agriculture and eucalypt forest. No economic valuations were used. Instead, agriculture was given an index of 1.0 per hectare allocated, and eucalypt forest an index of zero. The model was then run a large number of times at varying levels of salinity constraint while, in turn, maximizing and minimizing cleared area.

The results suggest that there is considerable scope for manipulating land use in order to achieve salinity targets over most of the range of possible salinity levels. The minimum salinity that can be achieved is 380 mg/l NaCl, and for this the entire catchment must be forested (see Figure 15.4). The present situation of the catchment within the feasible solution space is also shown. These results relate to the expected average salinity and assume linear relations between land allocation and the yields of water and salt.

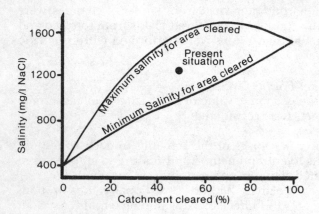

Figure 15.4: Solution space in terms of salinity and percentage clearing

In this catchment the release of salt from agricultural land far exceeds that associated with any possible amount of bauxite mining, even if mining contributes substantially to the spread of jarrah dieback disease, although this would probably not be true in some other local catchments in which there is little agricultural clearing. Thus, measures to improve water quality by choice of land use must concentrate on agricultural land.

Initial land allocation
Next, the "direct" net present values of land uses were used in the objective function. In the absence of water resource development, little change in land use was suggested by the model. In other words, current land use was close to the economically "optimal" allocation if recreation and water benefits and salt costs were ignored. A small area of some 40 km^2 was reallocated from agriculture to pine plantations, and a constraint based on refinery capacity allowed 200 km^2 of forest to be mined for bauxite. This very stable result was obtained because, according to the activity budgets, it would not pay to clear any more forested land for agriculture, while reforestation of agricultural land was limited

to the small areas recommended for pines. Table 15.1 shows that the value of the bauxite mining activity is large, but the refining capacity constraint keeps the allocated area small.

Table 15.1: Land allocation in absence of water development compared with existing land use

	Existing land use	Optimal allocation with no water resource development and no reserves
Areas (km^2 × 10):		
Agriculture	347	343
Forestry	306	300
Reserves	10	
Bauxite mining*		20
TOTAL	663	663
Aquastatistics		
Streamflow (10^6 m^3/yr)	318	328
Salinity (mg/l NaCl)	1,219	1,230
Net annual values (A\$ × 10^6)**		
Agriculture	5.14	5.07
Forestry	2.10	2.10
Bauxite mining* (followed by agriculture)		23.12
TOTAL	7.24	30.29

* Area of bauxite mining was constrained to be less than or equal to 200 km^2, this figure representing an upper limit in line with refinery production plans.
** Net annual values were calculated by expressing the net discounted value of the benefits minus costs over 120 years (using a 7% discount rate) as an annuity (at 7% discount rate over 50 years).

At the time the study was performed, public sector investment in softwood plantations was planned to be located outside the Murray catchment. Policies have since been changed. This and movements in relative commodity prices make it likely that larger areas of pine plantations and some agroforestry would now be selected, even if water and salt yields were valued at zero. Also, in the low rainfall zones, increasing attention has recently been paid to the economic benefits of planting salt-tolerant forage and crops that use greater amounts of water. These trends in what is being perceived as optimal planning for farm management might conceivably change the optimal enterprise budgets assumed in the study.

Addition of recreational values
The Murray catchment contains a great variety of landscapes with recreational potential. In order to include the benefits of recreation in the weighting of land uses, an estimate was made of the consumer surplus from recreation for each possible land use in a zone. This was based on a site-specific evaluation of willingness to pay, using the travel cost method. Some variants were also investigated. The method estimates the likely number of visits at each of a range of hypothetical entrance charges and imputes the excess of willingness to pay over actual entrance charge payments (of zero). From recent studies (Bishop and Heberlein 1979) we know that the method yields rough estimates of true willingness to pay, but can be subject to substantial error. Nevertheless, relative to the other benefits from land uses in the catchment, the likely error in recreational benefit estimates would not appear to be serious. Finally it was assumed that a sixfold growth in recreational visits would take place during the planning timescale.

In the absence of water resource development, inclusion of recreational values had two effects on the land allocation. First, national parks were selected for some 420 km² within the valley which had relatively low net present values for forestry. Second, a similar area of land in another part of the catchment was transferred from forest to agricultural use.

Providing for conservation objectives
Another major land use conflict in the catchment is between economic development and the conservation of flora and fauna. At the commencement of the study, an attempt was made to delineate sufficiently large reserves to achieve the ideal of covering the full range of ecosystems. It soon became obvious that this was no longer feasible, particularly in the eastern part of the catchment where the alienation and clearing of land has already progressed too far. However, reserves proposed by the WA Forests Department were incorporated as constraints on land allocation. No attempt was made to estimate option or existence values for these areas.

The costs of introducing conservation reserves were calculated as the change in net present values of other land uses. In the absence of water resource development, the reserves excised 480 km² from hardwood forestry and 170 km² from national parks. The new optimal location for mining was slightly farther inland and away from the aluminum refinery, in an area thought to have greater potential for raising salinity. The annual cost of proposed conservation areas expressed as an annuity over 50 years was A$l.7 million at 1976 prices. Of this figure, A$1 million would be incurred in forestry (reduced logging), A$0.5 million in net recreational benefits, and A$0.2 million would be borne by the mining industry for additional transport costs. The study concluded that the resulting addition to mining costs is not only small compared with the value of the bauxite, but may well be exceeded by the value of recreation alone. It was therefore concluded that taking advantage of the potential mobility of mining should be an important principle of efficient land use management in this and similar catchments.

No account is taken in this calculation of the costs (if any) that would result from the "sterilization" (non-use) of some bauxite deposits in the land allocated for conservation reserves. At planned capacity levels, however, alumina production would not be affected within the next 50 years. The preservation decision would be reversible if a sufficiently profitable aluminum industry still existed when local bauxite became scarce, and if the benefits from extraction were then considered to exceed the value placed on continued conservation.

Water resource development

Although the Murray River catchment contained a gazetted "water reserve" and was on the list of possible future development sources, it was not considered likely to be developed before the year 2000. Reduction of salinity itself would reclaim a large water resource. The Murray could yield about 250 million m³/yr, which is more than the hills reservoirs supply to either Perth or to coastal irrigation areas at present. Figure 15.5 shows the potential yields as a function of land use.

Economic justification for changes in land use that reduce salinity was sought by analysis of net benefits from water resource development and land use in the catchment at various scales and at alternative salinity levels. Thus, salinity was regarded as being reversible by vegetation change. The costs, which would fall mainly upon farmers, would depend on the efficacy of the particular changes.

The costs of producing water from the catchment were assessed as the opportunity costs of labour and capital needed to construct and operate dams, pipelines and pump stations. Each scheme was

Water yields from the Murray depend on the amount of the catchment covered by forest which evaporates water all year, as opposed to annual crops and pastures which only evaporate water during the wet winter and spring seasons. The more forest there is, the less water yield.

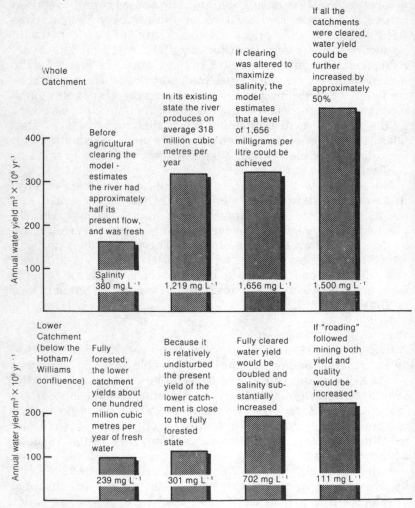

Whole Catchment

If all the catchments were cleared, water yield could be further increased by approximately 50%

If clearing was altered to maximize salinity, the model estimates that a level of 1,656 milligrams per litre could be achieved

In its existing state the river produces on average 318 million cubic metres per year

Before agricultural clearing the model - estimates the river had approximately half its present flow, and was fresh

Annual water yield m³ × 10⁶ yr⁻¹

Salinity 380 mg L⁻¹   1,219 mg L⁻¹   1,656 mg L⁻¹   1,500 mg L⁻¹

Lower Catchment (below the Hotham/ Williams confluence)

Fully forested, the lower catchment yields about one hundred million cubic metres per year of fresh water

Because it is relatively undisturbed the present yield of the lower catchment is close to the fully forested state

Fully cleared water yield would be doubled and salinity substantially increased

If "roading" followed mining both yield and quality would be increased*

Annual water yield m³ × 10⁶ yr⁻¹

239 mg L⁻¹   301 mg L⁻¹   702 mg L⁻¹   111 mg L⁻¹

*Because little research has been performed this assumption is subject to considerable uncertainty.

Figure 15.5: Water yields in the Murray catchment under different scenarios

then viewed in terms of an optimal allocation of land uses and the resulting levels of streamflow and salinity. It was then possible to examine the optimal pattern of land use under each water resource development as compared with a "no water development" alternative.

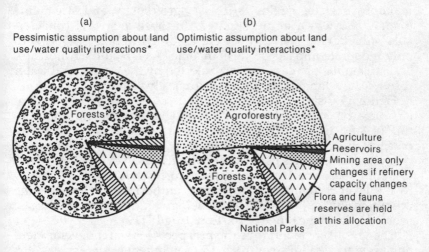

(a)
Pessimistic assumption about land use/water quality interactions*

(b)
Optimistic assumption about land use/water quality interactions*

*The "optimistic" assumption is that limited tree planting in agroforestry schemes would be effective in reducing salt flow from agricultural areas: the "pessimistic" assumption is that it is not possible to find land management schemes which achieve this, other than full reforestation of agricultural areas.

To meet the salinity standard nearly all the agricultural land has to be planted to plantations which lose money. Annual value of the catchment products falls to $25 million. Dam supplies, on average, 177 million cubic metres of water per year to Perth at 500 mg L^{-1} Total Dissolved Solids.

Agroforestry replaces money losing plantations. Annual value of the catchments products rises to $31 million. Dam supplies the same amount of water at the same quality standard.

Figure 15.6: One dam with land uses designed to meet the World Health Organization's standard of 500 mg/1 total dissolved solids (TDSs): pie charts show land allocation

Given the estimated values of water and salinity damage used in the study, the net social benefits of schemes involving extensive reforestation in agricultural areas or physical desalination would be either small or negative. Since agricultural income exceeded damages from salinity, the result was that little agricultural land was reassigned and resulting salinity of around 1,200 mg/l total dissolved salts (TDS) was much higher than would be acceptable to water suppliers.

The efficiency of possible new forms of land use designed to improve water quality, such as agroforestry and streamline plantations, was also investigated. In these analyses, considerable reductions in salt flows were assumed to be achieved with only moderate impacts on farm income. As a result, agroforestry and streamline plantations were selected by the model, and water resource development became economically viable.

Figure 15.6 shows that assumptions concerning the effects of land use on salinity have a profound impact on the optimum mix of land uses. With an optimistic assumption on the ability of agroforestry to reduce salinity, the net annual value of the catchment's products rises by more than 20%. Nevertheless, even under this scenario, it did not appear worthwhile to reduce salinity to the level recommended by water authorities (500 mg/l). The economically "optimal" salinity level, given the abatement costs, seemed to lie in the range of 700 to 800 mg/l TDS.

Changes likely to improve the prospects for water development and vegetative salinity control in this catchment include:

- higher regional price for water;
- higher price for softwoods relative to agricultural crops;
- improved technical efficiency of agroforestry production;
- viability of alternative grain crops; *and, possibly,*
- reduced use of subterranean clover pastures.

Water resource development would conflict with in-stream uses of the natural river valley. In-stream recreational values could, however, be partly maintained by flow regulation downstream of dams, while reservoir-oriented recreation would increase. The study shows that under certain conditions net benefits would be insufficient to justify water development, a result that would no doubt please users of the natural valley. Catchment-scale optimization would always need to be used as an input to broader scale assessments in considering statewide strategies for water development and environmental protection.

Impacts of variation of economic parameters

Given the number of land use options and externalities being considered, it is obvious that differing net benefit estimates could be generated for each land and water development plan by simple, yet plausible, variation of data values. This process, often referred to as "sensitivity analysis", in fact became a major learning activity. What emerged from this is that the solution surface, far from having prominent peaks or troughs (indicating a few very good or very bad solutions) in fact had gentle contours (indicating that solutions can be found for which there are small differences in net benefits but radically different land assignments).

In such situations, economic maximization will not give a clear lead as to which plan is "best", though it can yield a set of plans, each producing a similar overall net present value. Three aspects which might be of general interest are outlined below.

Discounting
An interesting result, which may possibly be counter-intuitive, was that the area of forest retained in the catchment was at a maximum when the real discount rate was 6%. At higher discount rates clearing for agriculture was less attractive than retaining forest, while at lower discount rates net agricultural benefits exceeded net forestry benefits for an increasing number of zones.

Timescale of water development
The model yielded the usual (and economical) conclusion that if growth in regional demand were moderate, thus leading to considerable lags before full utilization of large schemes, small-scale water resource developments would be preferable.

Salinity damage function
There was a critical level of damage cost per unit salinity at which large-scale reforestation and consequent improvement in water quality yielded larger net benefits than agricultural production.

Limitations of the analysis

The practical limitations of the modelling exercise mainly lie in restrictions on information. Much of the analysis had to rely on critical assumptions and sensitivity analysis:

- external benefits and costs were linear functions of land use activities;
- the "problem" could be moulded into the linear programming framework without total distortion of real conditions;
- water and salt yields were linearly related to the area each

land use occupied in a zone;
- stream salinity was reversible by planting trees;
- zones were sufficiently homogeneous to be treated as entities;
- orchards and other minor land uses could be ignored;
- there was no need to separate water yield into surface flows, varying according to season;
- water was yielded directly from each zone to the river when, in fact, it may flow across two or three other zones before entering;
- edge effects (e.g., spread of dieback around bauxite pits, or agricultural vermin spread from wooded areas or the aesthetic delights of a mixed landscape) could be ignored;
- market prices for catchment products would remain in the same ratios to each other;
- yields of products, water, salt and recreation would be as specified and that risk and uncertainty could be ignored; *and*
- land use budgets were reasonable even though some involved the estimation of growth rates for eucalypt plantations in areas where there was no experience of them, much less their commercial costs.

It should also be realized that market-based valuations, or approximations to them, might not be acceptable to interested parties. The legitimacy of the study could be questioned if the ethical or distributional assumptions were inappropriate.

Benefit-cost analysis is best viewed as a starting point for discussions on the ethical positions in the study. The role of benefit-cost analysis in helping society or the government to discover (or change) its values should be emphasized as much as its normative, prescriptive nature. The technique provides a means of weighing up (not weighting) options, which are often obscurely related to familiar yardsticks of value. The strength of this study lies in the attempt to estimate a salinity damage function and willingness to pay for recreation in the catchment, highlighting the economic importance of unpriced natural resource outputs.

Practical implications of the study

The case study was only one input to the political, administrative and community consideration of land use planning in the region. Some emerging policy directions in Western Australia are, however, consistent with the study conclusions. For example:

- Large-scale water resource development is no longer seen as an imminent possibility in the Murray catchment, by virtue of the costs of water quality improvement and development.
- Greater attention is being paid to the economic possibilities – from an agricultural, silvicultural, and water quality perspective – of forest management, agroforestry and modified cropping systems in this and other river basins (Treloar 1984; Malajczuk *et al*. 1984; Garland *et al*. 1984; Grieg and Devonshire 1981; Dumsday 1983; Sewell *et al*. 1985).
- Interdepartmental liaison with the mining industry has been much improved, and prospective mining plans within the mining lease areas are now subject to scrutiny and review.
- A larger area of land in the Murray catchment is now allocated for conservation and recreational use.
- Governmental authorities have been given greater powers to influence agricultural land use practices, and there has been greater financial support for community groups concerned with tree establishment and soil conservation in farming areas.
- Benefit-cost analysis within a regional environmental impact procedure has been mandated for all further proposals for release of new land for agriculture (McFadden *et al*. 1984).

An African comparison

Although the case study covers a semi-arid to humid region, which currently enjoys a high income level, it has some features that may be relevant to planning in other regions where there is rapid transition from subhumid to semi-arid conditions, or where development of dryland agriculture is liable to affect regional groundwater systems. To illustrate this, some comparisons are drawn with selected conclusions of the Advisory Committee on the West African Sahel (1983).

An early concern in this case study was with landform and vegetation mapping as a basis for land use planning. This may be compared with the Advisory Committee's recommendation (p. 45) for "the definition and identification of ecological provinces . . . as they constitute the basic physical units for analysis and rehabilitation . . . ." The links among land use, water resources and soil conservation are stressed in both cases.

The Advisory Committee also makes a number of recommendations for improving project assessment and design. In criticizing donor-assisted irrigation projects in sub-Saharan Africa, they conclude (p. 47), "Although many of the projects have been preceded by seemingly exhaustive studies, the studies . . . reveal little appreciation of the complex interrelationships among soil, water, vegetation, and other constituent elements of the river basin system." The case study methodology reported here recognizes such effects, though possibly in a simplistic way.

The potential of natural resources to yield multiple benefits is also a common concern of the two studies. It is now recognized – whether in Western Australia or the West African Sahel – that "the" natural resource base yields many different commodities and services. Economists think of this multiplicity as sets of demand and supply functions that may be interrelated. Emergence of a supply scarcity for one commodity (either through demand growth or resource failure) creates problems and opportunities for natural resource rehabilitation. In Western Australia, regional demand for fresh water provides economic justification for efforts to reduce stream salinity in some catchment areas; the changing mix of natural hardwood and softwood plantation forestry, which has resulted from growth in timber demand and hardwood supply constraints, provides opportunities for influencing regional groundwater recharge; and farm adjustment and diversification offer opportunities for soil conservation. Thus, from the perspective of this study it would seem that rectification of fuelwood shortages in Sahelian areas ought to be economically consistent with (rather than prejudicial to) dryland and rangeland improvement.

The Advisory Committee found that, "While donors spend substantial sums of money on plantation projects which often fail, the rehabilitation and conservation of natural forests stands costs very little and provides multiple benefits." An integrated economic approach should not fail to identify the comparative advantage of such indigenous forest management. In Western Australia, fresh water is a principal economic benefit derived from indigenous forest. The Advisory Committee recommended (p. 48) that "Sahelian governments and regionally-active donors cooperate in developing new multiple-use forest management strategies that permit both the conservation and increased utilization of forest resources," calling for "species trials to identify economically attractive, high yielding, drought resistant, multi-purpose trees." From experience in this study, imputation of scarcity values for unpriced natural resource outputs is a major step forward in coping with the problem of multiple uses of natural resources. Unpriced goods are prominent in the consumption patterns of low-income arid and semi-arid areas as well as in more affluent areas. Water, fuel and sometimes shelter are obvious examples. Greater attention to the means available for estimation of relative scarcity, and the recognition of these scarcity values in planning, are essential.

Distributional issues entered this case study to the limited extent that shadow prices based on perceived opportunity costs were used for mining and forestry labour. Also, the assumption of equal marginal utility of income between producer and consumer groups is implicit in the analysis. Such assumptions are often said to destroy the case for using benefit-cost analysis in low-income countries or in those with heavily skewed income distribution, situations common in many parts of Africa. The work of Helmers (1979) is pathbreaking in extending benefit-cost analysis to include income distribution objectives. Helmers's distributional weights could be incorporated within a case study methodology such as this.

Finally, it should be recognized that the social and political consensus often leaves enormous scope for consideration of radical alternatives for resource use. In Australia and elsewhere, project analysis has frequently paid insufficient attention to economic and environmental realities. Such realities increase rather than diminish the need for economic analysis of resource management options, particularly in dryland regions.

References

Advisory Committee on the Sahel *et al.* (Chairman, L. Berry), (1983),
   Environmental Change in the West African Sahel (Washington DC: National Academy Press).
Bennett, D., and J.F. Thomas (eds), (1982),
   On Rational Grounds – Systems Analysis in Catchment Land Use Planning (Amsterdam: Elsevier).
Bishop, R.C., and T.A. Heberlein (1979),
   "Measuring values of extra-market goods: are indirect measures biased?" *American Journal of Agricultural Economics*, vol.61, no.5, pp.926-30.
Dumsday, R.G. (1983),
   "The economics of dryland salinity", in *Proceedings of the Royal Society of Victoria* (June), Melbourne.
Garland, K.R., W.W. Fisher, and P.J. Grieg (1984),
   Agroforestry in Victoria, Technical Report Series no. 93, Victoria Department of Agriculture.
Greenwood, E.A.N., L. Klein, J.D. Beresford, and G.D. Watson (1985),
   "Differences in annual evaporation between grazed pasture and Eucalyptus species in plantations on a saline farm catchment", *Journal of Hydrology*, vol.78, pp.261-78.

Grieg, P.J., and P.G. Devonshire (1981),
"Tree removals and saline seepage in Victorian catchments: some hydrologic and economic results", *Australian Journal of Agricultural Economics*, vol.25,no.2,pp.134-48.

Helmers, F.L.C.H. (1979),
Project Planning and Income Distribution, Studies in Development Planning, vol. 9 (Boston: Martinus Nijhoff Publishing).

Leigh, J.H. (1981),
Rare or Threatened Australian Plants, ANPWS Special Publication no. 7 (Canberra: Australian National Parks and Wildlife Service).

Leigh, J.H., R.W. Boden, and J.D. Briggs (1983),
Extinct and Endangered Australian Plants (Melbourne: MacMillan).

Malajczuk, G., D.A. Morrison, G.W. Anderson, R.W. Moore, and J.J Havel (1984),
"An economic study of agroforestry on farmland in the Manjimup region of Western Australia", Technical Paper (Perth: Forests Department of WA).

McArthur, W.M., H.M. Churchward, and P.T. Hick (1977),
Landforms and Soils of the Murray River Catchment Area of Western Australia, Land Resources Management Series no. 3 (Perth: CSIRO Division of Land Resources Management).

McFadden, J.R., A.A. Burbridge, N. Orr, T.C. Stoneman, and J.F. Thomas (1984),
Report of the Working Party Assisting the Agricultural Land Release Review Committee (Perth: Western Australian Department of Lands and Surveys).

Peck, A.J., J.F. Thomas, and D.R. Williamson (1983),
Effects of Man on Salinity in Australia, Water 2000 Consultants Report no. 8: Salinity Issues, Department of Resources and Energy (Canberra: Australian Publishing Service).

Sewell, W.R.D., D.I. Smith, and J.W. Handmer (eds), (1985),
Water Planning in Australia: From Myths to Reality (Canberra: Centre for Resource and Environmental Studies, Australian National University).

Thomas, J.F., D. Bennett, and D.K. Macpherson (1985),
"Theory and practice in catchment land use planning: the Murray Valley of Western Australia" in *Proceedings of the Conservation and Economy Conference, Sydney, 1984* (Canberra: Australian Government Publishing Service).

Treloar, D.W.G. (1984),
Pilot Study of the Potential for Cooperative Ventures Between the Forests Department and Farmers in the Manjimup Region (Perth: Centre for Applied Business Research, University of Western Australia).

VI

Damage Cost Studies

Land degradation imposes costs on a wide range of resource users. Farmers and pastoralists see reduced productivity and others notice the effects of changes in water quality and quantity. The studies in this section view the problem from a socio-economic perspective that includes on-site as well as off-site effects within a social welfare framework.

Land and water are the principal resources involved, and resource degradation results in some or all of the following effects: reduced yields, vegetation degradation, soil acidity, salinity, sedimentation and changed water quality. Reduced air quality from dust and sandstorms is another consequence of the problem. By estimating the extent of these effects and the monetary costs involved, damage cost studies highlight the severity of the problem and identify important areas for government attention and intervention.

The three case studies in this section illustrate the application of damage cost analysis at regional and national levels. The first case by Sinden, Sutas and Yapp provides estimates of selected damage costs from various states in Australia. Though this paper does not attempt to provide a comprehensive estimate of all the costs of land degradation, it does give an order of magnitude estimate of the losses associated with various forms of land degradation in selected regions. It also examines the level of expenditures allocated by the government to combat these problems.

In the second study, Sinden takes a closer look at the costs of soil degradation in one part of the state of New South Wales, Australia. This study examines expected benefits and costs from undertaking soil conservation measures suggested by the Soil Conservation Service of New South Wales. Soil conservation to avoid losses in wheat production is clearly justified by the analysis.

In the Canadian study by Girt, both on-farm and off-farm costs are estimated. Wind and water erosion are shown to be the largest sources of damage in most areas of Canada. The study indicates that the magnitude of damages associated with land degradation may have substantial effects on national income and need to be prevented at the earliest possible stage.

16
Damage Costs of Land Degradation: an Australian Perspective

J.A. Sinden, A.R. Sutas and T.P. Yapp

Précis

Australia has extensive areas of dryland degradation. This paper examines the economic costs of land degradation, the so-called "damage costs", and the potential benefits (abatement costs avoided) to be derived from damage prevention and the rehabilitation of degraded areas.

Land degradation is seen as a complex interaction of soil, water and cultural practices. Major costs are associated with soil loss, sedimentation, decreased water quality and salinization. In New South Wales, annual expenditures on soil conservation and rehabilitation are but a fraction of estimated annual losses.

Introduction

Land degradation refers to a reduction in the quality of land that diminishes its usefulness to people. It is evidenced by reduced productivity, increased risks in land use, loss of genetic resources, and reduction in amenity or aesthetic values.

The basic physical and biological processes by which land degradation occurs are relatively well understood. Less well understood are the social, economic and political factors that determine how land is used. Although infrequent events such as droughts or heavy rains may trigger extensive damage, inappropriate land management or use of land beyond its capability frequently creates the conditions leading to degradation.

Indeed, land degradation rarely results from a single cause, but more often is the result of a combination of predisposing factors; complex interrelationships exist between cause and effect. For example, tree decline, itself a form of vegetation degradation, may result in soil erosion and salinity as well as affect the hydrologic cycle. On the other hand, soil erosion or salinity may cause tree decline. Figure 16.1 provides a simplified picture of some of the major linkages between different aspects of land degradation, and Table 16.1 further illustrates the complexity of the cause-and-effect

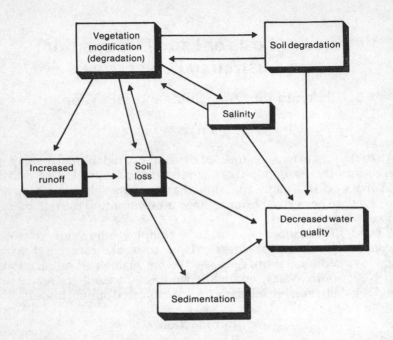

Figure 16.1: A simplified representation of some of the major pathways and the inter-relationships of land degradation

relationships involved.

To appreciate the complexity and dimensions of land degradation, it is useful to follow the processes as they occur within a catchment. Whatever its size or location, a catchment is a complete physiographic and hydrologic entity in which nature has packaged the inter-related problems of water, land, and people (Jackson 1982; Easter, Dixon, and Hufschmidt 1986).

Water is perhaps the most important natural agent in the process of land degradation. Water is usually the medium in which soil is moved downstream, creating off-site effects such as deposition of sediment, altered runoff patterns, streambank erosion, and damage within downstream ecosystems.

Land degradation within the upper catchment may impose extensive off-site costs as water passes downstream through towns and cities, dams, rivers, estuaries and then out to sea. Estuaries are highly susceptible to the effects of land degradation. Since the majority of the Australian population resides near the coast, the value of estuaries for recreation and as highly productive biologic zones means that the off-site effects of land degradation could involve very large costs.

Table 16.1: Consequences of the effects of land degradation

Increased runoff	Soil loss	Sedimentation	Decreased water quality	Soil degradation and salinity
Lower infiltration rates	Decreased value of land	Reduced stream-flow capacity	Reduced value of water resources	Reduced land productivity and capability
Increased streamflow	Sedimentation	Reduced water storage capacity of dams, lakes, etc.	Need for water treatment prior to use	Decreased water quality
Higher and earlier stream flood discharge peaks	Reduced water quality	Destroy estuaries, fauna, flora and habitat	Destruction of fauna and flora habitat	Destroy native flora habitat
Streambank erosion	Export of nutrients and other matter	Sediment damage to roads, culverts, drains, etc.	Decreased recreational value and amenities	Vegetation degradation
Greater soil loss potential	Damage to structures, e.g., roads and houses	Reduced navigation potential/ capability	Eutrophication	Alter runoff characteristics
Altered saline regimes for estuaries	Reduced land capability	Destruction of crops, etc.	Reduced aesthetic values	
Transport of organic material from land surface to water bodies				

Principles of damage cost estimation
Monetary damage estimates are one useful tool in the development

and implementation of environmental policy. However, they should not be regarded as an exclusive or perfect tool. Monetary damage estimates are useful in organizing and summarizing information on environmental effects that can facilitate better decision-making. Moreover, such estimates may remain useful even when they are not precise, and their use should be encouraged (Maler and Wyzga 1976).

Analysis of damage costs can be useful to identify the underlying causes of degradation, the significance of degradation, and alternative responses that may be made by land managers and policymakers.

Broad-scale, aggregate estimates inform policymakers, analysts and advisers of the economic dimensions of land degradation. By increasing awareness of the actual costs of degradation, they may play a useful role in helping to establish where government action is warranted in strengthening the political will to act, and in identifying the scale of resource commitment required.

On a regional or local level, damage cost estimates can help decision-makers determine priorities in selecting programmes and projects and in on-going management.

The level at which information on damage costs is to be employed, and the purpose for which it is intended, will influence the collection, presentation, and interpretation of data. Important considerations in any study of damage costs include identifying the costs of obtaining and using information, establishing appropriate boundaries for the analysis, and choosing an appropriate time frame.

Because of the complex physical and economic relationships involved in land degradation, successful damage cost estimation requires inputs from several disciplines. Application of the economist's analytical tools requires information on the physical damage relationships.

Damage costs may be broadly classified as resulting from either on-site or off-site effects of degradation. On-site costs include the direct loss of production due, for example, to changes in soil quality or quantity, and to increased costs of production incurred at the site of degradation. Off-site costs are those that occur or are experienced away from the site of the action causing degradation.

Off-site costs are nearly always externalities. They include, for example, off-site productivity losses, damages to public infrastructure, impaired aesthetics, ecological losses and increased hazards. Most on-site and some off-site effects can be measured and valued with relative ease, but some off-site effects are very difficult to measure and even more difficult to value in monetary terms. Recent thinking on the problem of valuation is summarized in Sinden and Worrell (1979), Hufschmidt *et al.* (1983), and Dixon and Hufschmidt (1986).

A further distinction can be drawn between damage costs that are readily recognized in the short term and others that are of a longer term nature and may not become apparent until a critical threshold level of degradation is passed.

A distinction is drawn between financial analysis and economic analysis. Financial analysis refers to monetary costs and benefits as perceived by an individual decision-maker or business entity. Economic analysis includes financial analysis but is much broader. It recognizes that not all costs and benefits are limited to the decision-maker, and that many costs and benefits are not readily expressed in monetary terms. Thus, economic analysis of land degradation encompasses consideration of both private and social costs and benefits, including priced and unpriced effects. Within this framework, estimates of damage costs would ideally capture the social opportunity costs of current land use management and policy decisions.

The measurement of damage costs can be undertaken in a number of ways. For example, the on-farm costs of soil degradation can be measured by loss of productivity, reduced land value (market value), and rehabilitation costs. The approach taken in a particular instance will depend largely on what data are available and on the purpose for which the estimate is made. Estimates may also involve different degrees of complexity and completeness.

Damage estimates based on rehabilitation costs may attract attention to the results of past land use policies and land management. However, such estimates tend to be static and backward looking. The total quantity of rehabilitation will almost inevitably exceed the amount of rehabilitation that is feasible and economic to undertake. Estimates of total necessary rehabilitation costs may do little to direct resources to soil conservation at the expense of other activities, and are of little help in making decisions about changing land use or allocating resources.

A more useful approach to measurement of damage costs from a dynamic, decision-oriented point of view is based on the opportunity cost concept, which is central to an economic analysis of land degradation. Land resources are scarce and can generally be put to alternative uses. The opportunity cost of choosing a particular use is the value placed on forgone benefits from the best alternative use. Taking this approach, the central question is what costs, in the form of forgone production or amenity benefits, are being incurred from current land management practices? How do these costs compare with current benefits derived and with the costs of further damage prevention or restoration? These terms can establish whether in fact the existing level or rate of land degradation constitutes a "problem" in economic terms.

In the context of on-farm costs of soil degradation, both the productivity loss and land value approaches are consistent with the opportunity cost approach. The two methods will yield different results, primarily from market imperfections including information deficiencies and unpriced effects, and from non-productivity damages which are captured in market land values.

The Australian situation

Overview of damage cost estimates
Within Australia, few broad-scale economic studies of land degradation have been attempted. Differences in criteria, methods and analysis make it difficult to compare results of those that have been undertaken. Therefore, it is also difficult to gain an understanding of the overall economic significance of land degradation.

One indicator of the seriousness of the problem as perceived by governments is the level of resources devoted to soil conservation. Total expenditure for all states was A$68.8 m in 1984 – 85, of which New South Wales accounted for A$39.9 m (58%). In contrast, a Commonwealth-State collaborative study conducted in 1975–77 (Department of Environment, Housing and Community Development 1978) concluded that the cost of required works was A$675 m (in 1975 dollars), or about 10 times the actual annual level of government expenditure on soil conservation 10 years later.

These large estimates are based on the rehabilitation cost concept, assuming reversal of all identified degradation. They provide no information on benefits forgone because of degradation, nor how much expenditure on rehabilitation may be justified in terms of generating net benefits to society.

The most reliable estimates of actual damage costs are probably those for regional production losses associated with salinization of agricultural land. In addition, isolated estimates exist for the costs of various off-site effects such as the increased costs of maintaining roads or the quality of municipal water supplies (see Upstill and Yapp 1987, and Table 16.2).

The scarcity of economic data is partially because for many

years resource managers were primarily concerned with unravelling the technical secrets of the unique Australian environment. Only recently the economic causes and consequences of land degradation and the potential contributions of an economic approach have begun to receive significant recognition (see Chisholm and Dumsday 1987).

Table 16.2: Illustrative Australian costs for selected aspects of land degradation

Annual cost	Description	Source
A$15 m (1983)	Cost to Victoria of human-induced salinity	Read and Associates (1984)
A$5-10 m (1983)	Cost to South Australia because of Victoria's salinity	Read and Associates (1984)
A$94 m	Cost of lost production in Western Australia due to land degradation	Robertson (1984)
A$7.5 m (average 1980-81 and 1982-83)	Cost for repair of damage to road surfaces, removal of waterbourne sediment, and other erosion damage (figure covers 46% of New South Wales municipal and shire councils)	Soil Conservation Service of New South Wales
A$40 m (1985)	Total costs to South Australia because of salinity	Easdown and King (1985)
A$40,000 (1982)	Cost of keeping sand off roads in Jerramungup district, Western Australia	Carder and Humphrey (1983)
A$1-2/ha	Costs of siltation and erosion of roads per hectare of cultivation in the Darling Downs	Alcock (1980)
A$1-2/ha	Costs of sediment in streams and dams per ha of cultivation in the Darling Downs	Alcock (1980)
A$4.40/ha	External cost of salinity from further clearing of Victoria's Loddon catchment	Grieg and Devonshire (1981)

Note: m = million

Many estimates of land degradation costs in Australia amount to little more than educated guesses. Accurate assessment often is not possible because of inadequate physical and economic data, but in many cases, as mentioned previously, pinpoint accuracy is not necessary for the estimates to be useful, provided their limitations are kept in mind.

Policy framework
Australia has a federal system of government with legislative authority divided between the Commonwealth and the states. Most decisions on environmental protection, nature conservation, land use, and land management in the states are primarily the responsibility of state governments.

The Commonwealth government, however, is capable of achieving an indirect but substantial effect on land use and management through its monetary and fiscal policies, particularly those related to trade and taxation. The most direct roles for Commonwealth government involvement are in the provision of direct financial assistance to the states and the co-ordination of Commonwealth and state actions.

Most of the state government organizations responsible for the management of natural resources were established at a time when natural resource systems were less well understood. The resulting structures consist of a number of agencies, each with responsibility for a single resource issue (i.e., soil, water, forest or land). Similar divisions of responsibility are evident at the Commonwealth level. The fragmentation and division of responsibilities cause difficulties in co-ordination of resource management, both within and between states. Junor and Watkins (1987) deal with these issues in some detail.

In a 1984 report on land use policy in Australia, the Senate Standing Committee on Science, Technology and the Environment stated that the natural resources humans seek to develop or use always occur in, and form part of, ecological and environmental systems which are not independent but interrelated; changes introduced to one resource can have repercussions on many others. The committee considered that a lack of co-ordination was evident, leading to duplication of effort within agencies, uncoordinated information on which to base land use decisions, and inconsistency in methods of management. Because degradation is a complex, multidisciplinary problem, the existing structure of management agencies is not able to achieve the necessary interrelationships and co-ordination.

Where states have mutual interests in areas of similar land use and land type (e.g., arid lands) and where natural resource issues cross state boundaries (e.g., River Murray), obvious benefits can be gained from co-ordination and co-operation by applying similar land management techniques, sharing technical information, and setting mutually beneficial standards of natural resource management.

In order to effectively address land degradation issues, an adequate statutory framework must be supported by a political and departmental will to move away from a predominantly corrective approach to land degradation control and to adopt instead long-sighted, multidisciplinary preventive actions.

Apparently some areas of government are starting to realize the importance of such an approach, as evidenced by the formal adoption of a state policy on Total Catchment Management by the New South Wales government in 1987. However, this type of action only establishes a foundation and must be followed by appropriate legislative and financial backing to be effective.

Land degradation in New South Wales

Within New South Wales, agriculture is the main land use that causes land degradation, but almost all land uses may be considered as contributing to degradation in some degree. In New South Wales, as elsewhere, there is growing realization that conservation of the land resource is vital in areas such as mining, urban and coastal environments, and infrastructure development. Although the distribution of damage costs is poorly recognized, both on-site and off-site effects can be shown to result in large economic losses.

Because of incomplete data on land degradation costs within New South Wales, no total estimate of damages can be made. However, an indication of the statewide expenditure in relation to combating degradation can be determined by selecting certain indicators of land degradation and collating the annual costs in relation to the land areas involved.

Within New South Wales, the following amounts were spent annually by state government departments and authorities in the mid-1980s (data extracted from relevant Annual Reports):

	A$m
Soil Conservation Service	
Soil conservation	22.4

Public Works Department

Floodplain management	6.5
Beach improvement	3.3
River management	3.6
Coastal protection	2.5

Maritime Services Board

Dredging ports and harbours	1.5 approx

Water Resources Commission

Urban flood mitigation	2.6
Floodplain and river management	5.6
Murray Valley salinity	3.8

Department of Main Roads

Road restoration – natural disaster	1.2 approx.

Local Government

Sediment damage	16.5

Further costs arise from activities such as water treatment works for urban and industrial uses and erosion control in relation to forestry and infrastructure development. The major forms of land degradation of concern in New South Wales are as follows.

Vegetation degradation
Vegetation degradation is an often forgotten aspect of land degradation. Examples of vegetation degradation occurring on a large scale within New South Wales include:

Tree decline. Since European settlement of Australia some 200 years ago, 45 to 50% of the forests and woodlands have been removed. The removal of trees as a precursor to agricultural development was necessary; however, in many areas of New South Wales, overclearing as well as clearing of land unsuitable to agriculture has occurred. The removal of trees contributes to salinity, wind erosion and water erosion.

Bitou bush. Bitou bush (*Chrysanthemoides monilifera*) was introduced from South Africa to assist in the stabilization of coastal dunes. However, it has become a problem because it excludes native species and does not satisfactorily stabilize dunes. Recent figures indicate that 21% (400 km) of the New South Wales coastline is now dominated by Bitou bush. Control has been estimated to cost A$1,800/ha/yr for the first three years and A$300/ha/yr for maintenance in subsequent years (Wickham and Stanley 1984).

The cost of eradication and re-establishment of alternative permanent vegetation would cost about A$5,000/ha.

Soil erosion
A Commonwealth-state collaborative study for New South Wales found that in 1975, more than 90% of the state's grazing and cropping land required treatment for land degradation with either erosion control works or land management practices. The total cost of implementing these works was estimated to be A$331 million in 1975 prices. At current prices, this figure would be approximately A$780 million. These estimates are subject to the qualifications mentioned earlier.

A number of other indicators of soil erosion costs are available. Studies of decreases in wheat yield and wheat quality resulting from sheet erosion were carried out at the Soil Conservation Service of New South Wales Gunnedah Research Centre from 1957 to 1960. Results indicated that following a soil loss of 75 mm, mean wheat yield decline was 9.5% while protein content declined by 21.5% (Junor 1984). When 150 mm of soil was removed, the mean decline of wheat yield was 29.1% and for protein, 24.2%. More recent trials conducted by the Soil Conservation Service from 1980 to 1984 resulted in crop yield losses of 39% in 1980 and 11% in 1981 following a soil loss of 30 mm. In 1984-85 the New South Wales wheat harvest was valued at A$1,079 million. The potential cost of declines in wheat yields is therefore very large.

Soil acidity
It is estimated that 2 million hectares of lightly textured soils within eastern Australia are already affected by soil acidity (Bromfield 1985). The cost to completely neutralize the acidity with the use of lime is approximately A$80/ha, or a total cost of A$160 million. Bromfield also considers that, if not addressed, the problem area could increase to 7 million hectares within 20 years, resulting in a remedial cost of A$560 million.

Salinity
In New South Wales, agriculture is the major human factor contributing to salinization. In 1982, a working party (Standing Committee on Soil Conservation Working Party on Dryland Salting in Australia 1982) estimated that 920,000 ha of the state were affected by saline scalding (primarily within the arid/semi-arid western region), and 4,000 ha were affected by saline seepage (primarily occurs within the eastern area). Some economic costs of saline seepage and scalding were also estimated and are shown in Table 16.3.

Table 16.3: Economic cost of saline scalding and saline seepage in New South Wales, 1982

Economic cost	Saline scalding (A$ million)	Saline seepage (A$ million)
Decline in capital value	3.7	2.0
Decline in annual productivity	2.0	0.4
Cost of restoration	1.5	0.5

Source: Standing Committee on Soil Conservation Working Party on Dryland Salting in Australia (1982)

Table 16.4: Estimated average annual costs (1982 prices) resulting from salinity in Australia for 1971–81 ($A million)

Type of cost	Households, industry and commerce	Agriculture	Government	TOTAL
Damage from salinity of water supplies	33	3	—	36
Damage from dryland salinization	—	22	—	22
Damage from irrigation soil salinity	—	6	—	6
Abatement of salinity in water supplies	—	—	13	13
Abatement of land salinization	—	1	9	10
Research and monitoring	—	—	6	6
Total damage and abatement costs	33	32	28	93

Source: Department of Resources and Energy (1983)

Salinization of irrigated lands is also significant within New South Wales. Although the area under irrigation is small, the potential productivity of these areas is high. Within the Riverina/Murrumbidgee Irrigation Area, salinity is a major cause of reduced productivity, but figures are not available. However, farther down the Murray River, loss of value of fruit production due to salinity of irrigation water within the South Australia Riverland in 1978 – 79 was A$4.3 million (1982 prices), (Department of Resources and Energy 1983).

Within New South Wales, salinity is a relatively minor problem compared with other states. Estimated average annual damage and abatement costs arising from land and water salinity within New South Wales from 1971 to 1981 were less than 5% of the national total of A$93 million. Of the A$93 million annual cost, about two-thirds were damage to production and one-third abatement costs. The total cost was shared almost equally by the government, agricultural and household-industry-commerce sectors (Table 16.4).

Sedimentation
Sedimentation rates within New South Wales are considered low compared with world standards; however, sedimentation still causes serious damage. The following sedimentation damage costs have been estimated within New South Wales:

- A survey of local governments, with a 46% reply, has indicated that an average of A$7.6 million was spent annually on removal of wind- and waterborne sediment from roads and culverts, repair of damage to council facilities, and repair of sediment damage to road surfaces (Morse and Outhet 1984). Extrapolated to cover all local government areas, this annual repair bill would amount to A$16.5 million.
- Lake Macquarie near Newcastle is currently losing 10 to 20 ha/yr from sedimentation. Based on estimated sediment loadings, the cost of removing such sediment would be A$637,500/yr (Morse and Outhet 1984). The impact of sediment upon ecological values of the natural environment, as well as upon aesthetic and recreational values of aquatic environments, can also be significant. Although data on the actual economic losses are not available, the effects of sediment upon estuarine fish nursery areas, freshwater fish habitats, recreationally important areas, and other significant resources have been documented.
- The impacts of land degradation, especially sedimentation,

are currently causing concern within the state's estuaries, from which more than A$30 million of fisheries products are harvested annually. The impact of sedimentation on navigation channels and ports and harbours is also noted; however, clear estimates of the costs involved are not available. A$1.3 million was spent in 1981 – 1982 on dredging operations by the Maritime Services Board as part of their port management operations (Maritime Services Board of New South Wales 1982).

Water quality
The impacts of land degradation upon water quality are also many and varied. The transport and retention of erosion products and salt by watercourses and water bodies are well known. The characteristics of a natural water body always reflect the characteristics of its catchment. Thus, when a catchment becomes degraded, so does the quality of its runoff water.

Mining operations often expose overburden and leave wastes to the effects of weathering, with subsequent release and transport of heavy metals to aquatic environments. The effects upon aquatic biota are usually detrimental. Rehabilitation at Captains Flat Mine near Canberra has cost A$3 million and was carried out to reduce the flow and accumulation of heavy metals into Canberra's Lake Burley Griffin.

Conclusions and recommendations

This paper has sought to determine an order of magnitude for various costs attributable to land degradation in answer to the question, "Is land degradation a serious problem in Australia?" Some conclusions can now be drawn.

1. Available estimates of damage costs are incomplete. Inconsistencies arise because of differences in conceptual bases, methodologies, and study objectives.
2. Notwithstanding point 1, the picture that emerges is of widespread losses due to both on-site and off-site effects of land degradation.
3. Notable losses include on-site losses of agricultural productivity due to soil erosion, soil degradation, and salinity and increased off-site costs of repairing siltation and erosion damage, and impaired water quality.
4. Estimates of opportunity costs are often quite high as compared with current levels of government expenditure on combative measures.

5. An analysis of the degradation processes suggests that political responses need to adopt more preventive, multidisciplinary, cross-resource approaches to land degradation.
6. One possible approach would focus on developing coordinated national policies for each of the principal types of land use, bringing together the resources and expertise of common value held throughout the states.
7. Given that most of the physical processes of land degradation are now fairly well understood and that technical solutions for a wide range of problems have been developed, it is necessary to focus on providing policy frameworks and incentives for improved land management.
8. There is a strong case for devoting resources to developing and applying economic techniques to the assessment of the causes and consequences of land degradation. This will assist policy decisions in relation to the level of funding which is justified, and in targeting combative programmes for greatest effectiveness.

References

Alcock, B.S. (1980),
  The Costs of Soil Erosion, Miscellaneous Bulletin no. 11, Economic Services Branch (Toowoomba, Queensland: Department of Primary Industries).
Bromfield, M. (1985),
  "CSIRO warning on soil – large land areas hurt by acid", quoted by Graeme O'Neill in *Canberra Times*, 30 September.
Carder, D.J., and M.G. Humphrey (1983),
  "The costs of land degradation", *Journal of Agriculture*, vol.24, no.2, pp.50-53.
Chisholm, A. and R. Dumsday (eds) (1987),
  Land Degradation: Problems and Policies (Cambridge: Cambridge University Press).
Department of Environment, Housing and Community Development (1978),
  A Basis for Soil Conservation Policy in Australia, Commonwealth and State Government Collaborative Soil Conservation Study 1975-77, report no. 1 (Canberra: Australian Government Publishing Service).
Department of Resources and Energy (1983),
  Salinity Issues: Effects of Man on Salinity in Australia, Water 2000: Consultants Report no.8 (Canberra: Australian Government Publishing Service).

Dixon, J.A., and M.M. Hufschmidt (eds) (1986),
   Economic Valuation Techniques for the Environment: A Case Study Workbook
   (Baltimore: Johns Hopkins University Press).
Easdown, G., and M. King (1985),
   "The Murray under threat", *Melbourne Herald*, 16 – 20 July.
Easter, K.W., J.A. Dixon, and M.M. Hufschmidt (1986),
   *Watershed Resources Management: An Integrated Framework with Studies
   from Asia and the Pacific* (Boulder: Westview Press).
Grieg, P.J., and P.G. Devonshire (1981),
   "Tree removals and saline seepage in Victoria catchments: some
   hydrologic and economic results", *Australian Journal of Agricultural
   Economics*, vol.25,no.2,pp.134-8.
Hufschmidt, M.M., D.E. James, A.M. Meister, B. Bower, and J.A. Dixon
   (1983),
   *Environment, Natural Systems, and Development: An Economic Valuation
   Guide* (Baltimore: Johns Hopkins University Press).
Jackson, E.M. (1982),
   Replenish the Earth (Albury: Catchment Education Trust).
Junor, R.S. (1984),
   "The extent of the degradation problem", paper presented at the con-
   ference on Soil Degradation – The Future of Our Land, 25 – 27 November
   (Canberra: Australian National University).
Junor, R.S., and W.A. Watkins (1987),
   "Policy agents: their interactions and effectiveness" in Anthony
   Chisholm and Robert Dumsday (eds), *Land Degradation: Problems and
   Policies* (Cambridge: Cambridge University Press).
Maler, K.G., and R.E. Wyzga (1976),
   Economic Measurement of Environmental Damage (Paris: OECD).
Maritime Services Board of New South Wales (1982),
   Annual Report 1981 – 82, Sydney.
Morse, R., and D. Outhet (1984),
   "Management of sediment in New South Wales, Australia", paper
   presented to Workshop on Management of River and Reservoir Sedi-
   mentation in Asian Countries, Honolulu, Hawaii.
Read, M., and Associates (1984),
   "Financing salinity control in Victoria", paper for the Salinity Commit-
   tee of the Victorian Parliament.
Robertson, G. (1984),
   Soil Conservation Districts: Their Role and Aims (Perth: Commissioner of
   Soil Conservation).
Sinden, J.A. (1984),
   *Estimation of the Opportunity Costs of National Resource Management Prac-
   tices*, report to the Department of Arts, Heritage and Environment,
   Canberra.
Sinden, J.A., and A.C. Worrell (1979),
   Unpriced Values: Decision Without Market Prices (New York: Wiley).
Standing Committee on Soil Conservation Working Party on Dryland

Salting in Australia (1982),
   Salting of Non-Irrigated Land in Australia (Melbourne: Soil Conservation
   Authority).
Upstill, H.G., and T.P. Yapp (1987),
   "Offsite costs of land degradation" in Anthony Chisholm and Robert
   Dumsday (eds), *Land Degradation: Problems and Policies* (Cambridge:
   Cambridge University Press).
Wickham, H.G., and R.J. Stanley (1984),
   "The role of Bitou bush (*Chrysanthemoides monilifera*) in the stability of
   coastal dunes", paper presented to a National Conference on Bitou
   Bush, August, Port Macquarie.

17
The Costs of Soil Degradation on the Northwest Slopes of New South Wales, Australia

J.A. Sinden

Précis

Estimates of the value of damages associated with dryland degradation are a key ingredient in determining the benefits of preventing damage and restoring land productivity. In this paper, a systems modelling approach is used to estimate the on-farm costs and benefits of a soil conservation programme in New South Wales.

Using a representative sample of farms in the area, the study estimates the regional costs and benefits of a soil conservation programme in terms of its effect on agricultural incomes. The results show that, over a 16-year period, such a programme would generate net benefits of more than A$100 million, for a benefit-cost ratio of 1.90.

Introduction

This study estimates the costs of soil degradation in the six shires of the northwest slopes of New South Wales using basic data from an intensive survey of 50 farms in one of the shires. The concept of well-conserved land as defined by the Soil Conservation Service (SCS) of New South Wales is taken as the technical standard implicit in the recommendations for conservation works in farm plans.

This region occupies some 22,311 km² and slopes from the New England Tableland in the east to the plains in the west. The steep hills and narrow valleys of the east are extensively grazed, while mixed farming occurs on the long slopes and shallow valleys in the west of the region. Average rainfall varies from 800 mm in the east to 200 mm in the west, and regional wheat yields average 1.5 t/ha. Since the survey area tends to be representative of the mixed farming area on the lower slopes of the region, the survey results are scaled up for the region.

The costs of soil degradation are measured in the following ways:

1. loss of agricultural output;
2. loss of annual agricultural income;
3. loss of long-term agricultural income;
4. total cost of the soil conservation works necessary to meet the standard;
5. total revenue from the necessary works as increased agricultural income;
6. net revenue of the necessary works; *and*
7. the benefit-cost ratio of these works.

Indicators 1 through 3 refer to the total amount of degradation at its current levels. Indicators 4 through 7 refer to the optimal quantity of restoration as defined in the next section.

Methodology

The general approach
The concepts of systems modelling were used to estimate the costs of degradation. The general procedure may be expressed in the following simple flow chart:

Objective *Select* conservation programmes and practices that maximize economic efficiency *given* inputs of natural resources, capital, labour, management and technology.

↓

Physical Changes *Estimate* physical changes in flows of goods and services, and changes in the condition of natural resources that follow restoration, or further degradation. In this step, physical damage functions are derived.

↓

Changes in Benefits and Costs *Calculate* the values of benefits and costs of specific restoration programmes from the physical changes and from financial data. Values of damage functions are derived from physical functions.

↓

Decision *Identify and execute* the most efficient programmes and practices.

The procedure may be summarized in a simple Natural Resource Damage Loss Equation, or NARDLE:

Expressed in terms of degradation:

Cost of   =   Physical decrease   ×   Value of a unit
degradation   in output   change in output

Expressed in terms of restoration:
Value of   =   Physical increase   ×   Value of a unit
restoration   in output   change in output

The general procedure and these specific NARDLEs were
tested in Sinden (1984) with data for the whole of New South
Wales. It is now applied, with more detailed data, to one region
of the state.

Data collection
Farm data were collected as part of a larger study to analyse the
influence of soil conservation and land condition on both land
value and wheat production in Manilla Shire, New South Wales.
Between December 1979 and October 1985, 70 properties in the
mixed farming part of the shire were sold. Fifty of these were sur-
veyed through interviews with buyers, and data were collected
for each from maps and from officers of the Soil Conservation
Service (SCS).

Farm planning is one of the services provided by the SCS. At the
request of the owner, the SCS sets out its expert recommendations
for various soil conservation works and land management practices on a farm plan. The works are the best practicable means of
conservation and, as a whole, provide the minimum requirements
to conserve the soil and mitigate erosion to acceptable levels as
perceived by the Service. In Manilla Shire, the main recommendations are for physical conservation works.

The SCS advises that the plan should be implemented as a
whole and, when farmers undertake the works at all, they tend
to complete the whole plan. Farmers do not appear to seek the
optimal economic plan for their property. In an economic sense,
therefore, the plan is a technical optimum that is implemented on
an all-or-nothing basis.

In the present study, the optimal amount of restoration is estimated on a regional basis. It is calculated by identifying those
properties for which total revenue per farm plan exceeds the
total costs for that plan. The optimal quantity of investment is
the investment required for all works on only those farms where
the revenues from the plan exceed the costs.

Partly because of this all-or-nothing/whole-farm implementation, and partly because of restoration to a common technical
optimum implicit in the farm plan, total revenues from restoration

are highest on the most degraded properties. Costs of restoration are, of course, highest on these properties also.

Estimation of the degradation/output relationship
Output is defined as wheat production in tonnes per hectare (W) over all the hectares of the purchased property. A simple production function to relate output to degradation would therefore be:

$$W = f \text{ (land condition)} \tag{1}$$

This model would imply that labour, capital, management and technology are all constant.

Two variables are specified for land condition: "PCAR", the arable percentage of each property; and "CCOST" equal to the cost per hectare of the conservation works recommended by the SCS in the farm plan. CCOST serves as a proxy for land degradation since the greater the degree of degradation, the greater will be the cost of conservation works. CCOST is measured as total costs per property divided by property area.

Smaller properties permit more careful management so the size of the property in hectares (SIZE) is included as a proxy for intensity of management. The more detailed production function is therefore:

$$W = f \text{ (PCAR, CCOST, SIZE)} \tag{2}$$

Available crop production technology can reasonably be considered constant so the main omissions from equation (2) are labour and capital.

Following theoretical expectations of diminishing returns to all factors of production, all explanatory variables were transformed to natural logarithms. The following production function was then estimated.

$$
\begin{aligned}
W = 0.279 &+ 0.484 \, \text{Ln(PCAR)} - 0.124 \, \text{Ln(CCOST)} \\
&\quad\;\; (4.7) \qquad\qquad\quad (1.3) \\
&- 0.122 \, \text{Ln(SIZE)} \\
&\quad\; (1.6)
\end{aligned}
\tag{3}
$$

n = 50
R^2 = 0.394
$\bar{R}^2$ = 0.355
F = 9.983 for 3, 46 degrees of freedom
t-statistics are in parentheses.

With PCAR and SIZE in linear form, the estimated model is:

$$W = 0.532 + 0.016\,PCAR - 0.104\,Ln(CCOST) - 0.0003\,SIZE \quad (4)$$
$$ (5.8) (1.3) (1.6)$$

n = 50
R^2 = 0.532
R^2 = 0.502
F = 17.4 for 3, 46 degrees of freedom

All independent variables in both equations (3) and (4) are significant at 10% or better. The damage costs are calculated from equation (3) because of its conceptual superiority and because a coefficient of determination of 0.394 is an acceptable level of explanation of variation in W. Higher levels would be welcome, but for a cross-section of farms where variations can be expected due to factors of biology, capital and labour, the ability of a model to explain 39.4% of the variation is a real achievement. Further, damage costs estimated from equation (4) are only some 20% higher than those estimated from equation (3).

Interpretation of the damage/output model
The general procedure for deriving changes in output from changes in land condition is now illustrated. The steps in this process are as follows:

1. The preferred production function is first simplified.
   The mean values of Ln(PCAR) and Ln(SIZE) are inserted into equation (3):
   W = 0.279 + 0.484 (4.019) − 0.124 Ln(CCOST) − 0.122 (5.437)
   = 0.279 + 1.945 − 0.124 Ln(CCOST) − 0.663
   = 1.561 − 0.124 Ln(CCOST)
2. The mean value of Ln(CCOST) is 3.953, corresponding to a cost of A$52/ha. At the mean, therefore:
   W = 1.561 − 0.124 (3.953)
   = 1.561 − 0.490
   = 1.071
   The output from land of mean size, arability and condition is therefore 1.071 t/ha.
3. If all the recommended conservation works had been undertaken, or if the land were already in "optimal" condition, CCOST would be A$0. The natural logarithm of 0 is minus infinity, a value that often complicates arithmetic. For convenience, let this desired level of land condition be denoted by a cost of $1/ha. The output from land in this desired condition is therefore:

W = 1.561 − 0.124 Ln (1)
  = 1.561 − 0.124 (0)
  = 1.561

4. If the A\$52 of works is undertaken (the mean cost of conservation works per hectare), the increase in wheat yield on this kind of property is therefore:
(1.561 − 1.071) = 0.490 t/ha

5. Because entire farm plans are undertaken and CCOST is the pro-rata cost of the entire plan, the increase in W can in fact also be calculated directly from the coefficient on Ln(CCOST) in equation (3). For the mean CCOST of A\$52, and its natural logarithm of (3.953), the increase is (0.124 x 3.953) or 0.490 t/ha.

The increases in annual yield per hectare were therefore calculated in this manner from the value of CCOST and equation (3). The per hectare values of CCOST and these increases are shown for 12 of the 50 farms in Table 17.1. The farms are listed in order of increasing CCOST; only the first five, last five and two farms near the middle are detailed.

Table 17.1: Calculation of the marginal costs of restoration

(1)	(2)	(3)	(4)	(5)	(6)	(7)
					Yield increase (tonnes)	
Farm no.	Purchased area (ha)	CCOST (A\$/ha)	Ln (CCOST)	per ha	per farm	Cumulative
1	272	10	2.30	0.285	78	78
2	92	10	2.30	0.285	26	104
3	54	10	2.30	0.285	15	119
4	113	11	2.40	0.298	34	153
5	91	11	2.40	0.298	27	180
23	41	50	3.91	0.485	20	3,988
24	40	55	4.01	0.497	20	4,008
46	130	137	4.91	0.609	79	8,105
47	518	140	4.94	0.613	318	8,423
48	80	142	4.96	0.615	49	8,472
49	430	157	5.06	0.627	270	8,742
50	53	190	5.25	0.651	35	8,777

Calculation of the revenues and costs of restoration

The damage/output model is now combined with basic survey data to calculate the revenues, costs, and net revenues of restoration. Revenues are considered first:

1. The annual yield increases per hectare are calculated as explained in the previous section and inserted in column 5 of Table 17.1.
2. The yield increases for the whole farm are simply the per hectare figures (column 5) times farm area (column 2).
3. The soil conservation works will provide a flow of benefits over time, but the flow will not start immediately. Following local practice, it was assumed that:

   - the works are undertaken equally over years 1 and 2;
   - no yield increases are obtained in years 1 and 2;
   - yields build up with one-third of the increase in year 3, two-thirds in year 4, and all from year 5 onward; *and*
   - there is a 14-year flow of increases (starting in year 3); thus, increases are obtained up to year 16.

4. The regional gross margin, or farm gate net income, from wheat is A$70/ha at a yield of 1.5 t/ha. The gross margin per tonne is therefore A$47 (70/1.5).
5. The present value of the total increase in revenue is calculated as $47/t times the discounted flow of yield increases over years 3 to 16. A discount rate of 5% per year is used. Total increased revenues for the 12 farms are listed in column 3 of Table 17.2.

The present values of costs were calculated as follows:

1. Following local practice, it was assumed that
   - the recommended works would be undertaken equally in years 1 and 2: *and*
   - maintenance is necessary every five years (years 6 and 11) at one-half of the original total cost.
2. The present value of this flow was obtained by discounting at 5%.
3. The total costs for each farm are shown in column 4 of Table 17.2, as present values per hectare.
4. The net revenues of column 5, Table 17.2, are simply revenues minus their respective costs. The flow of costs and revenues is depicted diagrammatically in Figure 17.1.

Table 17.2: Revenues and costs of restoration

(1) Farm no.	(2) CCOST (A$/ha)	(3) Total revenue (A$/ha)	(4) Total costs (A$/ha)	(5) Net revenue[a] (A$/ha)
1	10	103.7	16.0	87.7
2	10	103.7	16.0	87.7
3	10	103.7	16.0	87.7
4	11	108.4	17.5	90.9
5	11	108.4	17.5	90.9
23	50	176.4	79.8	96.6
24	55	180.8	87.3	93.5
46	137	221.5	218.5	30.0
47	140	223.1	223.3	–0.2
48	142	223.7	226.5	–2.8
49	157	228.1	250.4	–22.3
50	190	236.8	303.1	–66.3

Note
a = Net revenues rise to a maximum (at a CCOST of A$27 per ha) because total revenues are a logarithmic function of CCOST (rising at a decreasing rate) and total costs are an arithmetic function of CCOST.

The per hectare data were converted to per farm data by multiplying by farm SIZE. Then the per farm data were combined to give the following aggregate information for all 50 farms:

Present value of aggregate costs	A$1,808,457
Present value of aggregate revenues	A$3,193,973
Net present value (aggregate net revenues)	A$1,385,516

Results

Estimation of damage costs for Manilla Shire
The total possible increase in yield from the 17,681 ha of the 50 study properties is 8,777 t/yr (Table 17.1) – 46% of estimated 1984 – 85 total production. Associated increased revenues are A$3,193,973. The present value of aggregate costs to obtain this increase is A$1,808,457. Of this, the initial investment in works in

years 1 and 2 is A$1,133,663.

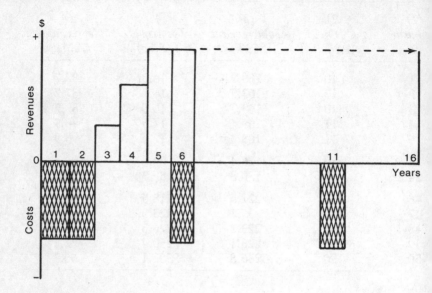

Figure 17.1: The flow of revenues and costs over time

Perhaps more interesting than these totals for restoration of all land are the results for the optimal amount of conservation works, because rarely is restoration of all degradation in the social interest. The optimal quantity of works, here defined as works only on those properties for which it is economically efficient to complete all the recommended works, is determined in the usual way by comparing revenues and costs.

Total revenues from implementing the farm plan exceed total costs for 46 of the 50 properties (Table 17.2). The optimal increase in output from these 46 farms is 8,105 t/yr. The aggregate costs of the recommended works for these farms is A$1,551,304, with an aggregate revenue of A$2,949,938, and an aggregate net revenue of A$1,398,634 – all as present values.

The benefit-cost ratio of this treatment is:

$$\frac{2,949,938}{1,551,304} = 1.90$$

Estimation of damage costs for the northwest slopes region
Manilla Shire is one of six shires comprising the northwest slopes
of New South Wales. The areas of these shires are as follows:

Barraba	3,075 km²
Bingara	2,389
Inverell	8,623
Manilla	2,245
Nundle	1,593
Parry	4,386
	22,311

The survey of 50 farms in Manilla was representative of the area
of mixed farming which covers some 64% of the shire. Since this
shire tends to be representative of all six, we take this survey to be
representative of 64% of the total area of the region. The total area of
the purchases is 17,681 ha. Thus, to represent the region, the shire
results can be scaled up by:

$$((2,231,100 \times 0.64) / 17,681) \text{ or } 80.8$$

Using this scaling factor of 80.8, we obtain the following regional
indicators of the severity of the degradation problem and the
economic potential for soil conservation to restore land condition.

1. Total annual opportunity cost, as lost wheat yield because
   land is currently "degraded"   709,182 tonnes
2. Total annual opportunity cost, as lost annual revenue (709,182
   x A$47 gross margin per tonne)   A$33.3 million
3. Total long-term opportunity cost, as the present value of lost
   long-term revenue (A$3,193,973 x 80.8)   A$258.1 million
4. Total costs of restoration (present value of installation and
   maintenance costs)   A$125.3 million
5. Total revenue of restoration (present value of 16-year stream
   of annual revenue at optimal level of restoration)
                                                 A$238.4 million
6. Net revenue of restoration (5 - 4) (present value)
                                                 A$113.1 million
7. Benefit-cost ratio of restoration   1.90

Indicators 1 through 3 refer to the total amount of degradation
at its current levels. Indicators 4 through 7 reflect only those farms
for which the present value of revenues from implementing the
farm plan exceeds the present value of costs.

Discussion

Reliability of the results

The gross margins, prices, costs and yield increases for the study region would seem to be representative of the whole region. The use of study area data for the region, therefore, should not be a major source of bias.

The on-farm revenues from soil conservation will be underestimated slightly because there will be increases in hay sales and livestock output, associated with the increase in wheat output. There will also be off-farm benefits through less silting and gullying of roads and rivers.

This "with project" analysis incorporates increased yields and assumes constant yields at the existing levels for the implicit "without project" situation. More likely, yields will decline without the project and so the project's true benefits are underestimated.

So far the analysis appears to be underestimating net revenues. However, a restoration programme of the scale envisaged may require a net addition to SCS staff and equipment of perhaps some 15%. The works themselves will reduce the available crop area slightly but probably by an insignificant amount.

The net effect of these sources of error would seem to be to underestimate true benefits to farmers and to society. In any event, the potential net revenue (of A\$113.1 m) is sufficiently large that a major decrease in revenue (or increase in cost) would be necessary before restoration loses its overall attractiveness.

Diminishing returns to soil conservation effort

The possibility of diminishing returns to conservation expenditures can be examined from the cross-sectional analysis of Tables 17.1 and 17.2. Following the normal presumptions of such analyses, the different CCOST expenditures that occur on different farms can be considered as different levels of expenditure on the representative property. On this representative property, therefore, the first \$10 investment returns a yield increase of 0.285 t/ha (Farm 1, column 5 of Table 17.1), or an average of 0.0285 t/ha/A\$1. The first \$50 returns a total increase of 0.485 t/ha (Farm 23), or 0.0097/t/ha/A\$1, while an investment of A\$190 returns 0.651, or 0.0034/t/ha/A\$1. The decline in average increase per A\$1 indicates diminishing marginal increases per A\$1 invested, as would be expected.

Acknowledgement

I gratefully acknowledge the financial assistance of the National Soil Conservation Programme, and the continued field assistance and encouragement of the Soil Conservation Service of New South Wales. Tim Yapp, Paul Sherman, and F. Poldi provided helpful comments on an earlier draft of this material.

Reference

Sinden, J.A. (1984),
   Estimation of the Opportunity Costs of National Resource Management Practices, Report to the Department of Arts, Heritage and Environment, Canberra.

18
Land Degradation Costs in Canada: a Recent Assessment

J. Girt

Précis

Canada has a large land area devoted to dryland agriculture and faces major land degradation problems from soil erosion, acidity and salinization. This paper examines the magnitude of the problems and the economic costs of present levels of degradation; it also makes projections of these costs for 1984 to 2008.

Even if the private and social costs of land degradation are known, it may not be economically efficient to prevent it in all areas. Government policies have a key role to play in helping to improve the situation. One goal is the sustainable use of agricultural soil and water resources in both the ecological and economic sense.

Introduction

During the past several years, the Canadian Department of Agriculture has commissioned or completed studies to assess physical and economic aspects of agricultural land degradation across Canada. Although these studies covered humid as well as dryland areas, this report focuses on conclusions from the dryland areas.

Two fundamental questions relate to soil degradation and public policy. First, how many resources can we realistically recommend that the public and private sectors put toward addressing this issue? Second, what policies unintentionally foster the spread of soil degradation and what positive adjustments can be made by way of modifying them or introducing new ones?

Knowing that topsoil is disappearing at a rate of X tonnes/hectare/year (t/ha/yr) does not help very much – at best it provides an ordinal ranking of problems. In order to manage the problem adequately, additional information is required:

1. the financial impact of degradation on farm profits;
2. the economic impact of degradation on total economy;
3. the reversibility of the degradation; *and*
4. the likely changes in 1 to 3 through time and between different cropping or production systems.

Table 18.1: Methodologies employed

	Prairie region	Eastern Canada and BC
Physical input	i) Salinity – soil surveys – subjective risk assessments by soil scientists at scale of 1:2.5 million ii) Erosion – subjective risk assessment by soil scientists at scale of 1:2.5 million	Base data – 2700 soil landscape units i) soil erosion estimated by USLE; ii) wind erosion by USDA Wind Erosion Equation; iii) compaction – susceptibility of soils by five classes; iv) acification – sensitivity of soil base status to exchangeable bases at the surface.
Yield assessment	Consultations with scientists who have recently completed experiments relating degradation and declines in wheat, barley, and canola yields regarding expected yield reductions by risk class in on-farm situations. Only small grains covered.	Structured regional meetings of scientists, farm advisers, concerned farmers to establish consensus of yield losses associated with specific regions of known degradation risk. All major crops covered.
Cost calculation	Use of census data on land use and current crop prices to infer revenue reductions for census divisions.	Use of census data on land use and current crop prices plus consensus estimates of increased fertilizer expenditures to infer revenue reductions for census enumeration areas.
Assessment of reversibility on and off farm	Not made. Probably limited on the farm.	Not made. As long as some soil depth retained may be possibilities.
Costs of reversal	Not assessed	Not assessed.
Off-farm costs	Not assessed	Some crude attempts made.
Expected rate of degradation	Crude but forecasts for 10 and 25 years made.	Crude estimate of current (i.e., 5 yr) trend made by panels; however, more refined predictions can be made if forecasts of future production shifts can be provided.

If this information can be linked with estimated costs of implementing remedial or preventive measures, it will form a base for addressing land management from an economic as well as a commercial approach (i.e., from both a public and a private perspective). Moreover, it will provide a framework for integrating environmental and developmental issues, and for addressing the intergenerational distribution of the benefits and costs of degradation. This approach will help to make the notion of sustainable use of agricultural soil and water resources viable in both the ecological and economic senses.

Table 18.1 presents a brief description of the methodologies used in the various studies carried out in the Prairie Region, Eastern Canada and British Columbia. The key points about this set of methodologies are as follows:

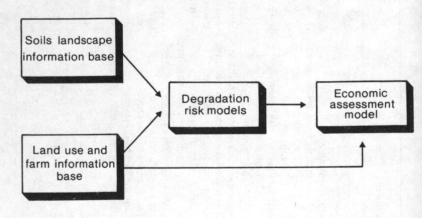

Figure 18.1: System to assess the economic impact of degradation

1. They are designed to reflect the state of knowledge of soil scientists and practicing agriculturalists in an integrated way.

2. They require two geographically consistent databases (see Figure 18.1):

- the costs and revenues of agricultural production;
- a soils landscape base from which information on soil, climate, and weather characteristics can be integrated with land use information to provide estimates of soil degradation risk. This can be provided through combinations of soil surveys, agricultural censuses, remote sensing databases, site investigations and extension service feedback.

3. The analysis should be conducted at the smallest feasible geographic scale of analysis; it is relatively simple to aggregate up to larger units, but quite difficult to disaggregate.

4. The weakest area is not likely to be either of the databases, but rather the means of inferring degradation risk and planning accordingly. For Canada at least, this may be a higher priority than national on-ground surveys of actual states of degradation and associated economic impacts. Some surveys, of course, will still be necessary to confirm estimates of risk and understanding of causal processes.

Prairie agriculture

Only 7% of Canada's total area is in farmland, and less than 70% of the farmland has been improved during the past decade. Most undeveloped lands for cropping lie in areas that are marginal in terms of economic returns and access to markets, or are physically too vulnerable to degradation for agricultural use. In the Prairie Region (Canada's most extensive dryland farming region), there has been some recent expansion in cropland area due to both relatively attractive forecasts for grain on world markets in the mid-1970s and economic pressures favouring a growth in the size of the farm unit.

Farmers in the Prairies practise large-scale dryland agriculture. Table 18.2 shows selected data for prairie agriculture. About 22 million ha are seeded in annual crops each year and another 8 or 9 million ha are summer-fallowed. Wheat is the major crop. Cropping is subject to the vagaries of weather and other environmental challenges (such as grasshoppers), as well as world grain prices, cash-flow problems associated with expansions in farm operations in the late 1970s, subsequent escalations in credit costs, and the market realities of the 1980s. Until recently, farmers have been

Table 18.2: Selected statistics on Prairie agricultural production

Land use 1983
  – seeded cropland 22 million ha
  – summer-fallow 9 million ha

Crop production (average annual production 1979–83)
  – 39 million tonnes small grains

  – wheat 20 million tonnes
  – barley 11 million tonnes
  – canola 2 million tonnes

  – 70% of national grain cash receipts

  – two-thirds of total Prairie farm cash receipts

Livestock production
  – one-third of national livestock receipts

  – in 1983, 2.5 million beef cows, 2.6 million pigs

Per farm statistics

		Manitoba	*Saskatchewan*	*Alberta*
No. of farms	1976	32,052	70,674	60,959
	1981	29,413	67,082	57,939
Average size	1976	240 ha	374 ha	331 ha
	1981	263 ha	394 ha	348 ha
Net farm income	1976	$6,203	$10,685	$ 7,354
(full-time farms)	1981	$8,021	$16,330	$11,516
(Canadian $)				

able to maintain or slightly increase yields despite the declining natural fertility of the soil by using more artificial inputs and improved varieties with greater yield potential. As a result, input costs are increasing at a faster rate than market revenues. The large number of livestock in the region are fed grain or graze on extensive rangeland. Forage production is not an economically viable alternative use for much of the grain-growing land. As the statistics in Table 18.2 show, from 1976 to 1981 the number of Prairie farms decreased, while average farm size and net farm income increased.

Grain land is predominantly used for spring-sown crops although fall-sown wheat is beginning to make significant inroads. Soils are frequently dry and are vulnerable to erosion in areas with moderate to steep slopes. Excessive tillage and summer-fallowing to build up soil moisture reserves and control weeds exacerbate the erosion problem. The time it takes Prairie soils to rebound from damages caused by wind and water erosion is long – too long, perhaps, to be considered reversible under conventional methods of economic assessment.

In addition, some Prairie farmers have to contend with increasing salinity. Some 6 to 8 million ha of soils in the Prairie Region are naturally saline, but it is estimated that another 2 million ha are undergoing so-called "secondary salinization", either as a consequence of dryland farming practices or from poorly understood fluctuations in the hydrologic regime.

Prairie farming practices have also consumed soil organic matter, bringing levels down to 40 to 50% of the levels found less than 80 years ago. The important question is whether, given present practices, soil organic matter levels will stabilize at a new equilibrium level that is high enough to maintain acceptable soil structure and water-holding capacity.

Table 18.3: Estimated on-farm costs of soil degradation, 1984 (in Canadian $m)

	Water erosion	Wind erosion	Salinity	Compaction	Acidification	Agric. GDP 1983
British Columbia	17–24	2	—	6–12	*	583
Prairies	468[1]	—	10–15	*	49	4,843
Ontario	69–157	1–8	—	71	*	2,689
Quebec	5–17	2	—	30–99	*	1,285
Atlantic	21–29	1	—	18	*	352
Canada				125–200		9,752

*Not estimated
1. The combined cost of water and wind erosion.

National impacts

In 1984, the Canadian Department of Agriculture identified the sustainability and enhancement of the natural resource base as a priority strategic issue for the agricultural sector. In that same year, the results of a parliamentary inquiry by the Standing Senate Committee on Agriculture, Fisheries and Forestry was published.

This study, *Soil at Risk* (Canada 1984), found that Canada was facing a serious agricultural crisis in all regions. The report stated that Canada risked permanently losing a large portion of its agricultural capability if a major commitment to conserving the soil is not made by all levels of government and by all Canadians.

National on-farm impacts from the Department of Agriculture's studies are summarized in Table 18.3. As a rough guide, net incomes from farming account for 40 to 50% of the gross domestic product (GDP). However, it must be stressed that on-farm impacts are more serious than these figures imply for a substantial proportion of the farm population (Girt 1986). In high risk areas, it is estimated that many farmers either have had their net returns from farming reduced by 50% or more, or have been forced to increase the size of their operation because of land degradation. This expansion has probably increased the rate of soil degradation as more fragile or marginal soils are brought under cultivation.

Another major aspect of national impacts are the off-farm effects. One crude estimate for Ontario shows that the off-farm

Table 18.4: Estimated annual off-farm costs of agricultural land degradation in Ontario (Canadian $m)

	Total costs 1984	% Attributed to agriculture	Agriculture's share (1984)
Dredging sediment from harbours	9.3	85	7.9
Sediment damage to inland lakes, reservoirs, channels	3.3	85	2.8
Water treatment costs	0.5	85	0.4
Sediment removal from road	3.8	50	2.0
Sediment removal from municipal drains	7.5	50	3.8
Recreational fisheries losses	87.4	85	74.3
TOTAL	111.8		91.2

costs are 60% of the on-farm costs (see Table 18.4). This is a lower percentage than found in recent US studies, but Canada has a lower population density and less infrastructure. Nevertheless, it is equivalent to about CN $10/ha under significant risk of degradation. This, plus the costs to the farmers as a consequence of continuing on-farm effects, forms the public cost of degradation, or the economic basis of public support for on-farm soil degradation control and prevention measures. Unfortunately, much uncertainty exists about future rates of degradation under existing or preventive crop production systems.

Regionally, some of the impacts of degradation on farm income are very considerable as most of the degradation occurs on only 20% of the cropland. Problems are very localized and to some extent crop specific. This points to the need for quite site-specific solutions as well as broader policy adjustments to allow the economic system to reflect public costs of degradation and public benefits of more sustainable on-farm practices. To make this transition from macro to micro effects, some researchers are using the same databases used to estimate macro-level impacts to examine expected net returns through time for individual farmers in specific degradation risk areas from different types of crop production systems (Secharan *et al*. 1986). This work can be used not only to advise farmers on production practices, but also to investigate how public costs of degradation and the public benefits of more sustainable practices can be linked. Based on this analysis, new management systems can be devised to support a switch to a more sustainable production system, while simultaneously reducing the national economic impact of soil degradation. This theme is explored in more detail in Girt (1986).

Although estimates of the current impact of soil degradation on agriculture provide an indication of the magnitude of the problem and the effect of years of uncontrolled degradation, they should not be used as a basis for funding future programmes to control and rehabilitate it. Funding decisions need to be based on the expected economic returns from proposed programmes. A proxy for this is the expected costs of further incremental degradation (costs that could be in part avoided), assuming that most of the damage which has occurred is to all intents irreversible over most planning horizons.

Estimates of the likely impacts of soil degradation on farming were made for the 25-year period, 1984 to 2008 (Table 18.5). These projections are based on 1984 prices and reflect the best judgements by the scientists involved in the study. Expected yield losses were then applied to the increments in soil degradation, leading to

Table 18.5: Prairies – 1984 to 2008 projections for annual degradation costs (Canadian $m)

	Wind and water erosion	Salinity	Acidification
1984	468	105	49
2008	558	128	132
Change	110	23	97
Percent change	23	36	198

Table 18.6: Net present value of predicted costs of Prairie soil degradation, 1984 to 2008 (Canadian $m)

	Discount rate	Wind and water erosion	Salinity	Acidification
Total on-farm costs				
	1	12,828	2,911	2,272
	5	6,990	1,606	1,060
	10	4,502	1,034	683
Incremental costs				
	1	90	24	83
	5	52	14	50
	10	34	9	32

an estimate of the degradation costs in 2008 if no changes in land use occur.

The net present value of all the annual impacts of degradation for the 1984 to 2008 period is substantial (see Table 18.6), and the net present value of the increments in degradation give a more realistic picture of what may be possible for degradation control (of course, assuming 100% success in programming and ignoring any off-farm effects). In the case of acidification, assuming an adequate supply of lime at competitive prices, it may be possible to aim for total rather than incremental reversal. There is still considerable uncertainty on salinity reversal.

Conclusions

Two conclusions can be drawn from this assessment. First, where soil degradation is occurring, it will be worth spending resources to stop it. These are areas where total expenditures will be less than the damages from soil degradation without rehabilitation techniques. Second, and more important, prevention is the only cure. Degradation prevention must be viewed as part of agricultural development, not an add-on at a later date.

In the past two years, progress has been made toward clearly articulating the public and private costs of soil degradation within the agricultural sector. A priority now is to define what is technically and economically feasible for degradation control. Information on yields and returns from different production practices under different environmental circumstances is needed, as well as a more detailed estimation of the off-farm costs of degradation. Research into alternatives to arrest or prevent degradation is obviously a high priority and should be focused on areas of high degradation risk that have been identified. Finally, there is a need for more work on policy instruments and policy development priorities. These might include market and price mechanisms that will encourage farmers to make the production decisions that they, as individuals, and society both want.

References

Canada (1984),
   Soil at Risk: Canada's Eroding Future, Standing Senate Committee on Agriculture, Fisheries and Forestry (Ottawa: Senate of Canada).
Girt, J. (1986),
   "The on-farm economics of sustainability and public intervention", *Canadian Farm Economics*, vol.20,no.2,pp.3-8.
Secharan, R., D. Culver, and D. Murray (1986),
   A Preliminary Economic Evaluation of Soil Erosion Technologies in Central Canada: Implications for Agricultural Development, Development Policy Directorate, Regional Development Branch, Agriculture Canada.

VII
Macro/Global Studies

Policymakers are unlikely to respond to calls for corrective action in dryland areas unless the benefits of public policy are demonstrated. Many national governments and international agencies still may not be convinced that the problem of dryland degradation is a serious one, or even have the means to assess the extent of the problem and the rate at which it might be growing. In the 1984 review of the Plan of Action to Combat Desertification, The United Nations Environment Programme (UNEP) attempted to derive some figures that would underline the full dimensions of the problem. Rough calculations suggested that, on a global scale, $26 billion of potential output was being lost each year from dryland degradation and that an annual investment of $4.5 billion over a 20-year period could prevent these losses. However, the reliability of these estimates has been widely questioned. There is a need for more data systems and analytical techniques that provide quantitative information on the economics of dryland degradation at national and international levels.

The case studies presented here give two quite different approaches to these problems. The Botswana case study by Gilbert exemplifies a new method to quantify changes in environmental conditions known as natural resource accounting. Designed to be applied mainly at the national level, natural resource accounts represent an extension of the System of National Accounts established by the United Nations in the late 1960s to identify changes in macro-economic variables. Natural resource accounts are intended to measure stocks and flows of key environmental and ecological resources. The underlying concepts are explained more fully in *The Economics of Dryland Management*.

The case study by Gigengack *et al.* demonstrates the application of systems analysis modelling to the problem of dryland degradation at the global level. Their model deals with relationships among key variables and regions, and endeavours to trace the effects of changes in economic activities and government policies on dryland areas. An important feature of such a model is its ability to identify system feedbacks and simulate changes over time.

19
Natural Resource Accounting: A Case Study of Botswana

A. Gilbert

Précis

Natural resource accounts (NRAs) are one way to explicitly incorporate environmental and resource information into an accounting framework. Based on the concept of the system of national accounts that monitors monetary flows, the natural resource accounts are designed to measure resource stocks and flows. In this case, the use of NRA is illustrated by data from Botswana. NRAs are composed of three interacting sets of accounts: Stock Accounts, Resource User Accounts, and Socio-Economic Accounts. Since NRAs are data-intensive and expensive to construct, care must be taken to develop accounts that are issue driven and can be integrated with other decision and policy analysis tools.

Introduction

Natural resource accounting (NRA) may be defined as a methodology for presenting environmental, resource and economic information. Its aim parallels and extends that of national income accounting (i.e., to provide an information framework suitable for analysing the performance of economic-environmental systems). This analysis is facilitated by:

- consistency in the presentation of diverse data;
- formation of a basis for a conceptual economic-environmental framework;
- provision of a common basis to facilitate discussion and the interchange of ideas; *and*
- description of the status quo.

A variety of approaches to NRA have been developed. These are reviewed in Gilbert and Hafkamp (1986), Braat *et al.* (1987), and in Gilbert and James (1988). Gilbert and Hafkamp (1986) outline a NRA framework developed within the design for a larger modelling and information system called IRENE (see also Roberts, Hafkamp *et al.* 1987). This case study elaborates further on this accounting framework using drylands issues in Botswana and assesses the value of natural resource accounts in drylands management.

This study constructs a set of natural resource accounts for Botswana using information and data derived primarily from Arntzen and Veenendaal (1986). The next section describes the accounting framework and discusses use of the resulting accounts. Drylands issues in Botswana are then discussed, followed by a preliminary set of accounts. In cases where data are not easily available, dummy numbers have been used; these are clearly indicated. The last section provides criteria for evaluation, a preliminary evaluation, and suggestions for further work.

The resource accounting framework

This NRA framework is modularized and consists of the following sets of accounts:

- Stock Accounts, describing the quantity and quality of natural resource stocks in physical units;
- Resource User Accounts, describing the use of these stocks within the economic-environmental interface in a mixture of physical and monetary units; *and*
- Socio-Economic Accounts, describing the movement of raw materials into the economy and other benefits from environmental use by human-oriented activities predominantly in monetary units.

The Resource User Accounts provide a bridge or link between the Stock and Socio-Economic Accounts (see Figure 19.1). Each of these accounts consists of sets of subaccounts, which are described in subsequent sections.

All accounts present information in the form of a "balance" where elements that contribute to (cause/input) or that derive from (effect/output) a particular production function are documented. Production functions are behind the generation of all commodities used directly and indirectly by society; these commodities include natural resource stocks, raw materials derived from these stocks, and environmental services, which include resource and environmental quality. The Socio-Economic Accounts are similar to the transactions matrix in traditional input-output analysis, where the inputs to and outputs from

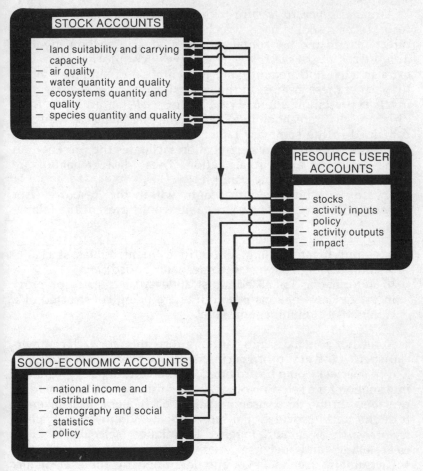

Figure 19.1: Links between stock, resource user and socio-economic accounts

each economic sector are documented. The Stock Accounts and Resource User Accounts adopt a different approach, largely because of the diversity of units and their non-additivity.

Here the subaccounts have a common structure based on "summary tables." These tables present aggregated information in the form of "characters" – key inputs to and outputs from a particular production function. Characters are usually but not always numerical and may not use the same unit of measurement. Consequently, the relationship between inputs and outputs or cause and effect – the production function – is implicit.

A *central summary table* provides an overview of a particular resource or resource user, which can be disaggregated in three directions. In the horizontal direction, disaggregation involves a *breakdown of the subaccount* (e.g., livestock into intensive and extensive livestock rearing) and presentation of summary tables for each of these groups. In the vertical direction, disaggregation involves presenting summary tables for *smaller areas*. In the third direction, disaggregation involves *detailing the individual characters* contained in the summary table. These characters may also be indicators, and so this disaggregation facilitates the presentation of all data used in their calculation. These disaggregations are illustrated in the following example.

Forestry constitutes a subaccount within the Resource User Accounts. The central summary table would present the following:

- inputs to forestry (e.g., effort, investment, quotas, stocks);
- outputs (e.g., harvest, income, value added); *and*
- information for all administrative areas – states or provinces, but also nations if accounts are being constructed at a continental or multinational level.

In the horizontal disaggregation, information for each commercial species (or group of species, such as hardwoods or broadleaved species) would be provided. In the vertical disaggregation, information for a selection of areas constituting a region would be provided. In the third disaggregation, each character is taken in turn and detail provided. For effort, this would involve detailing factors such as labour, logging techniques (selective logging, clear felling) and fuel use. A given table in a resource user subaccount is then defined and identified by three elements: species, region and character.

The Stock Accounts
The Stock Accounts are comprised of land, air, water, ecosystem and "component" subaccounts. Both quantity and quality of resource stocks and flows are addressed by a cause-and-effect approach. Minerals and energy would also constitute a subaccount, but the development of this accounting framework to date has not included nonrenewable resources.

The stock dynamics of the water and component subaccounts are documented using the following equation:

$$S_0 + I + N = C + E + M + S_1$$

where S_0 = stock at beginning of time period;
   I = imports (e.g., immigration or incoming flow of water);
   N = natural gain (e.g., growth, natality, run-off from rainfall);
   C = consumption
   E = exports (e.g., to other aquatic systems);
   M = natural loss (e.g., mortality, evaporation);
   S_1 = stock at end of time period

For water, only freshwater stocks are considered, distinguishing between ground and surface waters. "Component" species of interest include those exploited commercially such as livestock, fish and forests, although wildlife and pest species may also be included. The quality aspect of the Water and Air Subaccounts take into account natural and human-made emissions into water bodies (causes) and the resulting water quality (effects).

The Land Subaccounts combine quantity and quality issues by documenting land suitability and carrying capacity. Land suitability is defined according to characteristics such as chemical composition of soil, rainfall and topography. Existing and past land use also help to define land capability. Carrying capacity pertains only to grazers, and results from a combination of soil capability, plant cover and pasture quality. These latter aspects are also dealt with in the Ecosystem Subaccounts.

The Ecosystem Subaccounts describe the biotic structure of ecosystems and address both quantity and quality issues. Quantities of ecosystems are measured in terms of land area covered by the various vegetational units (e.g., shrub savanna, tree savanna, semi-arid shrub savanna, grass savanna, aquatic grasslands, dry deciduous forest, riparian forest, or woodland).

The Resource User Accounts
The Resource User Accounts are comprised of fisheries, livestock, crops, forestry, conservation, recreation (including tourism), water storage, urban and transport, and waste disposal subaccounts. Mining would constitute an additional subaccount but is not considered here. These users are largely consumptive, except for conservation and, to a variable extent, recreation.

These accounts adopt a simple "input-output" approach. Five categories of inputs are identified:

• stock, of primary resource (e.g., species) and land dedicated to that resource user;
• effort, subdivided into labour, fuel use, technology and equipment;

- infrastructure, subdivided into transport and storage;
- investment; *and*
- government policy.

Outputs are yield, income, value added, and environmental impact. This last character consists of two elements: current state of the environment resulting from use of that resource and future state of the environment. Both are aggregate, probably synthetic, indicators, with all the imperfections this implies.

Stock and yield are measured in physical units and are derived from the Component Subaccounts. Investment, income, and value added are derived from the Economic Subaccounts and are measured in monetary units. Government policy and the more demographic elements of effort are taken from the Social Subaccounts and use a mixture of units.

The Socio-Economic Accounts
The Socio-Economic Accounts consist of three separate modules. The first is the Economic Subaccounts, which are a modified version of the national accounts. Modifications include:

- adjustment of sectoral definitions so that all of the above resource users are explicitly documented;
- more detailed and explicit specification of expenditures within sectors such as waste disposal (and pollution control), conservation and recreation, particularly with regard to incentives, subsidies, and other investments into resource and environmental systems; *and*
- documentation of income distribution.

The second module is the Social Subaccounts providing demographic information. The emphasis is on interactions between the population and the environment, providing information on employment in the resource using sectors; tourism, recreational and leisure patterns in developed countries; and urban and rural population growth in developing countries. Social class information may also be included.

The third module is the Policy Subaccounts, which contain information on current environmental and resource policy.

Considerable work is being undertaken on modifying the national accounts to accommodate resource and environmental elements (e.g., Peskin 1981; Repetto 1986, and reviewed in Gilbert and Hafkamp 1986; and Gilbert and James 1988). The next review of the System of National Accounts probably will examine some of the suggested modifications for more explicit documentation of natural resources and environmental services.

Use of natural resource accounts

Natural resource accounts (NRAs) are useful in four particular areas: database, monitoring, conflict resolution, and integration.

Database. A comprehensive database lies behind the summary tables. Data availability is a major constraint to constructing natural resource accounts, despite large efforts directed toward the collection of environmental and economic statistics. An important role of the resource accounts is to identify data deficiencies and to provide some indication as to priorities in data collection. A second constraint is identifying key variables, since this requires intimate understanding of the system involved.

Monitoring. Resource accounts, like income accounts, are intended to be constructed on a regular basis. Since the data must be collected regularly, the accounts perform a monitoring function. Such time series are essential in the identification and evaluation of trends.

Conflict resolution. Management, whether of the economy, natural resources, or the environment, is multi-objective and requires resolution of conflicts between competing objectives. Management is also multidisciplinary, since no single discipline can provide both accurate and comprehensive information. NRAs, by providing a wide range of information and representing a diversity of disciplines and interest groups, can assist managers in the broader context of multi-objective analysis of resource issues.

A special problem area in natural resource management occurs where there is competition between different users for a resource, or where one resource user adversely affects another resource or resource user. Such cross-resource issues are difficult to manage because of the traditional, sectoral divisions in resource management. These competing interests are often resolved according to which manager has the greatest negotiating power, rather than which interest has the greatest benefit.

Integration. Integration pertains to interaction between accounts and other management tools. The greatest potential for effective interaction is in simulation models. Simulation models consist of equations describing essential production functions and relationships, and are used to estimate the future effects of select management inputs. Resource accounts can help overcome two constraints in simulation modelling: our knowledge of the production functions in the economic-environmental interface, and standardization of data presentation and collection. Not only can models make use of the data contained in the accounts and the information that accounts implicitly supply, but models in turn can generate estimates of future accounts. Model output is then in a familiar format, and so the results can be communicated to managers. Given that the accounting structure is understood, this greater consistency between data, information, model inputs and outputs encourages more effective communication at various levels of management, and between management and the development of management tools.

Resource management issues in Botswana

Ecological and economic problems in Botswana are closely linked, as they are in most developing countries where a large proportion of the population is directly dependent on the land for basic survival. Braat (1986) made the following general observations on Botswana, which serve to indicate this economic-environmental linkage:

- population growth is expected to continue at 2.75 to 3.75% per year;
- mining and secondary industries are not an important source of employment, and the potential for further industrial development is limited;
- livestock farming has traditionally been the major source of food and income, and its role is not expected to change in the future;
- livestock survival and quality depend on rangeland quality, over which there is only limited control;
- growing population and herd sizes are increasing the demands placed on rangelands and other natural resources, threatening both their quantity and quality; *and*
- an erratic rainfall pattern aggravates this situation.

Specific problem areas identified by Arntzen and Veenendaal (1986) are land degradation, competition for land and water, and water pollution.

Land degradation
Land degradation comprises all processes that cause deforestation, the encroachment of bush on grasslands, soil erosion, and ultimately desertification. The economic activities affected include livestock and crop production, wildlife, and wood consumption.

Overgrazing, combined with the effects of drought, causes range degradation throughout the country, but the total area of affected land and the intensity are as yet unknown. Only a small part of the livestock is managed in fenced, commercial farms; most animals graze and browse over an open, unfenced range. Control over the range and over livestock quality is limited. Stock numbers have increased rapidly over the past 20 years for technological and economic reasons. Consequently, areas under livestock production have expanded, and stocking rates now exceed carrying capacity throughout most of the country.

Crop production is not a major economic activity in Botswana – arable land constitutes only about 1% of land area. However, it is practised by most rural households and, until recently, Botswana was self-sufficient in food production. Crop production is a major cause of erosion (both gully and sheet), which may affect future production. Bush clearing and de-stumping, winter ploughing, bare fallowing, and large field sizes further enhance erosion.

Areas used by wildlife are also suffering from degradation, due to increased populations, less land available for wildlife, and drought effects, as well as increased activity of harvester termites.

Wood collection is a primary cause of deforestation, and when it occurs on hillsides, gully erosion can result. Simultaneous overgrazing and deforestation can exacerbate land degradation problems.

In the livestock sector, land degradation first affects cattle through higher mortality rates and lower birth rates. Conversely, goats – a species that does relatively well in degraded areas – tend to increase. The effects of land degradation are felt most by the smaller cattle owners who keep their cattle in congested mixed farming areas and have limited access to boreholes in grazing areas.

In the crop production sector, degradation is associated with soil erosion and reduced soil fertility, reduced rainfall infiltration into the soil, and difficulties in working the land due to the formation of gullies. Erosion may be enhanced by runoff from overgrazing and deforestation in adjacent areas.

Overgrazed wildlife areas probably encourage migration of wildlife into other areas, including those used by people. Where migration is not possible, a reduction in numbers as well as species will occur.

Competition for land
Land degradation is often the result of increased pressure on

land. However, competition for land does not necessarily cause degradation, and so can be considered as a separate issue. Arntzen and Veenendaal (1986) discuss three main forms of competition, namely:

- competition between cattle and wildlife;
- competition between livestock and crop production; *and*
- competition around large settlements.

Competition between cattle and wildlife occurs mainly in west and north Botswana, where grazing activities have penetrated into areas that were previously occupied by hunter-gatherers and wildlife. Wildlife survival is threatened, particularly during droughts. The gains to the livestock sector are not proportional to the expansion of grazing area, since the expansion is usually into areas of lower carrying capacity. The sustainable productivity of wildlife and cattle in these marginal areas has not yet been compared.

The encroachment of cropland into grazing land results directly from the expansion of cultivated areas and the trend toward mixed farming. Institutional regulations do not delineate mixed farming and grazing, and treat grazing claims as subordinate to arable claims. Consequently, land available for grazing is decreasing. This contributes to the drive toward exclusive rights in grazing areas, confinement of smaller herds to mixed farming areas, and expansion toward the north and west.

The number of large settlements is increasing, as is the percentage of the population living in them. This is causing increased competition for environmental resources between urban and adjacent areas. One impact of this is local depletion of resources such as wood and thatching grass. Another is the loss of cropland and rangeland through residential and infrastructure developments.

Pressure on water resources

Water is an obvious constraint to human activities in drylands. The major consumers of water in Botswana are livestock and irrigation, although mining is also an important user. The main water problem in Botswana is to satisfy the increasing demand in a sustainable and affordable manner. Water pollution does not yet affect water supply, but may in the future.

The effects of water shortages are partly known. Residential developments and economic activities have been hampered by water shortages, mainly in the southeast. Expansion of the livestock sector is dependent on suitable locations for new boreholes.

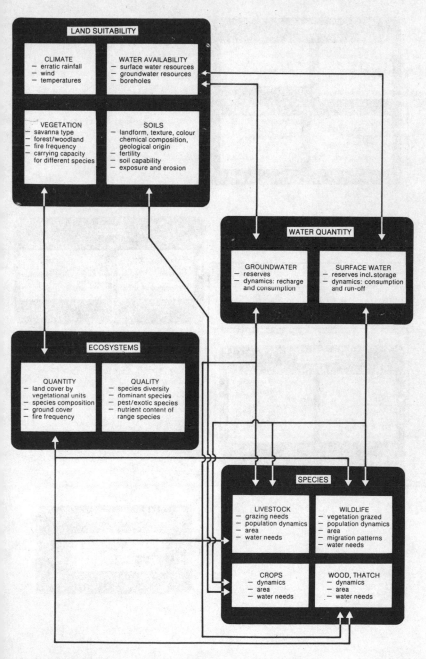

Figure 19.2: Resource and environmental stocks

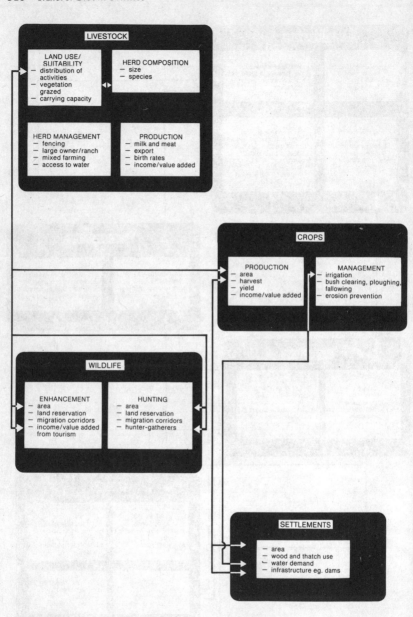

Figure 19.3: Resource use

Dams are often unsatisfactory forms of water storage since they tend to dry up during droughts, as well as taking up land and influencing vegetation and land use downstream.

All of these issues may be broken down and the elements grouped into the three categories used in the accounting framework (i.e., environmental stocks, resource use, and socio-economics). Figures 19.2 and 19.3 show a breakdown of issues within the first two categories. The socio-economic elements of major interest are already represented in the resource user accounts, and so this category is not expanded. Links between elements are indicated in these figures.

Natural resource accounts for Botswana

This section combines the accounting framework outlined earlier with the issues described to produce a preliminary set of stock and resource user accounts for Botswana. Data availability and consistency are variable, so in some places dummy numbers have been used. Such instances and the sources of data in general are clearly indicated. Readers are strongly recommended to refer to the original documents before using data from the following tables. Arntzen and Veenendaal (1986) is the major source of data and information.

Botswana is divided into ten administrative regions, coded as follows:

Southern	Sn
South-East	SE
Kweneng	Kw
Kgatleng	Kg
Central	Cl
North-East	NE
Ngamiland	Nd
Chobe	Ch
Ghanzi	Gh
Kgalagadi	Ki

Three main resource stocks are of interest: land, water and ecosystems. The main resource users or sectors are livestock, crops, wildlife and settlements. Summary tables for selected stocks and resource users, and their disaggregations, are discussed in the following sections.

Table 19.1: Summary table — Land Subaccounts

Character	Sn	SE	Kw	Kg	Cl	NE	Nd	Ch	Gh	Ki	Botswana
TOTAL AREA ('000km²)	27	1	38	8	148	5	109	21	118	110	585
SOIL CAPABILITY (%)[1]											
Class 1	15	39	24	29	31	39	30	26	34	24	25
Class 2	17	39	27	15	37	14	12	8	24	11	28
Class 3	38	13	26	9	25	15	28	55	5	15	49
Class n	0	0	0	5	3	16	12	19	10	2	1
LAND USE (%)[2]											
Communal	70	100	54	98	40	100	29	19	24	27	35
Cultivated	6	16	4	7	2	11	0	0	0	0	1
Traditional livestock	63	84	49	81	38	89	29	19	24	27	34
Commercial	20	0	22	0	14	0	7	14	0	14	10
Ranch livestock	19	0	21	0	14	0	7	14	0	14	10
Wildlife Management	9	0	17	0	4	0	15	0	19	24	15
Parks/Reserves	0	0	7	2	3	0	5	67	56	24	19
Unzoned	0	0	0	0	43	0	34	0	0	11	20
ENVIRONMENTAL QUALITY[2]											
Rangeland degradation											
Extensive	xx	xx	xx	x	xx	x	x	x	x	x	
Intensive	x	x			xx	x	x		x		
Desertification	x	x			xx		x			x	
LAND SUITABILITY(%)[1]											
Urban	1	2	1	3	0	1	0	0	0	0	0
Intensive agriculture	5	9	3	6	1	2	1	1	1	1	1
Extensive agriculture	20	45	36	19	15	22	5	5	2	0	18
Class m	0	0	0	5	0	3	5	1	75	95	55
POTENTIAL CARRYING CAPACITY (ha/LSU)[3]	14	12	12	12	16	24	12	10	21	40	

1. Data are totally fictitious.
2. Arntzen and Veenendaal (1986); livestock figures are fictitious.
3. Braat (1986) and derived from Field (1978); note that carrying capacity is greatest when this variable is lowest; LSU = livestock unit.

The Stock Accounts
Land Subaccounts. Table 19.1 presents a summary table for the Land Subaccounts, in which land suitability for various uses is addressed. Land suitability classes (e.g., most suitable for urban use, extensive agriculture, intensive agriculture, cultivation, forestry, recreation or conservation) are defined in terms of soil capability, existing land use and environmental quality. Soil capability addresses soil fertility and combines soil and geological characteristics with climatic features. Existing land use can constrain land suitability (e.g., urban development removes arable land from cultivation, reservation of land for wildlife precludes livestock activities, and forests can inhibit cultivation). Environmental quality relates primarily to rangeland degradation through overstocking.

Carrying capacity is a particular aspect of land suitability. Theoretical carrying capacity can be calculated under assumptions of average rainfall and may also be adjusted for evaporation, soil topography and vegetation type. Stocking rates that exceed the actual carrying capacity lead to rangeland degradation, lowering carrying capacity and reducing the land suitability for grazing.

Disaggregation of this summary table permits detailing of each character. The classes of soil capability and land suitability are based on quantitative information. Disaggregation permits presentation of this quantitative information.

Water Subaccounts. Water resources of interest are fresh (surface and ground) water and only in terms of quantity, not quality. A subaccounts summary table would present the dynamics of all fresh water stocks using the equation presented earlier. There is, however, inadequate knowledge of groundwater reserves and their rate of recharge in particular. Information on surface water stocks, runoff and water use are not available for each region and are not necessarily comprehensive.

Ecosystem Subaccounts. The Ecosystem Subaccounts begin with identifying the area covered by each of the nine major vegetation types (see Arntzen and Veenendaal 1986). Distribution of vegetation is typically presented in map rather than tabular form, and rarely on a regional basis; further effort is needed to construct a summary table for this subaccount.

Disaggregation in the Ecosystem Subaccounts provides detail on each vegetation unit and its grazers (drawn from the Component Subaccounts). Time series of this information signal changes in community structure, as occurs with rangeland degradation. Of prime importance here is any change in the nutritional status of rangelands, bush encroachment, and the links between vegetation, grazers and carrying capacity.

Component Subaccounts. The dynamics of crop, wood and grazing

---

Table 19.2a: Cattle Subaccount – summary table 1981

Character	Sn	SE	Kw	Kg	Cl	NE	Nd	Ch	Gh	Ki	Botswana
Stock t=0	333	23	252	110	1,174	141	255	5	43	59	2,395
Birth	74	6	53	27	283	34	80	1	12	11	581
Purchase	8	1	2	1	10	3	5	0	1	2	33
Off-take	20	2	16	8	94	9	36	0	6	5	194
Home Slaughter	3	1	1	1	7	4	2	1	1	1	19
Death	43	5	23	14	155	21	61	1	9	8	340
STOCK t=1	349	23	267	115	1,212	144	242	5	40	58	2,460

Table 19.2b: A time series of stock dynamics – Botswana

Character	1980	1981	1982	1983	1984
Stock	2,367	2,395	2,460	2,462	2,360
	(100)	(101)	(104)	(104)	(100)
Birth	582	581	604	521	502
	(100)	(100)	(104)	(90)	(86)
Purchase	41	33	53	37	31
	(100)	(75)	(129)	(90)	(76)
Off-take	190	194	205	205	169
	(100)	(102)	(108)	(108)	(89)
Home Slaughter	27	19	25	26	39
	(100)	(70)	(93)	(96)	(144)
Death	388	340	425	429	445
	(100)	(87)	(110)	(111)	(115)
Stock (t=1)	2,395	2,460	2,462	2,360	2,240
	(101)	(104)	(104)	(100)	(95)

Note:
Based on Braat (1986); all numbers not in brackets ×1,000.

ing species are important. Data on cattle are available and presented here. Information on wood resources and their dynamics are presented in Arntzen and Veenendaal (1986). Table 19.2a presents a summary table for cattle and Table 19.2b a time series of this information, both based on Braat (1986) and the equation presented in the second section. Numbers in brackets are an index, with 1980 as the base year. This permits a quick examination of trends in the variables. For example, the effects of the 1983 – 84 drought can be seen by increased death rates and decreased birth rates.

Disaggregation and detailing of each character in Table 19.2a would yield tables presenting the following data:

- stocking rates per management system – such as ranch, communal and cattlepost – compared with estimates of carrying capacity;
- calving rates, with comparisons between herd sizes and stock management systems;
- age, weight and destination of off-take (e.g., local consumption or export); *and*
- mortality rates and comparisons as for calving rates.

Table 19.3: Cattle productivity – communal, cattlepost and ranch systems

Character	Unit	Ranch	Communal	Cattlepost
Stocking rates				
Total	ha/LSU	11.6	6.0	
Cow	ha/cow	26.7	12.2	
Calving	%	74.0	50.0	47.3
Mortality	%	8.5	12.0	10.2
Weaning rate	%	67.7	44.4	42.5
Weight				
12 months calf	kg	200.0	132.5	123.5
12 months calf/ha/yr	kg	5.0	4.8	
12 months calf/cow/year	kg	135.4	58.3	52.5
Post-weaning gain	kg	105.9		89.7
18 month calf/cow/year	kg	195.8		90.6

Source: Arntzen and Veenendaal (1986).

Table 19.4: Livestock Subaccounts – summary table, time series

Character		Unit	1971	1976	1981	1984
STOCKS						
Grazing land		'000 ha	258	263	263	263
Cattle		'000	2,092	2,862	2,395	2,360
Smallstock		'000	1,391	1,820	761	1,105
Stocking rate		ha/LSU			7.6	9.3
EFFORT						
Rural population		'000	528		791	
1–10			5.0	2.5	3.4	3.9
11–20			13.0	9.9	8.5	7.6
21–40	Cattle herdsize	%	26.0	24.9	17.1	16.4
41–60			17.0	12.4	11.6	11.4
61–100			16.0	16.5	14.0	15.3
>100			23.0	33.8	45.4	45.0
1–10			27.7	16.7	23.2	29.7
11–20			24.6	25.0	24.3	20.7
21–40	No. Farms	%	26.8	32.2	25.5	23.8
41–60			11.2	9.5	10.0	9.5
61–100			6.5	8.3	7.8	8.0
>100			3.4	8.2	9.2	8.1
No. Ranches						
INVESTMENT						
Cattle purchased		'000			33	31
INFRASTRUCTURE						
Auctions		no				
Co-operatives		no				
Agents		no				
Abattoirs		no				
GOVERNMENT POLICY						
Livestock Development Programmes					x	x
Veterinary services					x	x
Borehole control				x	x	x
OFF-TAKE						
Total		% of herd	9.0	10.4	8.0	10.7
Local consumption		'000	40.0	50.0	35.8	46.9
Export		'000	156.5	212.0	205.0	169.0
NET INCOME		Pula				
Current prices				298.3	159.1	246.2
Constant prices (1978)				298.3	550.5	503.5
% AGRIC. INCOME						
Current				87.7	84.7	101.9
Constant				87.7	84.5	104.6
ENVIRONMENTAL IMPACT						
Carrying capacity indicator		index	1.0	0.98	0.95	0.83

Source: Based on Arntzen and Veenendaal (1986) and Braat (1986), but with some invention.

These data are collected and available in agricultural statistics.

The quality issues associated with cattle are stock productivity, rangeland degradation and the endangered, conservation, or pest status of species. Table 19.3 presents stock productivity from three livestock management systems. Information on rangeland quality and degradation is presented in the Ecosystem Subaccounts, but the specific link with livestock and stocking rates is to be made and documented here.

Resource User Accounts
Resource users or sectors include livestock, crops, wildlife and settlements. Information in the summary tables is presented in a diversity of units and, in some cases, the same information is presented in more than one unit. Information also overlaps with both the Stock Accounts and the Socio-Economic Accounts. Disaggregation of the summary table and detailing of each character specifies these overlaps and linkages.

Livestock Subaccounts. There is insufficient information in Arntzen and Veenendaal (1986) to present a summary table with a regional breakdown. Table 19.4 presents a time series of a summary table at the national level. Numbers are based on data presented in Arntzen and Veenendaal (1986) and Braat (1986), but required various "adjustments". The table is intended to be indicative only but shows that the livestock sector has been growing in herd size, number of large farms, number of small farms, and income. The number of cattle has varied since 1971.

Crop Subaccounts. A similar table could be devised for agricultural crop production. In this table a character of prime interest is "Effort". Detailing of this character should provide data on household participation in crop production, the mixture of livestock and cropping activities, and farming practices, particularly the use of draught power, seasonal labour, implements and seeds.

Links with other sectors are also of interest and should be detailed. These links are use of crop residues as fodder, crop damage by livestock, encroachment on grazing land, competition for water, and the impact on wood supply through the clearing of land and the need for fencing.

Wildlife Subaccounts. The emphasis of the Wildlife Subaccount is on wildlife utilization, which falls into three categories: tourism, recreational hunting and subsistence hunting. The regional breakdown used in previous accounts is not appropriate here, since these activities occur in select areas that may overlap regional boundaries. Table 19.5 is an attempt at a summary table. There is

Table 19.5: Wildlife Subaccounts – summary table

Character	Ki (south & central)	Ki (north & east)	Nd Okavango Delta	North	Tuli	Botswana
STOCKS ('000)						
Hartebeests	293	13				
Wildebeest	262	21	14			
Eland		2				
Springbok		44				
Elephant			4			
EFFORT						
No. hunters						
subsistence						10-20,000
recreational						1-2,000
Licences						6,491
No. tourists			8,136	14,551		
rooms		84		52	27	
Employment						230
GOVERNMENT POLICY – QUOTA						
Hartebeest				14,177		
Wildebeest				14,108		
Eland				1,290		
Springbok				3,615		
Elephant				0		
WILDLIFE KILLS						
Hartebeest				0		
Wildebeest				244		
Eland				14		
Springbok				6		
Elephant				–		
Poaching						13%
Game meat	670 tonnes					
large animals	16,000					
small animals	28,000					
INCOME						
government sector ('000 Pula)						348
private sector value added						11,850

Source: Data based on Arntzen and Veenendaal (1986).

a wide range of data to construct such a table, but its consistency is even poorer than that of previous summary tables.

Environmental impact is a particular problem. It is difficult to separate the impacts of direct wildlife use from other human activities (e.g., the expansion of grazing, fragmentation of grazing areas and migration routes, reduced access to water) and from droughts and habitat changes. However, detailing of these various impacts provides a more comprehensive and potentially integrated view of the state of the environment.

Settlements Subaccounts. The sector "Settlements" corresponds to households, secondary and tertiary industry, and includes infrastructure such as dams. Its consumption of natural resources has led to the following resource issues: sterilization of land, conflicts in water demand, and wood consumption for energy. Limited information is available, and almost none at a regional level.

The Settlements Subaccounts show the movement of raw materials into the economy and households and waste materials back into the environment.

Constraints

The major constraint in these accounts, as indicated by the preceding tables, is data. Arntzen and Veenendaal (1986) summarize and present only key data, indicating a wealth of data is available. However, this abundance does not extend across all issues.

Responsibilities for data collection in most countries is segregated along traditional sectoral lines, resulting in:

- irregular and unsystematic data collection;
- absence of complete sets of data for any one year;
- collection of data at varying spatial levels;
- absence of data adequately describing the multidisciplinary nature of resource and environmental issues; *and*
- absence of data adequately describing cross-sectoral or cross-resource issues.

For Botswana, further development of the accounts with access to more data and in co-operation with government authorities is needed to further expand the accounting structure and permit a more thorough evaluation.

Evaluation and recommendations

The Natural Resource Accounting framework discussed here was originally developed in the context of renewable resource management at the European level (Gilbert and Hafkamp 1986).

Development of these accounts is proceeding cautiously for two reasons: first, to ensure that the accounts are issue-driven and directed toward furthering our understanding of resource and environmental systems; second, to evaluate this benefit continuously and compare it to the cost of construction.

Accounts are data-intensive and expensive to construct, and the benefits to be gained from their use must outweigh the costs. These benefits can be enhanced if the accounts focus on key variables and relationships, monitoring trends in environmental and economic functions; if the accounting framework is internally consistent; and if the accounts can interact with other tools used in decision and policy analysis.

In addition, specific policy and management issues should be addressed or documented by the accounts. The following give an indication of such issues:

- stock depletion and enhancement;
- rates of resource use, particularly by economic sectors;
- control of resource characteristics such as age composition, carrying capacity, species compositions, ore grades, and sterilization of reserves;
- locational aspects of resources such as which resources should be used first, and where;
- temporal aspects such as rates of use over time, optimal turnover, or rotational times;
- substitution of resources in both production and consumption;
- conservation and/or recycling of materials and energy;
- international trade in natural resources and raw materials;
- pollution and other environmental impacts at regional, national, and international levels; *and*
- effects of fiscal instruments and policies on the natural resource base.

Integration with other tools used in management promises to be a major advantage of natural resource accounts. The next step in development and evaluation of this approach to natural resource accounting is to work directly with data generators, data analysts, and data users in the countries involved. This could also be combined with modellers and other researchers developing tools for policy analysis.

References

Arntzen, J.W., and E.M. Veenendaal (1986),
A Profile of Environment and Development in Botswana, report of a study conducted for the Environment-Development Linkages Project by the Institute for Environmental Studies, Free University, Amsterdam, and the National Institute of Development, Research and Documentation, University of Botswana, Gaborone.

Braat, L.C. (1986),
Risks in the Botswana Range-Cattle System: An Assessment by Scenario Analysis and Computer Simulation, report of a study conducted for the Environment-Development Linkages Project by the Institute for Environmental Studies, Free University, Amsterdam, and the National Institute of Development, Research and Documentation, University of Botswana, Gaborone.

Braat, L.C., F.M. Brouwer, A.J. Gilbert, E. Hulzebos, and W.A. Hafkamp (1987),
Integrated Modelling of Renewable Natural Resources: The Economic-Ecologic Interface, FAST Occasional Paper no. 172, Commission of the European Communities, Amsterdam/Gaborone.

Field, D.I. (1978),
A Handbook of Basic Ecology for Range Management in Botswana. Land Utilization Division, Ministry of Agriculture, Botswana.

Gilbert, A.J., and W.A. Hafkamp (1986),
"Natural resource accounting in a multi-objective context", *The Annals of Regional Science*, Special Edition – Environmental Conflict Analysis, vol.20, no.3, pp.10-37.

Gilbert, A.J., and D.E. James (1988),
Natural Resource Accounting: A Review of Current Activity and Its Application to Australia, Environment Paper Series (Canberra: Department of Arts, Heritage and Environment).

Peskin, H.M. (1981),
"National income accounts and the environment", *Natural Resources Journal*, vol.21, pp.511-37.

Repetto, R. (1986),
Natural Resource Accounting for Countries with Natural Resource-Based Economies, report prepared for the Australian Environment Council, Canberra.

Roberts, P.C., W.A. Hafkamp, *et al.* (1987),
Joint Final Report on the RES 2 and RES 3 FAST Activities: Models and Knowledge-Based Expert Systems for Policy Assessment in the Field of Renewable Natural Resources Management, FAST Occasional Paper no. 171 (Paris: Commission of the European Communities).

20
Global Modelling of Dryland Degradation

A.R. Gigengack, C.J. Jepma, D. MacRae and F. Poldy

Précis

This case study examines dryland degradation as an international problem. It maintains that land degradation assessment should include economic, social, ecological, and political factors. A detailed discussion is presented of the work carried out by the United Nations Environment Programme (UNEP) to assess the global costs of desertification, and the limitations of the UNEP approach are outlined. The use of global models is then explained. A brief description of the SARUM-AREAM global model is provided, including extensions of the model to study the effects of economic policies in developed countries on gross output, land use and land condition in Africa. The policies simulated include trade liberalization, trade restrictions, and trade preferences for African food exports, as well as various kinds of development assistance programmes. Sample results are presented. The model is at the pilot stage, and information generated is essentially qualitative. Further work will be required to improve the empirical foundations of the model before it is used for quantitative analysis.

Introduction

UNEP has stressed that "desertification is a world problem, not merely by reason of its scale and urgency but also through the universality of its impacts and causes, which extend far beyond the drylands more directly affected. Shared consequences include loss of the productive resource base; loss of valuable genetic resources; disruption of hydrological cycles; increase of atmospheric dust; loss of markets; threat to global security due to unrest and strife resulting from social and political breakdown. This globality of impact is a clear example of global interdependence and thus calls for worldwide co-operation and joint actions" (UNEP 1984).

Although it is clear that environmental conditions may be influenced directly and indirectly through all kinds of policy decisions, there has been only limited analysis of the relationship between policies and the environment, particularly at the global level (Bruckmann 1982; Leontief 1986a). Most analyses have been undertaken at the local, regional or national level. In addition, many analyses fail to account for the close connections among population, resources and the environment (Sachs and Levy 1985; Leontief 1986b; WCED 1987).

The role of international factors in causing dryland degradation can be illustrated by considering the problems of overgrazing and agricultural production in Third World countries. Because of population growth and a scarcity of grazing land, nomads may be forced to let their herds graze on the fallow fields of dryland farmers. With a deteriorating exchange ratio between agricultural products and imported industrial goods, farmers themselves may be forced to overcultivate the land, as well as moving onto marginal land previously used for grazing. A process of land degradation is thus initiated, leading to accelerated soil erosion and intensifying the problem of land shortage. The process will be exacerbated if nomads attempt to improve their economic position by increasing the number of cattle.

International factors may inhibit a reversal of this process. Limited export prospects for meat may preclude rapid destocking during times of drought. Attempts to improve export prospects for agricultural products may not improve the situation, especially if the emphasis is on cash cropping. Such policies can lead to "annexation" of land by those using it for production bound for the international agricultural market.

In the Sahel countries, the exchange ratio between the tropical agricultural export products (generally comprising almost all of their exports) and the necessary goods imported from the rest of the world (energy, fertilizer and machinery) appears to have an important impact on land use. Because these countries need a certain amount of foreign exchange (or barter equivalent) to finance their imports, a declining ratio generally leads to a policy to promote the cultivation of export products and increase the land area for commercial cropping by the market sector. The commercial export sector, often foreign-owned, requires the best available soils and, with the productivity attainable from modern agricultural techniques, it is able to pay for the best land. The result is that local farmers and nomads are increasingly "marginalized", being forced to use land of even lower quality, which is overexploited and eventually reduced to desert-like conditions.

Price and exchange rate policies and drought subsidies may be less effective in counteracting the problem than envisaged.

Price policies are often neutralized by the effects of "black market" exchange rates rather than the official rates. Official price movements may not be a proper allocative mechanism at the subsistence level. Drought subsidies may also be an ineffective policy instrument, e.g., in cases where cattle are retained during drought periods to maximize drought-relief payments. After a drought, high stocking levels may still be maintained because farmers expect to get a high price; thus, the recovery rate of the land is severely constrained.

The problem of farmers and nomads overusing rangelands might be solved locally if it were possible for them to find other ways of making a living rather than moving onto lands with lower productivity. Food needs could be met from imports bought with income earned in new economic activities. In fact, the process of finding alternative occupations to agriculture has been occurring in North America and Europe for the past two centuries. The use of land by the agricultural sector cannot be considered independently from developments in all other sectors of the national economy, which in turn cannot be considered independently from developments in the rest of the world.

Estimation of global damage and rehabilitation costs

UNEP is the only organization that has attempted to assess the global economic implications of desertification and its control. In 1981, UNEP expressed the view that "by various criteria, desertification control could reasonably hope to receive between 10% and 15% of such additional resources as may become available to meet developmental, environmental and other financial needs of the international community."

This assessment was based on the assumptions that 600 to 700 million people depend on desertification-prone areas for their livelihood, about 13% of world croplands is prone to desertification, and the rangeland areas prone to desertification represent 25% of the world's rangelands and produce 10% of the world's livestock products.

In another important endeavour, a group of high-level specialists in international financing convened by the Executive Director of UNEP attempted to identify current expenditures on desertification control, and put forward a financial plan outlining the costs of a programme to stop further desertification. This plan was designed to meet a minimum requirement of halting the spread of desertification and to provide further financial backing to the UN Plan of Action to Combat Desertification

(PACD). The group attempted to calculate the costs involved in stopping further desertification by determining the amount of land degraded and the restoration costs for several categories of land. The estimated costs of restoring land damaged by desertification ranged from US$1.5 to US$4 billion/yr, measured in 1980 dollars. It is interesting to note that the ratio of annual agricultural production forgone to the annual costs required to stop the desertification process during a 20-year interval is roughly 10 to 1.

The UNEP estimate of control costs was, in fact, somewhat limited. It covered the costs of corrective measures for desertified land in arid and semi-arid regions only, and excluded costs of developing new lands for agricultural production. The financial plan for desertification control, furthermore, was restricted to developing countries where GDP per capita is less than US$1,000/yr, and only in relation to irrigated lands, rangelands and rainfed croplands. Roughly half of the desertified land area of the world was thus left out of consideration in the financial plan. An even more restricted variant of the control plan was devised, requiring funding of US$1.3 billion/yr, in which attention was paid only to lands yielding zero or negative net returns.

Total costs involved in the plan were split according to the type of land. The costs of taking the necessary corrective measures for irrigated land and restoring it to a condition of optimum productivity were assumed to be, on the average, US$750/ha, with a variation between US$500 and US$1,200. These figures were based on information from the World Bank, the Inter-American Development Bank, the Food and Agriculture Organization (FAO), and other experts and referred to situations where tile drainage and leaching were needed but no pumping would be required. For the total relevant area of irrigated land, this implied costs ranging from US$8.2 to US$19.5 billion, with a mean estimate of US$12.3 billion. With total costs spread over 20 years, the mean annual costs were US$600 million.

Estimating the costs of desertification control in rangeland areas was a more complicated issue, if only because the area of affected rangelands is so vast. It was considered that only about one-fourth of all desertified rangeland area could be turned into land with positive economic returns. In the UNEP estimate of restoration costs for these rangelands, it was assumed that at least 50% of the relevant areas should be restored because of its significance for large population groups, especially in the least developed parts of the world. Based on this assumption, the annual restoration costs were estimated to vary between US$361 million and US$1.4 billion, with a mean value of about US$900 million. The figures on restoration costs per hectare were derived from consultations with FAO, the World Bank, and United Nations Development Programme (UNDP) staff, and independent experts.

The third category of land dealt with in the UNEP plan was rainfed cropland, with an estimated area affected by desertification of 100 million ha. It was assumed that about 70% of this area could be recovered with positive net economic returns at a cost of US$200–450/ha. Annual restoration costs varied from US$680 million to US$1.5 billion.

The UNEP plan was completed by estimating the costs to stabilize moving sand dunes in critical areas. The critical area of moving sand dunes was put at some 4.1 million ha, half of which was covered by the plan. The total costs involved in sand dune fixation in these areas were estimated at US$450 million/yr.

An analysis conducted by UNEP on spending by the World Bank, FAO, UNESCO, UNEP and USAID indicated that the greatest proportion of desertification funding was directed to projects that had only an indirect link with desertification, such as the construction of infrastructure or agricultural support, rather than land improvement. Although on paper the actual expenditures from bilateral and multilateral donor agencies on desertification projects came close to what was required according to UN estimates (some US$10 billion in 1978–83), only about 10% of this amount was spent on actual field control of the problem.

Use of a global model

The case for global modelling
It is legitimate to ask whether the UNEP approach satisfactorily deals with the basic causes of the desertification problem. As long as the economic processes which cause land over-use are not clearly analysed and understood, there is a risk that anti-desertification programmes will concentrate on symptoms rather than root causes. This consequently increases the chances that restoration programmes will help only in the short and medium term, without curing the problem in the long run.

The authors of this case study suggest that a more effective way of analysing the problem is to use a global model that accounts for major economic linkages and simulates the impacts of different combinations of policy instruments.

The model must be global in scope, and should distinguish various regions in the world, and preferably also basic sectors within the world economy. Furthermore, the model should be able to deal with "non-economic" issues like population growth, the depletion of natural resources, and land degradation processes in the various regions. The land degradation processes should be linked with economic processes and potential policy instruments. It is the authors' belief that, given the present state of the art, there is sufficient economic insight to deal with the desertification process by means of a global modelling approach.

The cost of different policy packages can be assessed by comparing their ultimate outcomes. Policymakers are not interested in costs alone, but also in resulting benefits, because only then can they judge whether incurring the costs is worthwhile. It also can be argued that costs involved in any economic programme should not simply be expressed in money terms, because the welfare implications of raising the funds to pay for the programme will differ depending on how and where the funds are raised. It makes quite a difference whether the funds are obtained by increasing import tariffs of affected developing countries, or by increased development aid from regular donors, even if the amount of money involved is the same. Some effects of policies, such as impacts on land condition, might be more usefully measured in physical, rather than monetary, units.

Every set of policy instruments can be analysed in terms of opportunity costs, by assessing the effects of allocating the same resources in alternative ways, such as on controlling population, increasing agricultural productivity, stimulating local food processing, or improving the standard of education. All these measures may, directly or indirectly, have some impact on the process of land degradation.

Description of the SARUM-AREAM world model
Simulation results presented here were obtained from a variant of the SARUM-AREAM global model. The results should not be considered final, but should be viewed as an illustration of the general approach.

SARUM-AREAM is an extension of SARUM, which stands for the Systems Analysis Research Unit Model. SARUM was constructed by a special research group within the UK's Departments of the Environment and Transport. Started in 1972, it was part of a project aimed at exploring the usefulness of world computer modelling for government policymaking. The model was completed in 1976, and later used in modified form by the Organization for Economic Co-operation and Development's (OECD's) "INTERFUTURES" project (OECD 1979). Since then, it has been used by various universities and government departments for both research and demonstration purposes. In particular, it was used

Table 20.1: SARUM regionalization

EURCOM – *Europe (Communist)*
Albania, Bulgaria, Czechoslovakia, German Democratic Republic, Hungary, Mongolia, Poland, Rumania, Soviet Union

WANA – *West Asia and Northern Africa*
Algeria, United Arab Emirates, Bahrain, Egypt, Iran, Iraq, Israel, Jordan, Kuwait, Lebanon, Libya, Morocco, Oman, Qatar, Saudi Arabia, Sudan, Syria, Tunisia, Yemen

NORAM – *North America*
United States, Canada

AUS – Australia

NZ – New Zealand

CHINA – China

LACARB – *Latin America and the Caribbean*
All of South and Central America

AFRICA – *Africa*
Africa except for certain northern countries included in WANA

EUR – *Europe (Western)*
Belgium, Denmark, France, West Germany, Ireland, Italy, Luxemburg, Netherlands, England, Malta, Switzerland, Austria, Cyprus, Finland, Greece, Iceland, Norway, Portugal, Spain, Sweden, Turkey, Yugoslavia

JAPAN – Japan

ESEA – *East and Southeast Asia*
Hong Kong, Indonesia, Kampuchea, North Korea, South Korea, Laos, Malaysia, Philippines, Singapore, Taiwan, Thailand, Vietnam

SASIA – *South Asia*
Afghanistan, Bangladesh, Bhutan, Brunei, India, Macao, Nepal, Maldive Islands, Pakistan, Sri Lanka

in the Australian Resources and Environmental Assessment Model (AREAM) project by Australia's Department of Arts, Heritage and Environment to assess environmental issues within Australia. The AREAM project added a post-processing stage to the use of SARUM, which coupled the output of SARUM to a more detailed model (Mula and Parker 1979). The model used in this case study does not make use of the post-processing capability, relying instead on the basic SARUM model as described elsewhere (DAHE 1986; Gigengack *et al*. 1985; SARU 1976, 1978).

Table 20.2: SARUM commodity disaggregation

MACHIN – *Capital equipment, traded*
SITC section 7, excluding passenger cars

CONSTR – *Construction*

OMANUF – *Other manufactures, traded, final demand good*
SITC sections 5 through 9, excluding capital goods and chemicals for agriculture

ENERGY – *Primary energy, traded, final demand good*
SITC section 3, excluding refined petroleum products

MINRAL – *Ore extraction, traded*
SITC divisions 27 and 28

OFLNP – *Other flow limited natural products, traded, final demand good*
SITC sections 1 through 4

SERVIS – *Services, final demand good*

FOOD – *Agricultural food production, traded, final demand good*
SITC section 0

LAND – *Development of arable land*

IRRIG – *Irrigation*

FERTIL – *Fertilizers and other chemicals for agriculture, traded*
SITC division 56

SARUM divides the world into twelve regions (see Table 20.1) based mainly on geographic and economic development criteria. Each of the regions contains eleven sectors, or industries (see Table 20.2). Of these commodities, eight are traded. The trading links, together with aid transfers, form the interconnections between the regions. Decisions on how much of each commodity to consume, produce, import, and export, for example, are functions of prices, income, production capacity and political/cultural aspects, and can be further influenced by population growth and income distribution. The form of the functions that relate these variables are largely rooted in neoclassical economic theory. For example, the demand for commodities classified as "final demand goods" are partly a function of Engel curves together with income and prices. The demand for commodities that serve as intermediate inputs for productive activities is codetermined by current production levels, a set of input/output tables, prices, and profit-seeking behaviour.

Use of SARUM for scenarios
Contrary to the better known macro-econometric models, a model such as SARUM is not intended to produce forecasts of specific variables. Central to any analysis using SARUM is the use of scenarios to embody alternative assumptions about the way future trends may develop. These trends can represent population growth, climate, trade, technological progress, and also certain policy decisions. The time interval that a simulation covers typically exceeds 15 to 20 years. Over such a period, many of the initial relationships can be significantly altered. For example, the decisions by private individuals can change as they become aware of a certain policy, and governments can adjust their behaviour in response to changes in observed international economic and/or political relations. In each case the reactions are motivated by opportunities to take advantage of the new policy, or to counteract or compensate for its expected effects.

This secondary and tertiary behaviour must be taken into consideration from the outset of scenario design. The need for these "coupled" assumptions becomes greater as the timespan increases. In practice, the presence of such adaptive behaviour can be reflected by altering the time paths of major scenario variables at regular intervals or by including a larger set of variables in the scenario design, especially during the later time intervals.

This case study is essentially a pilot study. The illustrations given do not fully reflect the richness that a scenario can and should contain. A practical application of the model would involve many more detailed assumptions than those presented here.

A distinction is made between environmental stress and environmental impact (Mula and Parker 1979). The former refers to existing conditions which are active sources of "strain" on the environment. For instance, return flows from irrigated agriculture may place an environmental stress on a river system by contributing to salinity levels. A steady-state condition in the river may, however, be reached within normal tolerance levels. An environmental impact results from a change in environmental stress that leads to a major change in the steady-state. For example, salinity may reach such high levels that it causes irreversible damage to vegetation and aquatic ecosystems.

The different stress levels which underlie such changes are caused by exogenous (policy or technical) factors and/or the workings of new endogenous relationships, such as resource degradation processes. For the model to be accurate, it is vital that these assumptions and relationships be specified realistically.

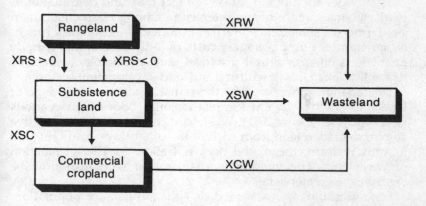

XRS   Transformation rate for rangeland to subsistence land; positive (rangeland is converted to subsistence land) if a shortage of the subsistence commodity exists; negative otherwise.

XSC   Transformation rate for subsistence land to commercial agricultural land.

XRW   Degradation rate for rangeland to wasteland; depends on the amount of rangeland vegetation cover.

XSW   Degradation rate for subsistence cropland to wasteland; depends on capital intensity of production in subsistence land.

XCW   Degradation rate for commercial cropland to wasteland.

Figure 20.1: Land types and transformation rates used in the model

Modelling land degradation
Results from land degradation modelling in this case study are

restricted to Africa, south of the Sahara. Four types of land are identified:

- rangeland, featuring mainly grazing and fuelwood collection;
- subsistence agricultural land, used mainly for rainfed cropping;
- commercial agricultural land, including irrigated agriculture; *and*
- wasteland.

The model attempts to reflect the fact that land degradation is partly a consequence of the interaction among people (commercial farmers, "subsistence" farmers, nomads), economics (prices of agricultural output, wages, costs of land development, trade restrictions on agricultural produce), and technology (especially its application in the agricultural and land development sectors).

Degradation processes and the transformation of one type of land into another govern the relationships between the various land types (see Figure 20.1). Wasteland consists of the cumulative sum of degraded land from each of the other three land types. In its present form, the model does not allow for the reclamation of wasteland. The various mechanisms at work can now be described in greater detail.

For rangeland, it is assumed that the subsistence population, through its grazing and firewood gathering activities, exerts a demand on existing vegetation cover. This harvesting, which is assumed to be proportional to the size of the subsistence population, is countered by a vegetation growth function dependent on rainfall. The net result of these two flows implies a vegetation density per unit area. The rate at which rangeland is transformed into wasteland is, in turn, a function of this vegetation cover.

The subsistence land is used for "subsistence agriculture", which is distinguished from commercial agriculture in that it does not employ large-scale, capital-intensive irrigation. It is largely rainfed, and does not make use of chemical fertilizers or pesticides in significant quantity. The subsistence land produces a subsistence commodity (a cheap foodstuff), the amount of which is determined as the minimum of actual yield and harvesting capacity. Associated with the subsistence sector is a fraction of the population, the size of which can vary according to employment opportunities in other sectors. The model can simulate different rates of population flow among the various sectors. Movement to or from the subsistence sector, for example, can be one-way or two-way, rapid or slow, depending on scenario assumptions.

A relationship exists between the amount of rangeland and the amount of land available for subsistence agriculture. They can be transformed depending on the shortage of the subsistence commodity. As this shortage rises, a tendency exists to convert rangeland to subsistence land, and vice versa. In addition, subsistence land can degrade directly to wasteland. This degradation rate is dependent on the amount of "capital" invested in the subsistence sector – terraces, windbreaks and earth works, for example. As the level of such conservation measures falls, the rate of subsistence land degradation rises.

Commercial cropland is distinguished by capital-intensive irrigation works and the use of chemical pesticides and fertilizers. The amount of land available to the commercial agriculture sector can be increased by upgrading subsistence land. It is assumed that rangeland will not be directly connected to commercial cropland. Consequently, subsistence land is subject to relatively severe pressure from degradation, commercialization, and possible transformation to rangeland. In this model, the commercial agriculture sector is constrained by the amount of subsistence land available. If the conversion of rangeland to subsistence land is low, it acts as a bottleneck, limiting commercial agricultural output.

Results

Scenario designs
The additional features incorporated in the model permit the construction of detailed scenarios for land and agricultural sectors in Africa. Simulation results were obtained for gross output (identified in the model by GSPS) and for the areas of different land types. Two regions, North America and Western Europe, serve as proxies for developed countries interacting with Africa. The simulations were carried out for 27 years, using 1973 as the base year.

The results presented here indicate the kinds of alternative "futures" that the model seeks to address. The first set, the "main scenarios", are simple first steps in designing alternative policy assumptions, whereas the secondary scenarios are intended to supplement the first by focusing on the behavioural response of the model to parameter changes.

Main scenarios
The main scenarios consist of the following:

1. Base run with standard assumptions and no explicit change in policies or parameters.
2. Across-the-board trade liberalization, in which all countries allow trade barriers on all commodities to begin falling after five years.
3. Across-the-board trade restrictions, in which all countries begin to raise existing trade barriers after 10 years.
4. Development assistance to commercial agriculture in Africa, in which net aid equaling 0.002% of total income in North America and Europe is diverted to capital investment in Africa's agricultural sector.
5. Development assistance to Africa, spread across general investment and consumer expenditure: 50% of the aid is directed to investment and 50% to consumption, maintaining existing proportions.
6. Development assistance to Africa, directed to the industrial sector: 25% to capital equipment, 25% to construction, and 50% to other manufactures.
7. Development assistance to all agriculture in Africa, as well as to consumer expenditure: the commercial and subsistence sectors each receive 25%, and 50% is allocated according to existing consumer expenditure patterns.

For scenarios 5, 6 and 7, the amount of development assistance is assumed to be 0.001% of total income in the two developed regions.

Secondary scenarios
The secondary scenarios reflect different assumptions about land conversion and degradation. One group of secondary scenarios comprises the following:

8.   Higher conversion rate of rangeland to subsistence land.
9–10.   Higher degradation rate of rangeland to wasteland.
11.   Higher degradation rate of subsistence land to wasteland.

Another set of secondary scenarios reflects possible responses by the developed countries to worsening conditions in Africa, by adjusting trade policies. These scenarios are identified as:

12–14. Developed country trade policies favouring Africa's food exports.

Scenarios 12-14 are designed to show the effects of lowering trade barriers on African food exports by the developed countries. This policy will soon have adverse economic impacts on national income and on the agricultural sectors of the developed countries. A reaction is assumed to set in. A reversal of the food export concessions to Africa is considered to be politically infeasible. Instead, the developed countries respond by raising trade barriers on manufactured imports from Africa. This has negligible impact, as Africa's trade in manufactured products with the developed countries is small. The adverse economic impacts continue in the developed countries, until eventually their governments are forced into beggar-thy-neighbour tactics, raising trade barriers on all imports of food and manufactured products.

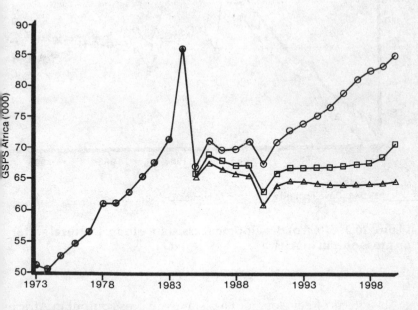

□   Base run
O   TL1   Trade liberalization
△   TB1   Trade restrictions

Figure 20.2: Effects of trade policies on gross output in Africa

Model results
Since lack of space rules out presentation of all the simulation results, only a few samples can be given.

Figure 20.2 shows the effects of trade liberalization (TL1) and trade restrictions (TB1) on gross output in Africa (GSPS) relative to a base run. Trade liberalization leads to an increase in output, and trade restrictions to a decrease. These results are for main scenarios 1, 2, and 3 described previously.

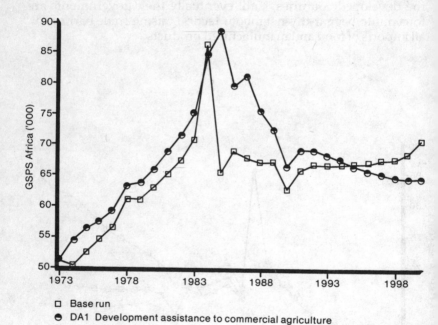

□ Base run
● DA1 Development assistance to commercial agriculture

Figure 20.3: Effect of development assistance to agricultural sector on gross output in Africa

The effects of development assistance on gross output in Africa are shown in Figures 20.3 and 20.4. Scenario 4 is indicated by the time path DA1. Other variants of development assistance are represented by DA2, DA3, and DA4, which correspond to scenarios 5, 6, and 7 respectively. An example of the effects of development assistance policies on the conversion rate of subsistence land to commercial cropland (XSC) is given in Figure 20.5. Figure 20.6 shows the effects on usable land area.

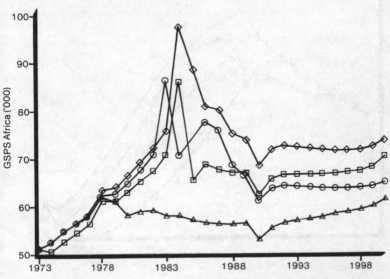

□ Base run
○ DA2 Development assistance to general investment and consumer expenditure
◇ DA3 Development assistance to industrial sectors
△ DA4 Development assistance to all agriculture and consumer expenditure

Figure 20.4: Effect of development assistance on gross output in Africa

Secondary scenarios 12, 13, and 14 are presented in Figure 20.7. The corresponding time paths are DES1a, DES1b, and DES1c. The effects are shown only in terms of gross output for Africa, but simulation results were obtained for additional variables, including land areas and land condition.

Conclusions

The modelling exercise conducted for this case study has demonstrated that it is possible to assess the effects of general economic policies on land degradation. The simulations, at this stage, produce essentially qualitative information. Further work is required to improve the database and fit the model to actual conditions.

With better quantitative information, new insights could be gained.

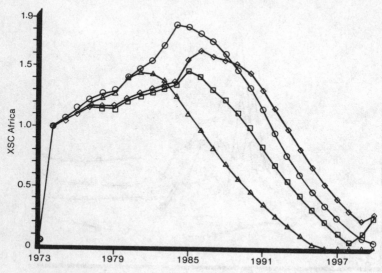

□ Base run
○ DA2 Development assistance to general investment and consumer expenditure
◇ DA3 Development assistance to industrial sectors
△ DA4 Development assistance to all agriculture and consumer expenditure

Figure 20.5: Effect of development assistance on transformation rate of subsistence land to commercial agricultural land in Africa

The results nevertheless suggest certain interesting conclusions. As is evident from the trade liberalization and trade preference scenarios, economic growth in Africa will tend to rise and fall in parallel with movements in general world trade. Also, contrary to popular opinion, Africa stands to gain more from an expansion of its industrial base than from agricultural support. Aid to agriculture delivers only short-term gains.

With respect to the dynamics of land degradation, the simulations suggest that increased world trade will lead to lower loss rates for undeveloped land in Africa, with slightly higher loss of developed land through commercial agriculture. Increased participation by Africa in world trade would benefit the subsistence population. Large increases in commercial agriculture, however, would be detrimental to the subsistence population, which would be forced to survive on an ever diminishing area of available subsistence land.

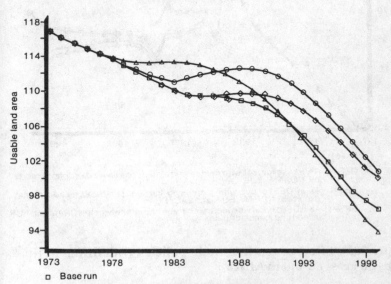

Figure 20.6: Effect of development assistance on usable land area in Africa

By simulating different rates of degradation, it was possible to demonstrate that Africa's economic performance is affected strongly by a rapid loss of subsistence land. Degradation of rangeland also has significant economic impacts, but less than those related to subsistence agriculture. The same can be said about reductions in total land area.

Tenuous though these conclusions may be, the results bear a strong resemblance to trends in Africa over the past 20 years.

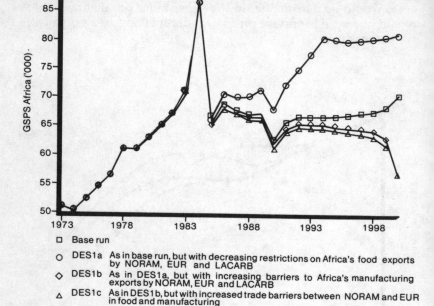

□   Base run

○   DES1a   As in base run, but with decreasing restrictions on Africa's food exports
              by NORAM, EUR and LACARB

◇   DES1b   As in DES1a, but with increasing barriers to Africa's manufacturing
              exports by NORAM, EUR and LACARB

△   DES1c   As in DES1b, but with increased trade barriers between NORAM and EUR
              in food and manufacturing

Figure 20.7: Effect of reactive trade policies with different time paths on gross output in Africa

References

Bruckmann, G., (ed.) (1982),
    Environmental Aspects in Global Modeling, Proceedings of the seventh
    IIASA Symposium on Global Modelling (Laxenburg, Austria: International Institute for Applied Systems Analysis).
Department of Arts, Heritage and Environment (DAHE), (1986),
    AREA Model Handbook (Canberra: Australian Government Publishing
    Service).
Dregne, H.E. (1983)
    Desertification of Arid Lands (New York: Harwood Academic Publishers).
Gigengack, A.R.,C.J. Jepma, G.J. Lanjouq, and C. Schweigman (eds),
    (1985),
    *The Use of a World Model for the Analysis of North-South Interdependence
    and Problems of Security and Development* (Groningen, The Netherlands:
    University of Groningen/Bureau Buitenland).

Leontief, W. (1986a),
"Environmental repercussions and the economic structure" in *Input-Output Economics* (2nd ed.), (New York: Oxford University Press).

Leontief, W. (1986b),
"Population growth and economic development: illustrative projections" in *Input-Output Economics* (2nd ed.), (New York: Oxford University Press).

Mula, J.M. (1978),
Conceptual Basis for an Environmental Sector of a World-Australia Model (Canberra: Department of Arts, Heritage and Environment).

Mula, J.M., and K.T. Parker (1979),
The Quantification of Environmental Stress Using the SARU/AREAM Global Model (Canberra: Department of Arts, Heritage and Environment). Also published in Bruckmann (1982).

Organization for Economic Co-operation and Development (OECD), (1979),
Facing the Future: Mastering the Probable and Managing the Unpredictable, INTERFUTURES (Paris: OECD).

Sachs, I., and M. Levy (Programme Directors), (1985),
Food-Energy Global Modelling Project, The United Nations University (London: Technical Change Centre).

Systems Analysis Research Unit (SARU), (1976),
Sarum 76 Global Modelling Project (London: Directorate General of Research, Department of the Environment and Transport).

Systems Analysis Research Unit (SARU), (1978),
SARUM Handbook 1978 (London: Departments of the Environment and Transport).

United Nations Environment Programme (UNEP), (1984),
General Assessment of Progress in the Implementation of the Plan of Action to Combat Desertification 1978-1984, Report of the Executive Director (Nairobi: UNEP).

World Commission on Environment and Development (WCED), (1987),
Our Common Future (Oxford: Oxford University Press).

Index

Figures in *italics*, tables in **bold**